KU-617-856

THE DECISION-MAKER'S HANDBOOK

ALEXANDER H. CORNELL

A SPECTRUM BOOK

Prentice-Hall, Inc. *Englewood Cliffs, New Jersey 07632*

Library of Congress Cataloging in Publication Data

CORNELL, ALEXANDER.
  The decision-maker's handbook.

  (A Spectrum Book)
  Bibliography: p.
  Includes index.
  1. Decision-making. 2. Systems analysis I. Title.
  HD30.23.C67   658.4'03   79-25530
  ISBN 0-13-198218-4
  ISBN 0-13-198200-1 pbk.

Editorial/production supervision by Betty Neville
Cover design by Tony Ferrara Studio, Inc.
Manufacturing buyer: Barbara A. Frick

© 1980 by Prentice-Hall, Inc., Englewood Cliffs, New Jersey 07632

A SPECTRUM BOOK

All rights reserved
No part of this book may be reproduced
in any form or by any means
without permission in writing from the publisher.

10 9 8 7 6 5 4 3 2

Printed in the United States of America

Prentice-Hall International, Inc., *London*
Prentice-Hall of Australia Pty. Limited, *Sidney*
Prentice-Hall of Canada, Ltd., *Toronto*
Prentice-Hall of India Private Limited, *New Delhi*
Prentice-Hall of Japan, Inc., *Tokyo*
Prentice-Hall of Southeast Asia Pte. Ltd., *Singapore*
Whitehall Books Limited, *Wellington, New Zealand*

Contents

Preface   v

Acknowledgments   ix

ONE
The Importance
of Decision Making   1

TWO
The Systems Analysis Approach   16

THREE
The Formulation Phase   38

FOUR
The Search Phase   57

FIVE
The Evaluation Phase   85

SIX
The Interpretation Phase   101

SEVEN
The Verification Phase   118

EIGHT
The Future of Systems Analysis
in Decision Making   127

APPENDIX I
The Downtown Parking Authority Case   136

APPENDIX II
Glossary of Analytical and Associated Terms   154

APPENDIX III
Some Popular
Quantitative and Other Techniques
and Tools Used in Analysis   176

APPENDIX IV
Two Case Studies for Analysis   248

Index   257

Preface

Although modern tools, techniques, and philosophies of management have helped enormously to facilitate good management, there remains the fundamental need to *use* them in a deliberate, analytical way in order to discover the real problems and opportunities, to develop the optimum alternative from among many, and to facilitate implementation of what is hopefully the best choice in our environment of shrinking resources. Still, as always, at the very heart of the entire matter lies the decision-making process. Of all the functions of management, *decision making* is still ranked number one by most scholars and practitioners.

As a technique aimed at attaining the optimum solution—the best decision—the Systems Analysis Approach (SA), the author feels, is one of the most comprehensive, the most inclusive of other good techniques, and the most orderly, rigorous, systematic method in use at the present time. It has proven its ability, when properly used, to shed a significant amount of light on decision making, primarily by reason of its *broader* use of quantitative, qualitative, and other dynamic judgment factors that do not fall into either category. Other approaches may not be broad enough to encompass the real objective or be capable of application because of their more limited scope or specialized areas of investigation. Systems Analysis not only provides for such scope and depth in problem solving, but offers an even more desirable product— *quality decisions.*

In pursuit of planning and teaching a different kind of "capstone" course for undergraduates in management and economics it became apparent to the author that there was a need for a single, useful handbook for students that would provide them with the broadest analytical approach to problem solving—specifically, the Systems Analysis Approach. They had mastered the tools and techniques, but "putting it all together" was a different matter and they needed a comprehensive text. That need has resulted in this basic handbook. It is intended for use at upper college levels, at a point where students have had a sufficient number of appropriate management, economics, and management-related courses to be able to apply the approach. It is also intended for their future use as managers, analysts, and decision makers and can be helpful to those already engaged in executive management in the business and organizational world. Hopefully, its simple but demanding and orderly stages of inquiry will provide the concise kind of guide needed in approaching problems and opportunities.

This simple procedural handbook is an attempt to demonstrate that Systems Analysis can serve many and varied users. In colleges it can be a basic text for a course in the decision-making process when coupled with any kind and number of case studies applying the Systems Analysis Approach. It can also be of value in a number of upper-level management courses such as business policy, planning and strategy, and advanced operational or strategic systems courses. It should have real application as a supplementary text for a variety of courses in management, finance, marketing, and other business subjects. Colleagues have voiced the need for such a supplemental guide to ensure that their courses tie in with the common denominator of all managerial functions—proper decision making.

In the vast, noncollege community of business executives and managers in all kinds of organizations, it should be a practical handbook that will improve their decision-making capabilities. It can serve as a text for in-house company training. It can supplement intuition and sound judgment and is not limited to purely quantifiable problems. The approach requires neither a college degree nor mathematical expertness. The facts will come from the problem, from the tools and techniques in the handbook, and perhaps from available assistants or any good math text, but the *will* to discover the facts and to use a simple, rigorous, and thorough method of solution lies with the individual user. To reemphasize, the organization and content of the handbook are directed toward satisfying the questions and needs of such users, whether sponsor, producer, evaluator, or implementor of Systems Analysis.

As an example of one intended use, it will serve for me as a companion piece to an outstanding refresher book written for college and noncollege users—*Management: A Basic Handbook* by Coventry and Burstiner, also a Prentice-Hall Spectrum book. With the two can be structured an invaluable "capstone course" in management in which the basics of the management book can be applied with the methodology of the Systems Analysis book to have students "create" a business or other enterprise of their own.

In sum, the handbook is intended for *all* those who may find themselves responsible for analysis and decision making in what the author firmly believes to be the most exciting and challenging profession—*management*—in its broadest concept.

A PREVIEW OF THE APPENDIXES

The appendixes in this book contain useful and condensed information which could not be incorporated into the text, such as a glossary of terms, examples of several tools and techniques used in Systems Analysis and two practice case studies. Brief descriptions of the appendixes follow.

I. The Text Case Study: The Downtown Parking Authority This appendix is a detailed case study used as an example throughout the handbook. It consists of both the case and the author's own solution. It will provide a continuing thread of application which will act as an illustration of the various phases, stages, techniques, and possibilities of analysis in a simple, yet provocative, case.

The case is, in my opinion, a classic and while not overly difficult, is an excellent vehicle for illustrative purposes. My sincere indebtedness and gratitude is extended to its author, Graeme M. Taylor, Senior Vice President of the Management Analysis Center, Inc., of Washington, D.C., for his kind permission to use it. Mr. Taylor is an author and practitioner of Systems Analysis whose professional expertise and leadership in the field is well known.

II. Glossary of Analytical and Associated Terms This appendix has been prepared to provide the student of decision making with a fairly comprehensive list and brief description of the terms, techniques, and tools used in the various approaches and steps in modern problem analysis and solving. Although all of them can apply to the Systems Analysis Approach, they have been broadly segregated beneath the analytic technique that best fits them. Thus, there are sections on economic reasoning; quantitative reasoning; analytical reasoning, processes, and techniques; and general management processes, techniques, and tools.

III. Some Popular Quantitative and Other Techniques and Tools Used in Analysis This appendix is a brief treatment of over thirty basic working tools and techniques together with the uses and examples of each. It is by no means intended to be a complete quantitative and/or statistical text but to serve as a convenient check-off list and example for the user when considering what might be appropriate for the analysis of a particular problem.

IV. Two Case Studies for Analysis This appendix contains two unsolved case studies for practice in analysis by the reader or by college classes or other training groups. One was prepared by Dr. William E. Turcotte, currently Chairman of the Department of Management at the U.S. Naval War College. It is called *Deepwater Ports* and, although it in no way represents official U.S. Government policy regarding an important energy-related situation, it is typical of the high range of important complex problems to which the Systems Analysis Approach may be applied.

The second is a case called *Swimming Pools*, prepared by Graeme M. Taylor, Senior Vice President of the Management Analysis Center, Inc., of Washington, D.C. It, too, is intended for class solution and discussion and, while it does not purport to be a statement of policy by the county involved, it is an excellent case for solution, involving a wide range of analytic techniques.

Teaching Notes for both cases for college teachers and other appropriate users, such as instructors of company/business/management courses, are available at a very nominal cost. Teaching notes for both cases may be purchased at a minimal cost from the Intercollegiate Case Clearing House, Soldiers Field, Boston, Mass. 02163, by written request containing appropriate identification and statement of use for instruction purposes.

A specialist in logistics and management, *Alexander H. Cornell* was engaged in high levels of decision making in the Industrial/Military/ Management Complex. In working with profit and nonprofit organizations in the private sector this experience, along with his knowledge of the Systems Analysis Approach, has been of great value. Through his college teaching—he is currently Professor of Economics and Management at Rhode Island College—Dr. Cornell shares his knowledge and experiences with those planning to enter the management profession, which he regards as the "most challenging and rewarding game in town."

As an officer in the U.S. Navy for 32 years, Professor Cornell headed schools and taught at all levels—from schools for enlisted men to the Naval War College, where he held the James V. Forrestal Chair of Military Management; he was the first active-duty officer to do so.

Acknowledgments

It is not necessary to reinvent the wheel. Good ideas and proven techniques should be used and built upon. This book lays no claim to invention, but merely to clarifying Systems Analysis and, hopefully, convincing the reader of its value in decision making.

My thanks and acknowledgments are first to all my colleagues, military and civilian, in Washington and especially in the Department of Management at the U.S. Naval War College. Their combined and inextricable notes, papers, techniques, and concepts produced much of what is in this handbook but is not easily attributable to a specific author. My thanks also to my good friend and economist, Professor Philip A. Gamble, for his contributions to the Glossary, which led to the section on examples of tools and techniques. Without his encouragement I would not have attempted the book. Thanks, too, to Commander Michael Gavlak, a great team instructor, for his notes.

Also, my thanks to Mrs. Mildred Imondi, an exceptional secretary whose rare abilities to proof, suggest, and type have me indebted to her a second time in my career. Having an English professor for a wife also helped an old warrior with writing. Thank you, Muriel.

My most sincere thanks to Graeme M. Taylor for the use of his classic case study *The Downtown Parking Authority* throughout this book and also for his unsolved case study *Swimming Pools*. Thanks also to Dr. William E. Turcotte, Chairman of the Management Department of the U.S. Naval War College, for letting me reprint his provocative *Deepwater Ports* case study as an unsolved exercise for classroom or individual use. Both cases are in Appendix IV. The last not least of my gratitude is offered to two professional analysts for their expert assistance with Appendix III: Dr. Richmond M. Lloyd, Professor of Management, U.S. Naval War College; and Dr. Peter A. Marks, Assistant Professor of Economics and Management, Rhode Island College. Commander William J. Roberts, U.S. Navy, also of the Naval War College faculty was most helpful in revisions.

Excerpts and Figures 6.1 and 6.2 from *Systems Analysis and Policy Planning: Applications in Defense,* E. S. Quade and W. I. Boucher, eds., are used by permission of Elsevier North Holland, Inc.

Table 1.1 is used by permission of The Institute of Management Sciences.

Figures 2.1 and 2.2 are modifications of illustrations appearing in *Conceptual Models of Organization* by George H. Rice and Dean W. Bishoprick. Copyright © 1971 by Prentice-Hall, Inc. They are used by permission of Prentice-Hall.

Figure 6.3 was derived from *Systematic Analysis* by Harley H. Hinrichs and Graeme M. Taylor. It is used by permission of Goodyear Publishing Company, Inc.

The excerpts and Figures III.5, III.6, and III.7 from *Management Science, Introductory Concepts and Applications* by David Heinze are used by permission of South-Western Publishing Co.

The following material is used with permission of McGraw-Hill Book Company:

Excerpts from *Quantitative Approaches to Management,* 2nd ed., by Richard I. Levin and Charles A. Kirkpatrick. Copyright © 1971 by McGraw-Hill Book Company.

The excerpt and Figures III.14 and III.15 from *Quantitative Methods in Management* by John E. Ullmann. Copyright © 1976 by McGraw-Hill Book Company.

Tables III.2, III.3, and III.4 and the excerpt surrounding them from *Accounting for Management, Planning and Control* by Richard M. Lynch and Robert W. Williamson. Copyright © 1976 by McGraw-Hill Book Company.

Tables III.5, III.6, III.7, and III.9 and adaptation of text from *Management Science: An Introduction to Modern Quantitative Analysis and Decision Making* by Gerald E. Thompson. Copyright © 1976 by McGraw-Hill Book Company.

Permission to use the "Downtown Parking Case" and the "Swimming Pools" case was granted by their author, Graeme M. Taylor.

1

The Importance
of Decision Making

During the past several decades, the "managerial revolution" has changed the status of management from amateur to professional. . . . Management can no longer fly by the seat of its pants; it must use instead more accurate instruments, and vastly improved techniques. . . . Quantitative techniques are, therefore, much in vogue. Nevertheless, there is still room for the inspirational hunch, though backed today by probability theory decision-making. Happily, too, most managers still regard people as more important than things. A place exists for the social or behavioral specialist, as well as for the accountant.[1]

This *handbook* on decision making is based on the same premises and perceptions of Coventry and Burstiner and is an attempt to develop them in a systematic way in order to help in problem solving and to choose opportunities—the primary tasks of management. As one is exposed more and more to the recent outpourings of many excellent management texts and applications, it is quite apparent that (1) we now have been presented with a need for better managerial professionalism as the result of a highly competitive, complex, and resource-scarce environment; (2) the expertise, techniques, and tools are available to apply better managerial professionalism; and (3) we need a healthy regard for *both* the quantitative and nonquantitative, as well as for the human aspects of problems and choices. There has been an equally impressive outpouring of several excellent problem-solving approaches designed to use the tools and techniques in various ways, usually toward specific desired results. Some of these are outlined

[1] W.F. Coventry and Irving Burstiner, *Management: A Basic Handbook* (Englewood Cliffs, N.J.: Prentice-Hall, 1977), p. 1.

1

later in this chapter. The real challenge now is up to all practitioners, students, business and organization executives, and even amateurs to become more actively aware of these systematic methods and, most importantly, to use them deliberately, faithfully, and properly. Of all of them, the more comprehensive and systematic approach described in this handbook is the most complete. Yet, in many ways, it is one of the simplest and best quality-producing decision approaches. The author has chosen to capitalize the name in order to deliberately single it out from among others. It is the *Systems Analysis Approach*. Within its scope and depth, all other approaches are encompassed as parts of its thorough and systematic phases and steps. It certainly is not new. It certainly is not perfect. It certainly does not guarantee the one best solution or opportunity. But its very *inclusiveness* goes a long way toward obtaining the best solution. The approach has been used successfully by governments (national, state, and local components), by managerial consultation firms, by some businesses, and even by individuals in solving personal problems or choosing opportunities. It is this author's opinion that its full uses have not yet been attempted. Surely not *all* of its phases or steps need be used in *all* situations, but the framework, the mental processes, the deliberate consideration of every conceivable factor, make it universally applicable to a much broader range of objectives in all business and organization, and in personal problems and opportunities.

Systems Analysis has sometimes been described as the application of the scientific method to problems of choice. Perhaps so. But it does not employ pure scientific research in its *uses*. In contrast to pure sciences, its objectives are to *recommend*, to *suggest*, rather than only to understand and predict. Quade and Boucher see it almost as a form of "engineering."[2] They recognize it as an approach not to be interpreted narrowly; not merely the application of quantitative economic, statistical, and mathematical analysis but to uses ranging from decisions about weapons design to toy manufacturing to simple choices of the best use of funds for household applications.

> Systems analysis is really not a single method or technique nor is it a fixed set of techniques. They can differ from problem to problem, but it is the thread that holds them all together. It is simply that of a systematic approach to helping a decision-maker choose a course of action by investigating his *full* problem, searching out objectives and alternatives, and comparing them in the light of their consequences, using an appro-

[2] E. S. Quade And W. I. Boucher, eds., *Systems Analysis and Policy Planning: Applications in Defense* (New York: Elsevier, 1968), p. 3.

priate framework—in so far as possible analytic—to bring expert judgment and intuition to bear on the problem.[3]

Hitch, one of the earliest proponents of analysis, describes it as a continuous cycle of defining objectives, designing alternative systems to achieve those objectives, evaluating the alternatives in terms of their effectiveness and cost, questioning the objectives and other assumptions underlying the analysis, opening new alternatives and establishing new objectives—and so on indefinitely. This seems to bear out the idea of utlimate *use* as well as application of *rational methodology* to problems of choice. As such, it can be seen as going beyond the scientific method.[4]

INHERENT PROBLEMS AND REALITIES OF DECISION MAKING

As all professionals know, every business and organizational policy, strategy, short-range plans, long-range plans, and day-to-day operations, are made up of real, hard decisions and even harder predictions. Ideally, these decisions and predictions should be the best ones. But the realities of what is *available* to do the job continue to prevail. Constraints of funds, of materials, of existing organization, of intelligence, of personalities and politics, of resource problems of all kinds, and especially of time, are some of those realities. It is almost axiomatic that decisions and predictions can never be based on *all* the information that is desired or even required. Decisions and predictions of major importance are made every day without benefit of all the data or information a decision maker would like to have. But when viewed as part of the accepted risks, the gambles, the anticipations, the joys or disappointments of managerial life, such decisions are acceptable. To wait for *all* the facts before taking action would be to perish on the tree of success. To make the best, systematically-arrived-at decisions, with an awareness of the constraints, is to flourish on the tree.

What is more, all problems and opportunities, like life itself, are filled with uncertainties and assumptions. They exist and they must be recognized explicitly. But once having done the best one can in reducing them to manageable proportions, or at least facing up to them, there is no reason not to proceed along systematic lines to

---

[3] *Ibid.*, pp. 1–2.
[4] Charles J. Hitch, *Decision-Making for Defense* (Berkeley and Los Angeles: University of California Press, 1966), p. 52.

develop alternatives and to arrive at a solution. Uncertainties may not be capable of becoming certainties and assumptions may not be correct, but Systems Analysis requires they be brought out clearly into the reasoning process. Systems Analysis goes further and insists upon *reexamining* uncertainties and assumptions and trying for a solution based upon new or modified ones. It is this iterative process inherent in all its stages and steps which makes Systems Analysis the thorough technique it is. The hope and possibility of producing something as correct as humanly possible, something really constructive, something really needed, lies with its proper use, despite seemingly overwhelming unknowns and assumptions.

The uses of Systems Analysis will be addressed more fully later. However, at this point it is appropriate to give the reader a feel for the range of its applications:

1. It can be used to *manage operations*. Through quantitative techniques it can be used, for example, to determine inventory levels, or optimum sales, or adequate sampling of a product, or the cost of levels of upkeep.
2. It can be used to *choose alternatives*. Through identification of the most *effective* alternative (be it the longest-lasting, most repair-proof, etc.) product to accomplish the job.
3. It can be used to *design* and *develop* products. Through determination of *need* for a product, or the competition, or its role and design in the market.
4. It can be used to determine major *policy alternatives*. System Analysis is not merely quantitative but embraces qualitative measurement as well. For example, the determination of a business to be "number one" or "number two" and the policy decisions which must be made to reach that position.
5. It can be used to help determine *how much is enough?* Through its open, demanding self-criticism, Systems Analysis can help determine "how much" of a weapons system, a commercial product, a welfare program, or a personal desire or need is "enough." We all know the usual answer to such a penetrating question is "more." But tools such as marginal analysis, costs, return, optimum product production, and even optimum "mixes" of these when plural items or means are the problem—these and others can *help* clarify how far to proceed. The question of whether extra cost is *worth* the extra effectiveness is addressed and made explicit.

Hitch includes in his philosophy an appropriate warning about System Analysis when he points out that cost effectiveness and related approaches are not a panacea for *all* problems. Problems can be of such a nature that they should not be forced to fit the analytic or quantitative molds. If something is completely nonquantifiable, reasonable steps leading to a good intuitive judgmental answer are sufficient. More will be written in a later chapter on this and other caveats. Suffice it to state here that the author, as an amateur but avid behavioralist, is the last one to believe that optimal solutions to everything can be calculated on high-speed computers.

Systems Analysis is an *open* challenge and opportunity to get at the real objective, to define the relevant, to evaluate and test reliability, and to invent new alternatives. It is a part of many kinds of information needed, including judgment and a knowledge of a world full of realities, in order to reach good decisions. The very fact that it is always open to criticism, not merely by other analysts but by everyone engaged in its use, means it must "remain open, verifiable, explicit and self-correcting," as Hitch observed.[5]

Deeply rooted in the feelings of many people is the idea that what they are after is far too important a matter to be inhibited by cost. This is true of the public sector, defense particularly, and to a lesser extent in the minds of some businessmen and the buying public. To anyone trained in economics or the hard school of competition in business, it is well known that the act of making a choice involves weighing the usefulness or benefit to be gained against the costs incurred. It is a simple fact that benefits cost resources —and the world has limited resources. What we use for one purpose leaves less or none for other purposes. Where a decision situation exists choice is as inevitable as death and taxes. Economic choice and Systems Analysis choice are ways of looking at problems. Neither depends entirely on quantitative, computer, or other aids. Choice involves judgment in designing the analysis, choosing the alternatives to develop and compare, and selecting one's measure of effectiveness or cost (one's criterion). As Hitch concludes, "Except where there is a completely satisfactory one-dimensional measurable objective (a rare circumstance), judgment must supplement the quantitative analysis before a choice can be recommended."[6]

Analysis and cost effectiveness do not lead solely to decisions favoring the cheapest product. Analysis is neutral with respect to unit cost. It is concerned with finding the unit which offers the greatest amount of effectiveness for a *given* outlay, or, the unit which can offer a *prescribed* effectiveness to be achieved at least cost. The fact that one machine can produce twice as much or twice as fast as another must be weighted against its additional cost where profit is the

[5] *Ibid.*
[6] *Ibid.*, p. 57.

criterion. The fact is that a cheaper and less efficient unit may also be a choice simply because its lower costs permit it to be made in much greater numbers, and numbers in this case equal greater effectiveness.

THE NEED FOR COMPLETE INQUIRY

Every business policy, plan, or strategy, as well as day-to-day operational problems, is made up of complex quantitative inputs, qualitative inputs, and decision outputs. The amount and complexity vary, depending on the scope and depth of the problem, but nevertheless they are present. The demand for new and better quantitative and qualitative tools and techniques has been met with a sizable outpouring of such techniques and tools, which are now literally and actually well ahead of our capacity to use them properly. One of the features of the Systems Analysis Approach is to ensure that none of them is overlooked. If one simply follows the outline of systematic analysis procedures faithfully, *deliberately* referring in this book to the listing, descriptions, and possible uses of such techniques and tools that do exist, the problem can be not one of recall but of recognition and application. Simply stated, it "systematizes" the way toward solving problems or deciding upon opportunities by its requirement for a deliberate process and deliberate consideration of all possible alternatives and decisions along the way, as well as the appropriate choice of techniques and tools to help illuminate them. It is a blueprint of direction, a road map of variable routes, a memory bank of tools and techniques.

Even today one hears the continuing request of managers to "give me some analytical tools to help me do this or that." They usually know of Systems Analysis and other techniques such as operations analysis and economic analysis but seem to be less aware that the analytical tools are there, waiting to be used properly. The tools are available. The processes are available. It takes some effort to put them together. The real key is as old as the scientific method itself, perhaps older. It is to ask oneself simply *what, where, when,* and *how* to use them. The real judgment is in first adopting the technique and then determining which mathematical or statistical tools to use *and* which judgmental techniques are appropriate to the problem at hand. It becomes a more simple matter of proper recognition and selection.

For example, what at first appears to be an impossible situation can become manageable by running down the repertoire of tools and techniques and by continually asking oneself questions—Is a technique of "sampling" useful here? Or is regression analysis? Or sensitivity analysis? Or the "Delphi" technique? And so on. It doesn't take an expert analyst to apply common sense and a little knowledge of what such techniques can do for one in making decisions. One need not run down the entire list; with practice and experience the obvious techniques will come to mind at once. With further skill and application the choices are apparent quite soon.

The most difficult part of the approach is to beware of the interrelationships of the tools and their possible effect upon one another as the total problem becomes clearer. A nonquantitative factor, such as an assumption, will affect every quantitative or qualitative factor that follows.

The need for completeness in an inquiry is not merely a phrase. Systems Analysis is not merely a "numbers game," not merely a "judgmental game," and above all not "paralysis by analysis." These and other pitfalls will be covered later. Completeness means considering *all* valid information to help reduce those inevitable uncertainties and assumptions to an *acceptable* level. They cannot be reduced to zero, but through intelligence and an orderly process, they can be reduced. At the very least they can be made explicit.

DECISION MAKING DEFINED

In recent years a growing body of research and literature has been concerned with the process called *decision making* and its conceptual twin, *decision theory*. Not too long ago the so-called economic man concept was the focal point of what was and still is called *economic decision making* or *economic analysis*.

Admittedly, economic analysis was in use before the broader Systems Analysis Approach became popular. It still is very much in use. Hitch, as a pioneer in both areas, in his description of the purpose of economic analysis reveals the proper use of the more quantitative applications. In the quest to get simply the *most* out of any *given level of available resources*, or, the logical alternative, to achieve a *given level of effectiveness* (or product, or service) at the *least* cost, it is *economic analysis* that is best used. His description of approaching the problem from either point of view is of interest here. If the problem is approached from a *given level of resources*, one works in terms of marginal rates of transformation and substitution. If the problem is approached from the achievement of something at *least cost*, one works in terms of marginal products and marginal costs. This is economic analysis.

He then goes on to expand the approach to other problems, which is to optimize the allocation of resources across the entire spectrum of needs, be they national, local, business, or private—and this means exercising choice among *many* desirable objectives. This is Systems Analysis, because it includes both economic analysis *and* the goal of proper allocation of resources.

Economic analysis still remains an excellent and thorough approach for those problems and opportunities which lend themselves to purely economic and quantitative techniques and tools. Economic analysis stands with Systems Analysis in its emphasis on the fact that judgments or measurements of *gains* are just as important as measurements of *costs*. Resources can be used for other purposes and other alternative gains can be obtained. Therefore, a decision should not be made on the basis of either costs or gains alone. To achieve an objective it may be the minimization *or* maximization of either one that is important.

Economic analysis is more concerned with cost effectiveness alone, however, than is Systems Analysis. A homey example of the difference is this one from Quade and Boucher:

> Suppose T. C. Mits has decided to buy a washing machine for his wife. His objective is fairly clear and the alternatives are probably well-defined. If so, the situation is one for a cost-effectiveness analysis. The available machines have differences in both performance and cost. With a little care, making due allowance for uncertainty about maintenance, water, and electrical costs, he can then estimate, say, the five-year procurement and operating cost of any particular machine, and do so with a feeling that he is well inside the ball park. He will discover, of course, that finding a standard for measuring the effectiveness of the various machines is somewhat more difficult. For one thing, the problem is multidimensional—Mr. Mits must consider convenience, length of cycle, load capacity, residual water in the clothes, and so forth. But ordinarily one consideration—perhaps capacity—dominates. On this basis, he can go look at some machines, compare costs against capacity, and finally determine a best buy.
>
> Now suppose Mr. Mits has simply decided to spend more money and thus increase his family's standard of living—a decision similar to one to strengthen the U.S. defense posture by increasing the military budget. How can he decide how to allocate the money among various possibilities? This is a situation for systems analysis, and he should probably call in his wife. Together, they first would need to investigate their goals or objectives, and then establish criteria, determine measures of effectiveness, look into a full range of alternatives — a new car, a piano, a trip to Europe. Here because the alternatives are so dissimilar, determining what they want to do is the major problem; determining what it costs and how to attain it may become a comparatively minor one.[7]

---

[7] Quade and Boucher, eds., *Systems Analysis and Policy Planning*, p. 5.

The decision-making process of today more often than not transcends the boundaries of purely quantitative solutions and cost effectiveness. It is this fact that leads economic analysis into the broader Systems Analysis Approach.

As for decision theory, there remains a division of another kind, the *normative* and *descriptive* approaches. Most of the normative type (i.e., what *ought* to be) has been concerned with quantification and monetary prescriptions and has enjoyed the progress of contributions by the government, business, and economists. The purely descriptive type of research (i.e., what *is*) has had a somewhat slower growth because complex processes involving judgments made, as well as economic *faits accomplis,* are more difficult to unravel or to trace. True, the historian can help here, but the "why" of most events leads to human judgments not always clear to later generations. Really good universal generalizations of cogency to a given time, place, events, judgments, and decisions are hard to discover. The reason is that "the real world is a messy place" as someone once appropriately observed.

Yet even a messy place can be attacked systematically. In the case of decision making, it is *planning* which is the common sense prelude—planning the attack on the problem which has given rise to opportunities for decision making. Planning is the major source of identifying and providing all the *inputs* that serve to establish some kind of desired goals, some kind of a beginning to the entire process. Moreover, planning is a key function that appears and reappears throughout an entire solution as it does when it touches on every function of the total management process. Planning is facilitated, at least the mechanical steps, with Systems Analysis, if the process is followed faithfully. It does not, however, take the place of that step which is the essence of problem solving, the making of a decision. This is still the arena of sound judgment based upon the unfolding and use of the total approach.

What is a *decision?* A somewhat simple definition would be that it is a settlement, a fixed intention, used to bring a conclusive result. It could also be called a resolution or a judgment to bring on a conclusive result. Webster's dictionary, among its several meanings, contains two that, when put together, are applicable to what we are after. To paraphrase and combine them, a decision is the act of deciding or settling a dispute or question by giving a judgment or conclusion reached or given. The key phrases are "the act" and "a judgment" or "a conclusion" which *settle* a question.

A decision is therefore first of all an act, but an *act* requiring judgment. A *judgment* requires a choice to become a decision. For if there is no choice, the decision already has been made. It is where alternatives exist that the act of decision making becomes meaningful.

The act of deciding then becomes one of first becoming aware that possible alternatives exist and thus leads into the entire process of making lesser decisions to be applied throughout the fundamental procedural steps. John Dewey is credited with perhaps the most succinct list of procedural decisions to be made:

- What is the problem?
- What are the alternatives?
- Which alternative is best?[8]

Those three questions might have been enough for most practitioners, but they have been vastly improved upon today with the more thorough, methodical procedures, coupled with quantitative and qualitative techniques to ensure the inquiry is conducted correctly.

Others have gradually enlarged upon Dewey's fundamental decision steps to make more complete ones such as this useful five-step concept:

- Recognize the need for decision making (a decision in itself)
- Consider and analyze alternatives (replete with decisions)
- Select an alternative to attain a goal (*the* decision)
- Communicate and implement the decision (involving the decision to *whom* to communicate and how to communicate and especially the decision *how* to implement)
- Evaluate and review (decisions again as to criteria and the need for further study).

The conceptual model for the Systems Analysis Approach is presented at the end of this chapter. For now, it is interesting to see from just the above three-step and five-step models how the focus has become broader, the depth greater, the decision points more recognizable.

Before moving on to the challenges inherent in decision making and to round out this introductory chapter on its importance, a brief word on who makes decisions is in order. Most feel that, ordinarily, decisions are made only by top executives. They may be correct for those decisions that rightfully belong "at the top." But the truth is that a great many decisions are made by middle and lower management and even lower operative groups and individuals. This may be heresy, but the author has often seen good decisions offered by staff analysts, planners, quantitative specialists, judgmental specialists, and others who are supposed to be only contributors to the creation of alternatives. The very act of coming up with alternatives involves choice, a choice

[8] John Dewey, *How We Think* (New York: D.C. Heath & Co., 1910), chap. 8.

more often than not made by the analyst. There is nothing wrong with this, provided *all* choices and how they were arrived at are given to the decision maker. To attempt a rigid division between analyst and decision maker has always seemed to this practitioner to be artificial, especially if the decision maker gets into the act, as he should. As decisions are woven into process and process into structure and structure into alternatives, it is inevitable that the analyst will be making decisions. Indeed, the objective is to provide a busy decision maker with alternatives *based* upon decisions from which the decision maker actually judges one to be best. Even in the important and often little regarded implementation phase of decision making one finds a whole new set of decisions having to be made by the implementers. These are not usually the decision makers, either!

In sum, although there are those who justifiably caution us against mixing analysis and decision making, the fact that they are combined cannot be ignored in real life.

THE CHALLENGE
OF DECISION MAKING

Before the various other approaches are set forth to complete the stage for the Systems Analysis Approach, perhaps a final word or two is in order about the challenge of being an analyst or a decision maker.

Analysis is a *creative* as well as a procedural process. Analytical techniques involve not only a logical attack on problems or opportunities but a searching, probing, imaginative, and creative mind to isolate major ideas and techniques, to define objectives that defy objectivity, to brainstorm the idea—generation stages of all phases of Systems Analysis, to "create" a creative climate or environment within which *everyone* feels free to participate to avoid stifling originality—in short, to insist on creative decision making at every step of every phase of analysis and of change. Decision making is risky. Decision making is fraught with perils and pitfalls. Decision making is avoided by many. Yet good decision making also pays off and can be made less risky by deliberate, proven steps in preparation. It is also exciting and satisfying. It is where the action is, as the popular phrase goes. Making simple decisions is easy. Making hard decisions, especially in a win-lose or possible lose-lose situation, is not easy. The act requires application, strength, and often courage, especially if careers are at stake. It is hardest where human welfare or lives are at stake.

Decision making is a *creative* thing requiring exceptional diligence, intelligence, application, and time. The last requirement alone dissuades or prevents many otherwise well-meaning executives from giving decisions the time they require. There never will be enough time and the question of "how much is enough" becomes even more one of human judgment. Decision making is more often than not very *complex,* so complex that one may not know its exact shape or at what point the crucial decision has been made. It is *iterative,* demanding repetition of processes with changing variables. It is *fluid* and purports to base itself on rational thinking. Rationality is not easy to achieve. It means different things to different people. For example, to an economist something may be rational if it maximizes profit. To a business executive it may be the assurance of communication, controls, and motivation, as the management pioneer Chester Barnard visualized. To a mathematician or management scientist it may be rational only if it optimizes output per unit of input. To the behavioral scientist it may be rational only if it meets human needs. And so on, reflecting the interests of different kinds of decision makers and analysts of different backgrounds and objectives.

Indeed, one may wonder after reading the above brief listing of the challenges, whether there can really be a rational decision, based upon logical, systematic processes. The writer believes there can be, and the challenges have been emphasized by keeping the whole process explicit. If one looks upon "rational" as a *sensible process* and *also* as a *goal* which may and can vary according to the context of the problem being confronted, then a frame of mind and a work procedure can be put together and applied in any mix of the two. Again, it is believed the Systems Analysis Approach provides the broadest rational vehicle for applying rational means toward rational goals.

OTHER APPROACHES
TO DECISION MAKING

The author would indeed be remiss if, before plunging into the subject approach of this book, he did not give recognition to other approaches to decision making. These methods or processes are in use and are useful for their purposes. They lack only the universality of application which SA offers.

The first two such approaches or "models," if one were to employ that popular term, have been explained in the preceding pages. The three-question model of John Dewey is one, and the five-step model is the other.

Continuing along the growing spectrum of such general and some more specialized models, one finds good ones tailored to specific functions such as the problems of acquisition, investments, pricing, and market strategy.

Here in Table 1.1 are some approaches which Smalter has already compared, showing the similarities in their major steps.[9]

Column G is the Systems Analysis Approach which was not treated as such in Smalter's step illustration but was used in part in his systems engineering model.

The chart reveals some interesting comparisons. All the methods start from about the same place in time and nearly all go through most steps even though different descriptions are used. Second, the use of the term Systems Analysis in systems engineering first appears, but only as a step in the model. If expanded in both directions, as will soon be seen, the term covers all the steps in a complete approach.

Third, the inclusive steps in SA are found somewhat scattered, emphasized, or left out in the other approaches. Finally, it is offered that the SA Approach contains all the other steps within its purview, its broad scope—the subject of the chapters which follow.

SUMMARY

Of all the managerial functions which executives perform, whether at top, middle, lower, or even worker levels, the act of making a decision is without equal in importance—that is to say, the act of making the *right* decision about the *right* problem or opportunity.

This is not meant to downgrade the ever-needed and classical functions of planning, organizing, staffing, operating, controlling, appraising, and numerous others which must be carried on. A case could very well be made for planning, for example, as the primary function of management. But the approach in this book includes planning and recognizes it as absolutely necessary from beginning to end and then over again in the decision-making process.

This is also not meant to downgrade the necessity of management having to deal on a daily basis with technical skills, human skills, conceptual skills, and even imagination and risk. It does mean that in these, too, decision making is inherent in every interrelationship of men, machines, material, and technology.

If one sees decision making clearly as the heart of executive functioning, then the philosophy of this book really affects all mana-

---

[9] Donald J. Smalter, "The Influence of Department of Defense Practices on Corporate Planning," *Management Technology*, Vol. 4, No. 2, December 1964, pp. 131–32.

TABLE 1.1 Approaches and Steps in Planning and Problem Solving

Major Steps (A)	Managerial Planning (B)	Military Strategy (C)	Operations Research (D)	DOD Weapons Systems (E)	Systems Engineering (F)	Systems Analysis Approach (G)	Phase
1	Plan the plan	—	—	Strategy and Tactics Analysis	—	Decision situation presents itself. Plan the plan.	Problem/Opportunity
2	Study opportunities, threats and prepare other premises	Situation observed	—	—	Environmental Needs Research	A problem, need, situation, or opportunity exists	A — *Formulation Phase*
3	—	—	Problem Identification	Military need identified	Identified to a system	Identified to a system	
4	—	Mission Description	Problem Formulation	Specified Need	Problem Definition	Assumptions Clarified	
5	Set objectives	Situation Objectives	Construct Model	Objectives Defined	Select Objective Criteria	Select an Objective(s)	
6	Identify Alternative Courses of action to achieve objectives	Identify all feasible courses of action	Derive model solution	Concept proposals solicited	System synthesis alternatives	Alternatives determined	
7	Examine alternatives	Analysis of each course	Test model and solution	Conceptual and feasibility studies	Systems Analysis	Measure effectiveness of alternatives	B — *Search Phase*
8	Choose alternatives to follow	Compare	—	Cost/Effectiveness comparison	Comparison	Measure cost of alternatives	
9	Develop detailed plans	Decision on best	Establish controls	Selection of best	Selection	Construct model(s)	
10	Organize to carry out plans	—	Report results	System Package plan defined	Communicating results in prospective	Establish a criterion and apply	C — *Evaluation Phase*
11	Carry out plans	—	—	—	—	Decisions or Conclusions Recommendations Implementation	D — *Interpretation Phase*
12	Review and evaluate results	Action plan assembled	—	Action-planning	Action-planning	Verification of Results or Iteration	E — *Verification Phase*
13	Recycle planning program	—	—	—	—		
14	—					Other Effects, Incommensurables, Spill-overs, Unknowns	

gerial actions. It is an inclusive method, more complete in its requirements and steps for the purpose of really shedding more light on the problem at hand. It recognizes the need for a technique embracing orderliness, rationality, sequential progress, and thoroughness in the search for top-quality, optimum decisions. One of the aims of this book is to recommend professionalism via the decision-making function which can be attained by the SA approach.

Systems Analysis can and does include the steps of other approaches. For example, cost effectiveness is often properly looked upon as the correct approach to problems of limited costs and achieving the most effectiveness for these costs. It is properly used for such purposes. However, cost effectiveness is but one of the techniques contained in the SA approach, which ensures that nothing is overlooked and recognizes tools and techniques for what they are—parts of the total system problem to be solved.

Systems Analysis can either emphasize, delete, or combine whatever steps are essential to the current problem. Its universality is its strength. It does take effort and time and it will continue to do so, but payoffs today are becoming increasingly very personal and societal matters of importance. It behooves us to use the best possible means of ensuring that they are optimum ones.

SUGGESTED FURTHER READING

COVENTRY, W.F., and BURSTINER, IRVING. *Management: A Basic Handbook*. Englewood Cliffs, N.J.: Prentice-Hall, 1977.

HITCH, CHARLES J. *Decision Making for Defense*. Berkeley and Los Angeles: University of California Press, 1966.

OPTNER, STANDFORD L. *Systems Analysis for Business Management*. Englewood Cliffs, N.J.: Prentice-Hall, 1968.

QUADE, E.S., and BOUCHER, W.I., eds. *Systems Analysis and Policy Planning: Applications in Defense*. New York: Elsevier, 1968. Chapter I.

STEINER, GEORGE A., and MINER, JOHN B. *Management Policy and Strategy*. New York: Macmillan, 1977.

2

The Systems Analysis Approach

EARLY MILITARY AND GOVERNMENTAL
BACKGROUND

In describing the Systems Analysis Approach, due credit must be given to the leadership and the example set by the United States Department of Defense. By this I mean the department's acceptance and development of problem solving and opportunity decision making in matters ranging all the way from global strategy to the choice of weapons systems to new military building construction or the cessation or modification of military strategy, weapons systems, or constructions. There are those who see its roots going back to the "Operations Research" of World War II, when quantitative methods and techniques were systematically applied to tactical and strategic problems. Indeed, operations research is with us today and is applied by many experts in appropriate cases.

But, as for the broader-visioned Systems Analysis Approach, 1961, when Defense Secretary Robert S. McNamara brought a new group of visionary analysts to the Pentagon to help approach the massive weapons systems problems, is perhaps the first time that Systems Analysis with its present connotations was introduced.

Not only did the technique help shed light on many complex problems of an organization of, at that time, 4 million people with a budget of over $50 billion, but its unique approach was noted by President Lyndon B. Johnson, and he directed that it become a model for the civilian governmental agencies. Thus, Systems Analysis is in use today in the so-called Planning, Programming, and Budgeting System (PPBS) of federal agencies and departments and is widely used

at state and some local levels of government. It is being used to attack
health and education problems and pollution, among other things. It
is also used in the business and private sectors. Appropriately, it has
been called the "big-think-way to solve problems by observers."[1]

WHAT IS SYSTEMS ANALYSIS?

The real goal of Systems Analysis is to teach decision makers to
think in a special, orderly, and thorough way. It is more than formulas,
figures, and computers; it is the ability to use them creatively and to
rely on both quantitative methods and human judgments about problems and opportunities. It is the identification of the truly key objec-
tive(s) and not merely the contributing, less important one(s). Once
the big objective or problem has been identified, the lesser, contributing ones are not ignored but are recognized for what they are—
suboptimized problems that may contribute to the larger system
problem. They are then used to systematically attack contributing
components in a controlled manner for which suboptimization is
intended. However, the main point is to be concerned with the right
question, the right problem, realizing that there almost always will be
associated problems requiring solution.

Quade and Boucher put it this way: "The idea of an analysis to
provide advice is not new and, in concept, what needs to be done is
simple and rather obvious. One strives to look at an entire problem, as
a whole, in context, and to compare alternative choices in the light of
their possible outcomes."[2] They go on to list three basics as key
ingredients: (1) a systematic investigation of the decision-maker's
objectives and the relevant criteria for deciding the ones that promise
to achieve those objectives are needed; (2) the alternatives must be
clearly defined, fully explored, examined for feasibility and then and
only then compared in terms of effectiveness and cost, taking time and
risk always into account. It is well to look first for *gross* differences in
the alternatives in terms of cost and effectiveness, and specifically for
differences of the sort that have a chance of surviving the quantitative
tests and the various uncertainties and intangibles; and (3) finally,
every attempt must be made to design better alternatives and select
other goals if those previously examined are unsatisfactory.

The approach that makes this possible is to construct and operate

---

[1] "Systems Analysis, What's That?" *Changing Times*, August 1969, p. 1.
[2] E. S. Quade and W. I. Boucher, eds., *Systems Analysis and Policy Planning: Applications in Defense* (New York: Elsevier, 1968), p. 11.

a correct model. A model is one of the essential parts of Systems Analysis. It may well range from a broad, elaborate, computerized one to a simple, specific drawing of a way to off-load cargo or supplies, to a model of only words or to one of symbolic functions. We will explore models more closely later.

Another listing of the critical steps of Systems Analysis is this version which is shorter than the annotated outline at the end of this chapter.

Systems Analysis is a *cycle* of:

1. Defining objectives (problems and opportunities),
2. Designing alternative systems to achieve those objectives,
3. Evaluating the alternatives in terms of effectiveness and costs,
4. Questioning the objectives and all assumptions,
5. Opening up new alternatives,
6. Establishing new objectives,
7. Repeating the cycle until a satisfactory solution is reached; hopefully, the optimum solution, whether it be in keeping with the criteria of effectiveness, cost, or both.

SYSTEMS ANALYSIS AND OPEN AND CLOSED SYSTEMS

Recent interest in so-called open systems and closed systems prompts a brief consideration of the two as they may be affected by Systems Analysis.

A *closed system* is considered to be one in which only the components within the system are assumed to exist. All other influences or variables from *outside* the system are considered to be nonexistent or insignificant. It is a hypothetical, assumptive system, really, as there probably never was a completely closed system. Components within a system are always subjected to outside forces.

It has been of use in the pure sciences, the social sciences, and in organizational decision making to *assume* a closed system and to consider that the environment will remain constant in order to permit manipulation of its variables within the closed system. Statements such as "assuming all other variables are constant, then a change in this or that variable will have such and such an effect." Figure 2.1 is a simple model of a closed system derived from Rice and Bishoprick and modified by me.[3]

[3] George H. Rice, Jr. and Dean W. Bishoprick, *Conceptual Models of Organization* (Englewood Cliffs) N.J.: Prentice-Hall, 1971), p. 177. (Modified to use some flow chart symbols.)

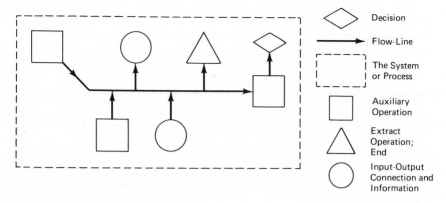

FIGURE 2.1 Model of a Closed System.

Relating the closed system to Systems Analysis is the simplest and perhaps easiest application of the latter to the former. That is, performing a Systems Analysis of a closed system permits one to study the effect of each component on other components within the (artificial) isolation of only the system under analysis. Systems Analysis is designed to go well beyond closed systems, but it can be used in such applications.

The basic elements of a model of an *open system* can be expressed in many ways, but they basically involve inputs (the importation of energy), through-puts (processing and using up some of that energy), and outputs (producing units of some kind). Adding to their "openness" are other characteristics such as the cyclical nature of their events, the internal attributes that add to the continuity, or life, of open systems, a differentiation of functions, and a variety of ways to carry out those functions.

An open system recognizes and permits all interactions of components to take place across the boundaries of the system. It is realistic, much more complex, and therefore more difficult to control or analyze. Components from without and outward thrusting components are characteristic of an open system. It has not been very long since we have finally come to realize in management that businesses or organizations are really open systems. The planning and operation of enterprises no longer can be under the sole control of their designers, or administrators. Today we know that outside forces such as customs, laws, consumer preferences, the elements of nature, personalities, governments, ecological considerations, and competition, to name but a few, influence organizations more and more. Rice and Bishoprick

19

use their same closed system model to indicate some of these influences which make a system an open one in Figure 2.2.[4]

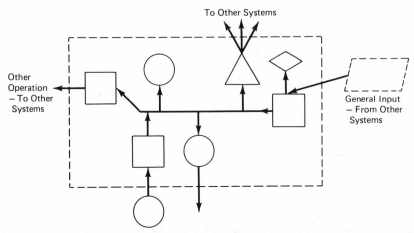

FIGURE 2.2 Model of an Open System.

Systems Analysis is right at home with the task of analyzing open systems, as Systems Analysis *itself* is an open system. It is dedicated to the whole concept of complete exploration, discovery, and application of outside influences and components as well as those which are generated and move outward beyond the particular system to affect and be affected by other systems and subsystems. Thus, it is sufficient for purposes of this brief consideration of open and closed systems to recognize they exist and to emphasize their compatibility with Systems Analysis, which is itself an open system of enquiry.[5]

Figure 2.3 is a simple diagram of the system, showing it as an ongoing process of a set of elements, each of which is functionally and operationally united in the achievement of an objective. It is especially useful to visualize the interrelatedness and constant feedback inherent in a productive system. The analyst's services, purchased or directed by the decision maker, would be concerned with all the processes, even including the formulation of the proper objective.

[4] *Ibid.* (Modified to use some flow chart symbols.)
[5] For a theoretical treatment of the study of closed and open systems and especially the study of social organizations as systems, the reader is referred to a work by Daniel Katz and Robert L. Kahn, *The Social Psychology of Organizations,* which is included as suggested further reading at the end of this chapter.

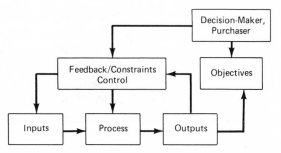

FIGURE 2.3 The Basic Concept of a Productive System.

SOME SYSTEMS ILLUSTRATIONS

Let's take a simple example to illuminate an SA Approach, your automobile. To begin with, how would you describe it as a "system"? There is first a "total" system, an automobile, made up of a combination of interacting and supportive subsystems such as its wheels, steering mechanism, engine, body, electrical system, cooling system, and so on. It is beautiful, useful, and seen by most of us as an "automobile." However, the subsystems may be beautiful to a first-class mechanic rather than to the owner. To an owner it is a system to be used for transportation—a necessity to get people from one place to another. At this point our automobile becomes part of an even larger system, the system of roads and transportation. Immediately, if it has not already been recognized at the first system stage, the problems of efficiency and effectiveness of such a means of transportation become foremost, not only for the individual but for the community as a whole.

Next, after looking at the auto as an efficient and effective means of transportation, an analyst would consider the travelling the owner must do and start to explore various alternatives; in this case the routes, time, comfort, costs, benefits, and safety factors are some examples. Then, the owner would consider all possible other means to accomplish the travel, other systems, such as buses, trains, subways, monorails, taxis, motor bikes, or even walking. If the automobile survives the competition with these systems, the next investigation would be to determine the best route by an analysis of each one in terms of the kinds of variables mentioned above. A route may be shorter but the roads unsatisfactory. A route may be faster but the amount of gas used and tolls too expensive. A route may be longer and the roads good with no tolls, but the mileage and time prove prohibitive for the individual concerned. Time may well be a key variable to the individual in relation to his or her value in terms of hours at work. Each of these in itself is a system of getting there. Each illustrates a point made in chapter 1, especially that the objective and the chosen alternative vary depending on the individual. From the point of view of the executive, his or her time is so valuable that the choice of the more costly but fastest route is appropriate. For the student, the least expensive may be appropriate. For the professor, the most comfortable and reliable may be his criteria.

In sum, the example illustrates the systems approach and its careful selection of alternatives and decisions as part of a larger system, connected to other systems, and, within those systems, the need to isolate the proper objective. If one wishes, the identification of the highway systems of a community as the proper focus might be in order, or the highway systems' effect on the cities, the environment, or the energy problem.

Approaching a problem presents very much the same effect as a stone thrown into a quiet pond. As the ripples move outward and get larger, so too does the problem of isolating the proper system which, when analyzed, will give the right choice for the problem at hand. If one were to keep on expanding the possible systems which are affected, perhaps nothing would get done. The same reasoning applies in reverse. Taking too narrow a systems view will not adequately help the situation. This is the initial step in Systems Analysis which requires sound judgment and practicality. A good analysis must start with its focus on the entire problem and then attempt to work back from what might be identified as one far too large to be attempted with available effort and resources to one which is smaller but will solve the problem adequately if correctly completed. Conversely, if the system involved in a given problem produces an analysis which initially falls short of the real objective, then the scope must be broadened until the *right* system level is reached. All this sounds reasonable and possible but it is difficult to achieve by the average practitioner. So, before we plunge into an outline of the Systems Analysis Approach, which thereafter will be followed and illustrated throughout the book, let's pause to focus on the subject of *who* uses the approach.

WHO USES SYSTEMS ANALYSIS?

Although some mention has been made above of the users, more should be said in order to help new practitioners to understand who uses Systems Analysis. It might be well to eliminate first those who do not use Systems Analysis or any other of the approaches. That includes those who still believe in the strictly intuitive method of decision making despite the complexities and uncertainties in modern organizations and management, to say nothing of the high failure rate of businesses. If such "seat-of-the-pants" individuals would employ *any* systematic process or analysis, it would be better than intuition alone. This is *not* to say that creative, intuitive judgments are to be ignored, as we shall see.

Today, although called by other names, Systems Analysis is practiced by large organizations having to cope with the problems of scarce resources and strong competition. The author recently reviewed such an analysis carried out by the marketing executives who were attempting to penetrate the "one-stop" home construction industry chain of stores which has become popular with builders or do-it-yourselfers. The analysis was correct in its objective, in its alternatives, and in the decision to go ahead. The corporation has already realized a 20 percent increase in business at this writing. But the increase did *not* come without cost and effort. It will take a year or more to recoup the resources put into the decision and its implementation, but the payback should be all that is expected.

Systems Analysis has become the method not only for market managers, but for scientists, engineers, production managers, planners, finance directors, and chief executive officers of all kinds. It ranks with automation, management science, computers, nuclear power, and similar wonders of our age simply because it helps solve problems and often *uses* the other "wonders" to solve other problems.

It is a personal as well as a big organizational technique. The author found it useful to solve the very problem described above, the problem of the optimum means of transportation to meet his objectives. Cooperative groups of individuals have used it to determine the optimum way to obtain food of their liking, for instance health food co-ops. It is applicable to a college graduate who attempts to come to grips with his or her real career objective at that point in life and to determine in a deliberate fashion the alternatives and costs of getting there. For example, a recent graduate was faced with the problem of whether to continue making sacrifices in order to obtain his master's degree in a year, or to take a relatively attractive job and then spend six to eight years getting the degree in an extension program. His reasoning, for *his* objectives, was to make the sacrifice and then be educationally a step ahead of his baccalaureate competitors. The decision paid off. The individual is now four to five years ahead of his colleagues in the banking business in terms of promotion and compensation. But be assured the decision was one that carried him through the whole system of analyzing objectives, costs, alternatives, and implementation problems (to say nothing of family problems).

SYSTEMS ANALYSIS AND INDIVIDUAL
AND GROUP DECISION MAKING

Before leaving the matter of who uses Systems Analysis, or any systematic approach, a few words on the subject of individual versus group or committee decision making are necessary. There is no doubt that, as problems increase in complexity, the group method is better. Moreover, there is no doubt that for either an individual or group, an analytical procedure of any kind is better. In a minor decision or one in which a single individual has all the necessary skills to make an analysis, a group approach may be wasteful. No one needs a group approach, for example, to analyze his personal transportation problem, to discover the alternative ways to go to work, and to select the one way which best fits his objectives.

However, when a problem involves management scientists, planners, statisticians, behavioral scientists, administrators, historians, and other distinct disciplines, no one individual can be expected to provide all the inputs and process them. Systems Analysis used in problems at the higher levels invariably requires a team made up of people with several skills and varied experience. Today, we know enough about the benefits and pitfalls of group decisionmaking to take advantage of the former and avoid the latter. This handbook cannot include the wealth of information about groups which has become available in recent years. Perhaps the most important ingredient for group decision-making success is the individual in charge. A strong individual with a broad background who displays consistent behavior, who avoids any imbalance taking place in the process, who can resolve conflicts without destroying things of value, who can discern imperfections, and who can see and direct the total problem better than any of the specialists involved, is the best single guarantee of success.

In any decision-making process, there are bound to be some *administrative constraints*. Problems to be solved and solutions implemented require people. Trained, capable, task-oriented people are essential. But, as in most all efforts, it is not always possible to get the top-flight team of experts one may desire. Indeed, there are many who believe this constraint is the greatest limitation in carrying out good Systems Analysis. This has been true in federal government; hence, one can see that it is even more of a constraint in organizations not having the vast manpower resources and expertise the federal government can afford.

As for a hierarchy of decision makers, it seems automatically to suggest *itself* as a problem or opportunity arises. At the top levels of management, the decisions are less numerous but important and far-reaching in their effects. Although the greatest amount of decision making is done at lower levels, the moment it results in policy decisions with significant effects, it is passed upwards.

The decision maker himself, as contrasted with the analysis group leader described earlier, is obviously important in the decision as to whether a group or an individual approach will be used or at what level the problem will be located for resolution. It is here that those who would help should look to the individual's temperament, biases, values, outlook on life, and his preferences for intuitive or systematic analysis, all of which will put their mark on the total effort. Of all the arguments for a group, task force, or committee approach, perhaps the insurance factor of *not* having the decision be the result of one man's character and ability is the best case for a group approach, despite the arguments against group action. Analysis can be as valuable a technique to someone facing his or her own personal challenge in a competitive world as it is to a corporate planning group.

THE POPULARITY AND EFFECTIVENESS OF SYSTEMS ANALYSIS

As stated earlier, the government and the military found its Systems Analysis roots in the early World War II era when radar was developing. The vast technical possibilities of radar were unfolding as a group of foresighted scientists saw the operational uses of turning the data produced into probabilities and the probabilities into better ways to save precious cargoes. The information developed by radar was broadened to include application to and evaluation of allied bombing raids and antisubmarine warfare. With the outpouring of techniques and tools to provide more and better quantitative data, analysts, who had taken the name Operations Researchers (OR) became adept at systematically and objectively processing it through the steps of analysis to an extent that included entire systems of warfare. It was an inevitable step to including the remainder of the modern Systems Analysis Approach, the uses for which are almost limitless. They seemed only constrained by time, for the most part. The federal government then espoused the technique and made it mandatory, calling it the Planning, Programming and Budgeting System (PPBS), with many states and some local governments soon following suit.

Today, no industry, large or small, would act without performing an analytic approach. *Changing Times* gives an example of the case of the International Business Machines Corporation and the air freight operation at Heathrow Airport. It took six days, on the average, to unload a package, process it, and deliver it to the consignee. A businessman could stand at the airport and actually see his package come off the plane. But then it would disappear into the maw of the establishment. Neither he nor the airport manager could determine where it was or how soon to expect delivery.

> Systems Analysis determined that the problem was not one of handling so much as knowing what was going on. Eventually, each sub-system was identified, captured, and confined to its own "black box." When the new system became operational, at each stage of processing, unloading, conveying, stamping at customs, conveying to storage, etc., the person in charge had a small computer input device. By a system of simple punching the information after the actions—the result is that every morning the manager can ask the computer anything he wants to know about the total operation or a single package. The problem of *where* and *how long* regarding packages was solved.[6]

Today, the Heathrow Airport routine has been reduced to two days and the report predicts it will soon be one day. In short, the problems of the system of total package handling were analyzed and solved. The system is now in use in many busy airports. It was another example of a good Systems Analysis Approach by an electronics and computer industry.

Locally, as this is being written, another airport problem may serve as a useful example. Engineers have determined that adding two thousand feet to a local runway would permit a through-put of twenty more flights a day and the through-put would be possible by heavier, multiengined aircraft. The nearest cities would welcome this as a service and potential for business. The nearby residents would not. A systems analyst would consider not only the additional through-put and business but the broader problems involved. In addition to more revenue he would consider the real costs of the benefit, such as the noise pollution, air pollution, discomfort, hazards, depressed real estate values, homes destroyed, historic landmarks lost, feeder roads needed

[6] "Systems Analysis, What's That?" *Changing Times*, pp. 4–5.

to service the airport, and auto and truck congestion. A good analyst would look into alternatives, ranging from the buildup or use of neighboring airports not located so close to the population centers, the possible need for new and faster connecting roads, or even a brand new airport sufficiently far away but not so far as to be of little use. He would look into what other side effects or trade-offs are possible, and he would attempt to cost out these variables as well as determine their effectiveness measured against the objective of effectiveness, of economy, of human considerations, or even of ecological considerations. Costs and effectiveness, quantified where possible, would be two major considerations, but by no means the only ones in Systems Analysis. Meanwhile, the controversy between the "through-putters" versus the potentially disturbed homeowners captures the limelight of the whole controversy and, as in so many instances, nothing has been done and when it will it may involve lose-lose results which make no one happy. How many times has the reader come across similar community problems which seem to produce only a controversial two-sided debate in which neither party has really attempted to understand the other. There is a ray of hope, however. Recent news of ecologists and coal producers cooperating in pursuing a solution to a nationwide problem is most encouraging. They have met not to debate, not as antagonists, but to reach some accord. The next step is to employ true analysis.

Finally, the leadership of the federal government and particularly the Department of Defense has led to massive departments such as the Post Office and Health, Education, and Welfare putting analysis to use. Even problems of mental retardation, air and water pollution, welfare, and other subsystems of the total system of human welfare and health control are now put to penetrating analysis.

There have been bonuses or spin-offs from its use in government, also. For many federal programs it was the first time consideration had to be given to programs, not as *ends* in themselves but as a *means* of attaining longer-term, greater-size objectives. Still another bonus has been the total costing of a solution, or weapons system or program or project, something which forces the consideration of the cost and effectiveness of the solution from its very beginning to its very end—even to the point of requiring that programs or projects be resubmitted under zero-based budgeting each year. It really can be used by anyone, any organization, any government, any agency trying to find a logical answer to problems which are the result of chaos, and trial and error in the past. Even in an era of increasing lose-lose situations, it can at least help arrive at the least-loss answer.

AN OUTLINE OF THE SYSTEMS ANALYSIS APPROACH

INTRODUCTION

It is now time to develop a working outline of the Systems Analysis Approach for use in the chapters that follow and to illustrate its application to a case study. In teaching the subject, the author has found it useful to plunge first into an outline which gives the reader a feel for the approach as a whole. As a matter of fact, it one were to put more flesh on the bony framework that follows, a fairly good grasp of the approach, its potential and use, is quite possible. Thus, the annotated outline with its brief remarks will be offered now and referred to during our inquiry. Such a return to the framework outline becomes a simple, clarifying exposition to the necessary jargon as well as to the phases and the steps to be followed.

Phase I
Formulation

A. *System*—an entity which is an assembly of interrelated components which together serve a common purpose or objective.

1. Understanding the *system* is the whole foundation for Systems Analysis and is the basis for *models*.
2. The focus of decision making should be on *productive systems*.
3. Productive systems are those considered in terms of *input–process–output* relationships.
4. *Feedback* and *control* are essential to the effective performance of a system.
5. Effective performance in the operation of a system toward a *productive objective* is *effective management*.

B. *Decision Situation*—a condition that presents a decision maker with the opportunity to decide among alternative courses of action.

1. A *decision situation* may be the result of the recognition of an existing *problem*, or it may be the result of the desire to take advantage of an unforeseen *opportunity*. Correct diagnosis of the system and the key decision situation is mandatory at this point.
2. For a decision situation to exist, a decision maker with

the *authority* to act must be *cognizant* of the problem or opportunity.

C. *Objective (or Problem)*—a definitive statement of what the *decision maker* wishes to achieve with the system being analyzed. Again, this involves correct diagnosis based on the first two steps.

   1. An analyst should always *question* the objective, i.e., be sure that both the decision maker and he are studying the *right* problem.
   2. The development of an objective may in itself involve an *iterative process*.
   3. The stated objective must be *consistent* with higher level objectives, i.e., with the objectives of higher level systems.
   4. In reality, all objectives are suboptimizations of higher level objectives.
   5. A good objective will suggest its own appropriate *measure of effectiveness* (MOE).

D. *Assumptions*—an agreed-upon position, worth, or effect of a *variable* which may be difficult to quantify or relate subjectively. Assumptions are used to treat *uncertainty* in problem solving.

   1. Assumptions can also be used to *limit* the *scope* of the problem, objective, or alternatives.
   2. They must be *explicitly stated* throughout the analysis.

Phase II
   Search

A. *Alternatives*—the means of *achieving* the *objective*.

   1. They need not be *obvious* substitutes for one another, i.e., they may be entirely different.
   2. They may be *given* to an analyst to employ in an analysis, or may be *developed* or *discovered* by the analyst.
   3. They are likely to be discovered by *iteration*, i.e., *repeating again* the search for other means of achieving the objective.

B. *Measures of Costs* (MOCs)—measures of the benefits foregone or the opportunities lost for each of the alternatives.

   1. They are the *consequences* of decisions.

2. Some ways of *measuring* costs:

   a. By the *resources required.*
      Raw materials—100,000 lbs. of steel; 10 acres, etc.
      Manpower—20,000 man-hours; kind of skill, etc.
      Facilities—5,000 square feet of production space, etc.
   b. By determining *alternative* uses (opportunities lost) of resources.
      The cost of an aircraft carrier is two-hundred grammar schools.
      The cost of building a new thruway may be the cost of building a mass transit system.
   c. By estimates of the *values* of the alternative uses of resources. This is also a highly *judgmental* estimate.
      Value of twenty grammar schools in terms of educational benefits lost to society by reason of selecting the aircraft carrier alternative.
   d. By estimating the *actual dollar value* required by each alternative.
      The cost of the aircraft carrier is $1,100,000,000.
      The cost of twenty schools is $1,200,000,000.
      Beware of accepting any dollar value as a *true* reflection of the cost of each alternative.

3. Some categories and characteristics of costs.

   a. Dollar expenditures:
      One must be careful to include only those dollar *expenditures* which are *altered* by the decision at hand and exclude all expenditures that would have been incurred *regardless* of the decision made.
   b. Other costs that can be evaluated in dollars:
      This category includes the consumption or utilization of many resources which might *not immediately* or directly affect dollar expenditures but which can be conveniently evaluated in dollars.
      Dollar valuation should reflect *replacement cost* not *historical cost.*
      Manpower requirements, office space, materials required, etc., may fall in this category.
      Costs allocated should reflect the *best* or *most likely alternative* use of these resources.
   c. Other costs that can be *quantified:*

Lives lost; persons injured or wounded, time lost, etc.
d. Other, *nonquantifiable* costs:
Loss of goodwill, morale, credibility, public confidence, or support, etc.
These always should at least be cited by the analyst. They must not be ignored.

4. In *measuring costs* the real objective is to measure the probable *resource drain* on the economy that would result by selection of each alternative.

   a. In the *short run,* e.g., as in the case of a business which wants to take advantage of a tactical situation in a competitive market, the critical element may be the *availability of resources.*
   b. In the *long run,* simply for ease of analysis and decision, it is frequently necessary to use *dollars* as a convenient common denominator.

5. *Relevant costs* lie in the future, not in the past.

   a. Past costs are *sunk costs* and are not meaningful.
   b. *Relevant costs* are those costs that depend upon the *choice* made.

6. *Discounting* must be taken into consideration.

   a. Time is valuable.
   b. *Future* dollars must be discounted, for they are worth *less* than *current* dollars.
   c. A proper discount rate depends on the alternative uses of the money.

C. *Measure of Effectiveness*—a measurement of the *degree* to which each of the alternatives *satisfies* the objective.

1. Effectiveness must be defined in some term(s) that is(are) measurable.
2. There may be a requirement for more than one measure of effectiveness (MOE).
3. An analyst may have to rely on the decision maker to *establish* the MOE; i.e., the professional expertise of the decision maker can help here.
4. Frequently, an MOE will only be *approximate.*
5. There is *no one best way* to arrive at an MOE. Here

again the process is iterative and depends on the good judgment of both decision makers and analysts.

D. *Models*—abstractions of the real world which permit the comparison of the *cost and effectiveness* of each alternative.

1. *Cost comparisons* have been covered above.
   They usually will depend on the method used in the measuring of cost. Most frequent MOC is in dollars. Cost comparisons may require more than one MOC.

2. *Effectiveness comparisons* have been covered above.
   The model permits using both the MOC and the MOE to measure the degree that each satisfies the objective, i.e., so much effectiveness for so many dollars or vice versa. It really provides a measurement vehicle to reveal the degrees of satisfaction—that satisfaction or objective determined in the first place.

Phase III
   Evaluation

A. *Criterion*—this relates the MOE to the MOC by stating a *decision rule* for selecting among alternatives whose *costs and effectiveness* have been determined, usually with the help of a model.

1. Frequently, like costs and effectiveness, it too is only proximate.

2. Whatever criterion is chosen which must be met, it should be related to and be consistent with *higher level* criteria.

3. Examples of some *frequently used* criteria:

   a. *Maximize effectiveness* for a given cost.
      If an effectiveness model is used, then *costs* are *fixed* for one iteration. This is also known as the fixed budget/cost approach.

   b. *Minimize cost* for a given level of effectiveness.
      If a cost model is used, then effectiveness is usually constant for one iteration. Also known as the fixed effectiveness approach.

   c. *Maximum gains-minus costs.*
      An acceptable approach only if gains and costs can be measured in the same units. This approach assumes that there are no constraints on either cost or

effectiveness. (An extremely rare situation. The author knows of only two weapons systems which enjoyed such a status—the Manhattan Project, or development of the atomic bomb, and the Polaris Missile Program.)

d. *Minimax.*

This means *minimizing* the worst possible outcome. It is a most conservative decision rule and most likely to be inappropriate.

e. *Maximizing the ratio* of effectiveness to cost.

This approach assumes no constraints and may tend to drive one to a low-cost solution which may not be the best one.

f. *The maximin criterion.*

Consider for each available strategy or set of alternatives only the worst possible outcomes; then choose that alternative with the *best* of these *worst* outcomes. That is, maximize the minimum outcome. This implies that the world is against the decision maker and no matter which alternative he selects, he believes he will be dealt the worst possible outcome. This would appear to a reasonable person to be too cautious a stance under most situations.

g. *The maximax criterion.*

This is for the incurable optimist who does not consider losses. This sanguine criterion is that for each available alternative, consider only the best possible outcome; then choose that alternative with the best of the best outcomes. That is, maximize the maximum outcome. Most decision makers would consider this too audacious.

h. *The principle of indifference.*

This calls for reasoning that if there are no possible outcomes and a decision maker has no prior knowledge or experience, then perhaps he should assign *equal* probability to each. Complete ignorance in this method could lead to paradoxical choices.

i. *The optimism index.*

If maximin and maximax are extreme cases, some argue that taking some weighted average of the best and worst to come up with an index of optimism would be a good compromise. This gets us into the

study of not only this theory but others concerning probability which cannot be treated in this handbook.
j. *Maximizing* the *expected value.*
This is useful in situations of uncertainty where it is possible to assign some value of worth to each possible outcome and where the probability of each outcome is known.

4. The danger of *overspecification* of the *criterion.*

a. It is impossible to *maximize* effectiveness at *minimum* cost or to achieve a *given* level of effectiveness at a *given* cost, thus avoiding the specification of both cost and effectiveness. This approach would be *maximin,* or enjoying *both maximum* effectiveness at *minimum* cost—a feat I have yet to be shown.

Phase IV
Interpretation

A. *The Decision*—the act of making a choice from among the alternatives that satisfies the objective of the decison maker.

1. Ideally, decisions are made from an array of "same level" effectiveness results and the least cost one selected. Usually, however, there are maximum and minimum standards for both cost and effectiveness, and incremental analysis techniques have been used to reduce the scope of the analysis and the range of choice.
2. After utilizing these aids in developing *quantitative* measures of effectiveness, the *qualitative* factors or subjective considerations often become the deciding factor.
3. Decisions are rarely irrevocable except in extreme circumstances. Indeed, in Systems Analysis, they usually lead to another round of iteration to ensure their correctness or to come up with a different decision.
4. Decision making should be the final province of the authority who set forth the objective. It is here that the analyst, having done all he can and clarified all alternatives, must leave the final choice to that authority.

B. *Recommendation*—the act of decision may well be in the form of a recommendation to a higher authority.

1. The *decision maker* may *not* be the one who must

implement the decision. It may hinge on the approval of corporate or political bodies. Hence, the place for recommendation, prior to approach and implementation.

It is not wrong for an *analyst,* moreover, to *offer* his *recommendation* if requested by the decision maker.

2. *Recommendations* should be *backed up* by a frank presentation of the major assumptions, uncertainties, and sensitive variables that went into the analysis. The act of recommendation should not be a "sales job" but a step wherein explicitness and honesty are the keynotes.

C. *Implementation*—although this is contained in the interpretation phase, it is so important that it ranks with the decision phase and is one of the most difficult tasks of total analysis.

1. *Implementation* means *commitment.* Commitment means the expenditure of resources. Implementation puts the decision to the acid test—Was it *correct* or *not?*

2. Implementation can and usually does involve a whole new set of *individuals*—planners, operators, and controllers who have the monumental job of giving life to what until then has been a model.

Implementation often is a *one-shot deal;* that is, the consequences being what they are, full implementation may not be pursued until the first one is verified by its results.

Implementation can be one of the most exasperating steps, especially if the implementors are determined to thwart the decision being carried out. Politics, personalities, attitudes, selfishness, ambitions, individual and group values or beliefs—all these and many others come into play. Implementation is a whole new ball game deserving of much more study than it has received in the past.

Phase V

Verification

A. *Verification of Results*—the result of evaluating the initial implementation. It is exactly what it implies—a "go" or "no go" decision.

1. Verification may well bring out significant omissions or several other unforeseen relationships and effects such as *incommensurables, unmeasurables, spillovers,* and *un-*

knowns. Hopefully, these had been found and treated at least subjectively in the analysis and fully illuminated for the decision maker.

Incommensurables refer to those aspects of the system which cannot be treated in common terms.

Unmeasurables are those aspects that defy any kind of meaningful measurement.

Spillovers are the *unintended benefits* or *bad effects* which result from the selection of an alternative.

Unknowns refer to those elements of the problem which are not and cannot be known or predicted with any degree of certainty.

2. The best advice or rule in handling all factors or results of the verification process, especially those described above, is *do not ignore them.*

SUMMARY

With its roots in good scientific analytical reasoning and armed with the latest available data, the Systems Analysis Approach had a beginning in World War II as operations research. It has since out-reached the OR approach and today can be used to go beyond purely quantitative problems, a situation which rarely obtains. It is now in use under the same name or through a similar approach by the federal government, state government, business and industry, (large and small), local governments and agencies, and can even be applied on a much more personal level, if time and the importance of the problem dictate.

It has moreover, yielded some important spin-off benefits in requiring proper planning for true objectives, the search for real alternatives, self-examination, and above all, cost awareness that is sorely needed in today's complex society of ever-scarce resources and never-scarce needs.

Its basic phases of defining the system within which the problem lies, the formulation phase, the search phase, the evaluation, and interpretation phases, and verification through decision implementation, each with its several creative, diagnostic, and sensible steps, are the building blocks with which we will next be concerned.

We will now proceed in detail with these phases and steps, applying them to the case study.

SUGGESTED FURTHER READING

BIERMAN, H., JR. et al. *Quantitative Analysis for Business Decisions.* 4th ed. Homewood, Ill.: Richard D. Irwin, 1973.

CLELAND, DAVID E., and KING, W.R. *Management: A Systems Approach.* New York: McGraw-Hill, 1973.

HARRISON, E.F. *The Managerial Decision-Making Process.* Boston: Houghton Mifflin, 1975.

HITCH, CHARLES J., and McKEAN, ROLAND N. *Elements of Defense Economics.* Washington, D.C.: Industrial College of the Armed Forces, 1969. Chapter 1.

KATZ, DANIEL, and KAHN, ROBERT L. *The Social Psychology of Organizations.* New York: John Wiley & Sons, 1966.

QUADE, E.S., and BOUCHER, W.I. *Systems Analysis and Policy Planning: Applications in Defense.* New York: Elsevier, 1968. Chapter I.

RAIA, A.P. *Managing by Objectives.* Glenview, Ill.: Scott Foresman, 1974.

RICE, GEORGE H., JR., and BISHOPRICK, DEAN W. *Conceptual Models of Organization.* Englewood Cliffs, N.J.: Prentice-Hall, 1971.

3

The Formulation Phase

UNCERTAINTIES AND SYSTEMS ANALYSIS

Decision makers face uncertainty far more than certainty in attempting to solve their problems or in taking advantage of opportunities simply because more uncertainties exist in the world or organization and management than do certainties.

In management, the exercise becomes one of probability judging and risk taking at all levels. The higher the level, the greater the uncertainties, the risks, and the consequences. But managers, like rational people, do not simply give up in the face of uncertainties and retreat into a state of inaction.

It is in the conceptual phase of formulation that the decision maker, very much like a medical doctor, is faced head-on with the problems of diagnosing the system involved, the cause of the problem, the objective which, if attained, will cure it, and the uncertainties and assumptions which must be dealt with to proceed with a cure. It is in this formulation phase that the crucial step of *localizing* and *limiting* the problem is essential to coping with it. Some practitioners aptly call this the critical step of *diagnosing* the problem. These are really difficult jobs, the jobs of isolating the real issue, of seeing it in total context with other problems, of facing up to its solvability, of being capable of solution in time and within available resources. To literally get a feel of all the variables operating within and upon the problem is no mean accomplishment. Difficult, yes, but resolvable. If the variables were not resolvable, we would not be where we are today.

Uncertainties enter the picture again and again from the point of isolating the system and the objectives within it, all the way through quantitative and qualitative judgments, and not ending until the point of decision. If the uncertainties are recognized and admitted, the inquiry can get off to a proper start. Using a systematic process and encompassing full use of analytic techniques is the best way to help reduce uncertainties to an acceptable point. The primary purpose of Systems Analysis is to advise a decision maker in determining the best possible alternatives to the correct question, in developing good alternatives, in sharpening his intuition and adding to his basis for judgment, and then in exposing and exploring uncertainties. The analyst must not only recognize and reveal the uncertainties each step of the way but also do the job of reducing them to some manageable and acceptable size. The reason that the subject of uncertainties has been used to introduce this phase is to impress on the practitioner that they are common to every step in every phase of Systems Analysis or any other analytical process and should not be avoided or overlooked. They have been dealt with successfully in past decisions and can be in the future.

THE SYSTEM AND SUBSYSTEMS

Recognition of a system and subsystem of all organized effort is the first step in the formulation phase once the presence of uncertainties has been accepted as a fact of life and progress. The first question to be asked is whether something with which we are concerned *is* a system, subsystem, or subsystems. As was pointed out earlier, *all* systems are really subsystems of something larger. The object of properly locating an inquiry is to direct it toward the subsystem that is the most sensible, most manageable, and most capable of examination; it should be the least complex to get the job done—and yet be the right one. Let us just focus on the *manageable* one, the one capable of being examined. Is the problem, objective, or question we are attempting to resolve within our *competence* to handle? If the answer is yes, then the next question arises. Will the solution really contribute to the resolution of the major problem or objective? If the answer is also yes, then there is hope that the solution process will yield meaningful, applicable decision situations and alternatives from which to choose.

It is something like delegation in management. Delegation is the fine art of getting the job done at the optimum level, one which is more often than not at a much lower level than imagined. Good delegation is exemplified when decision making is thrust *downward*

to the lowest level of individual *competence* that includes willingness
as well. Without proper delegation, precious time is wasted by the top
decision maker, to say nothing of the adverse effects upon those
subordinates who are quite competent to make lower level decisions.
Similarly, it is important to strive for the optimum level in the search
for a system which will adequately satisfy the level of inquiry into the
main problem.

SYSTEMS AND THE CASE STUDY

Now to use our case study as a simple but provocative illustration
of the first of five main phases of the Systems Analysis Approach.
Addendum I to this handbook is a scenario of a situation which is both
a problem and an opportunity for a typical city administration. "The
Downtown Parking Authority Case" is perhaps one of the best of many
cases that might have been chosen to illustrate the analytical approach.

At this point it is suggested that the reader turn to the case,
first read it through, and then reread it with the purpose in mind of
considering only the possible different and related systems involved
in it. Do not read the suggested solution at this time. It will be
covered step by step as we proceed.

After carefully reading the case and recalling the information
regarding systems thus far in the handbook, it should become apparent
to you that several systems and subsystems are involved. The problem/
opportunity of a new city-owned parking facility is a subsystem of a
larger system, namely, the proper use of an available downtown area
of a large metropolis. In turn, the latter is but a subsystem of a larger
system, e.g., the proper use of the whole downtown development of a
city, of its suburbs, and even of its economic, social, and cultural way
of life. Even these systems can be visualized as subsystems within a
greater system of regional size with its economic, social, cultural,
political, and ecological interrelationships. There are others, if we
were to enlarge our scope.

If we move toward the other end of the spectrum of systems, the
subsystems grow narrower in scope. For example, there are the
subsystems involved in the problem of whether to construct and
operate a city-owned system at the site or to have one privately owned
and operated. Or, to move even farther in the narrower direction, is
the subsystem to be involved in demolishing the theatre for no other
purpose than to remove a danger or to speculate in future land values?
Or, is it to be concerned only with the taxation system or a system of
city parks?

In short, the seemingly single-purpose system of a parking facility as initially proposed overlaps and interrelates with other systems in both directions, outward or inward. If the parking facility system is regarded correctly as a subsystem or larger system as compared to other components and their interrelationships, it takes its rightful place as one system to be considered as long as we are aware of the others. Once an awareness of the several systems has been gained, the optimum choice becomes one which is most in keeping with the objective (already becoming evident as the systems are recognized) and is the proper focus for the next related steps.

At this point there is neither the need nor the capability for the city to attempt to resolve the problems of the entire region, the area, or the total city problem itself, especially given this particular case. Also, at the other extreme, the subsystems of private versus public ownership of the facility, taxation, park, and so forth, are included in the system involved in determining the proper or best use of the Elm Street site. The optimum system appears to fall somewhere between that of solely a parking facility and the best use of all downtown areas. Hence, it becomes more workable to consider the system and objective to be the best use of the Elm Street site. However, Dick Stockton has been given a narrower objective and its analysis should be the springboard to move higher on the systems spectrum or options. This first look at most of the systems involved will prove to be time well spent as our next step focuses more on objectives in the decision process. For now, let's start with the three objectives given to Dick Stockton by the city fathers and let's see what latitude they permit in considering the systems involved.

1. Using the information presented, should the city of Oakton construct the proposed garage?
2. What rates should be charged?
3. What additional information, if any, should be obtained before making a final decision?

Looking at the first charge, Dick's initial system to keep in mind has already been prescribed—a system of construction and operating (albeit through a contractor) a parking facility. The construction part involves one system and related objectives, namely demolition and construction of a particular kind of structure. The objective is clear, a parking facility, even though couched in the words, "should the city of Oakton construct the proposed garage?"

The second charge opens up the objective of making a profit or at least of breaking even and thus involves a business system. The third objective is the one which allows Dick to consider several other relevant systems and their objectives. It allows for more than one decision situation. It allows him to move "upward and outward" or "downward and inward" in his investigations if time and resources are available. Indeed, in Dick's final report, the closing observations are about a host of other and related objectives, all of them greater in depth and scope than only the parking facility and many of them highly judgmental wherein the worth to the city is of main concern.

When it comes to assembling all conceivable interrelated components which comprise the system of best using the city property, Systems Analysis lends more insight into the *totality* of the problem because it insists upon first deliberately thinking in *systems terms,* and then identifying the *decision situation* that exists at the heart of the system, and then, the *objectives* for which to strive. In our case, it has raised the sights of the opportunity to one of bettering Oakton's economy and way of life should we so desire to broaden the scope of the inquiry.

SOME SYSTEMS CHARACTERISTICS APPLIED TO THE CASE

Next, a brief development of the essentials of a system and their applicability to the case is in order.

1. A system should have several components or subsystem elements.

The case is an excellent example of the first generalization about a system. The system of Oakton's typical way of life in modern times, namely, that of expanding the suburbs while trying to attract business to the city and to recapture the beauty of the inner city—is one almost every metropolis attempts. Suburbia is needed for homes and "escape," the inner city for businesses, shoppers, and those who cannot move to the suburbs. Without suburbia providing it with workers and shoppers, the city would fall into decay. Hence, to remain alive it must be made accessible and attractive. Subsystems or subcomponents are also evident. For example, there is the vital system of *transportation* to emphasize and maintain. In this case study there are two, the subway and the *real* mass transit system of America, the automobile! There is the subsystem involved in meeting the parking requirements for the suburbanites and other business people. There is the dilemma, too, of providing for parking while possibly harming the subway system.

2. In a system, there should be a relationship between the component elements.

Such a relationship is present in our case. There are relationships between the city's entire transportation facilities system involving the subway, automobiles, and possibly buses and taxicabs, and the business system of the city.

3. A system transcends any of its parts.

This is self-evident in our case.

4. Systems are usually complex.

The complexities already mentioned could be expanded to include other systems affected by the parking facility and its clientele. Added complexities might include air and noise pollution systems, ecological systems, beauty, human safety and welfare systems, maintenance and repair systems, and of course the political system.

5. A system has a singleness of purpose which permits and dominates all of its parts.

The singleness of purpose, a municipally built and leased garage, is evident from the case. Whether it *remains* the single purpose is another matter. As it stands, the purpose will inevitably carry the investigation into problems of funding, demolition, building, ownership, operation by others and renting by others (a landlord system), a system of tariffs, and so on.

6. If it is a system, does it offer alternatives?

Obviously, the possibility of pursuing a number of objectives within a number of systems exists in our case.

7. A system should assist in the accomplishment of a given objective.

Again, the answer here is in the affirmative, as the parking system will contribute to the economic welfare of the city. However, we know now that there are other systems, other decision situations, other objectives and choices that may be just as important.

8. Is the system capable of being understood?

Yes, it is, especially at its point of introduction to our analysis. Those in charge understand the particular system they wish to have analyzed. As yet, however, the broad range of other quantitative and qualitative factors is not well known.

9. *Is the system a productive one?*

Yes, for this point. The decision makers will receive a calculation of the necessary inputs, processes, and outputs. Chapter 4 is almost entirely devoted to the productive (cost/benefit) aspects in detail.[1]

It is fairly safe to say, then, that our case and our systems inherent in the case fit the above definitive statements of a system. They are complex, related components, functioning together, and they fulfill a singular productive purpose (of our choice).

SYSTEMS—SOME FINAL CAVEATS

Before moving from system considerations to the decision situation, a final caveat is in order. When we contemplate the time and effort which can be (and unfortunately is) expended in solving the wrong problem, the formulation phase initial step of determining which is the *proper* system to be studied is a very important one.

Perhaps an appropriate illustration from the author's war years will serve to highlight the need to pursue the *right* objective, the *right* problem. During the Vietnam War, the breakdown of heavy duty military trucks was a problem to the United States forces. Specifically, the clutches and transmissions were failing on otherwise satisfactory equipment, built to rigorous specifications. Those in charge of repairs believed that the problem was due to either the quality of the workmanship or more likely, the peculiar nature of the Vietnamese terrain and the unusual demands being placed upon the equipment. As a result, efforts were directed toward improving the overhaul and repair record at the repair center. One ambitious goal after another was set and achieved to "get those trucks back on the line." It occurred to someone that the real cause might be something else and that we were treating the symptoms rather than the cause. To be brief, the inquiry led to the discovery that most of the vehicles were driven by Vietnamese civilian drivers, whose average height was about a foot less than that of Americans. As a consequence, the civilian drivers could only depress the clutch pedal part way and had to "ride the clutch" in going through multiple gears or speeds. We all know that such a practice, if done around the clock, can cause trouble with the

---

[1] Most of the definitions about what constitutes a true "system" have been adapted to our case from Robert E. Schmaltz, "Systems Evaluation," *A Compendium of Systems Analysis and Operations Research Methodology*, Vol. 1 (Washington, D.C.: U.S. Air Force, Asst. Chief of Staff, Studies and Analysis, 15 July 1968), p. 1.

clutch and transmission. The solution—attach a block of wood to the clutch pedal to permit the driver with short legs to depress it to the floor as required. It worked. The real problem was solved, not the symptom.

At its best, the formulation phase and its emphasis on isolation of the pertinent system will prove to be subjective in several respects. It is for this reason that an analyst should not blindly accept the decision-maker's original idea of the system and objective to explore. Not to question the objective is an injustice to the decision maker as well as to the analyst. Perhaps Dick Stockton should have made this clear before proceeding with the given objectives. However, his solution does reveal his concern with other ramifications, as does his list of alternatives in building the parking facility.

Very much akin to a municipally owned garage is this illustration of systems and objectives. Suppose a state were in the process of determining the need for five or six new, state-owned vehicle garages and repair facilities. Is the problem merely one of setting up a state-owned system or is it one of the *strategic* location of that system? Land, building, and equipment costs are going to be pretty much the same (land may vary more), but isn't the overriding problem selecting the location so that the state will do the most efficient job where needed? Or is the system to explore one of a "mix" of state-owned garages to be operated with those already in place and operational, i.e., one of supporting each other? Or is a system of joint operations with commercially owned garages a better one to investigate? Or is it best to leave the system entirely in the hands of contractors and existing commercial garages? Our city-owned system of a parking facility is much the same mix of systems.

To summarize, systems are very closely tied to decision situations. To change the system goal or focus is to change the decision situation and obviously the objectives. Systems, decision situations, and objectives are very flexible and can be enlarged or limited in scope. Their direction may also be changed. The skills and judgments involved in carrying out the early steps of the formulation phase will affect the remainder of the problem solution or the opportunity involved. So, with this in mind, it is time to examine the decision situation. In our case, an obvious decision situation exists; as a matter of fact, more than one exists. But dealing openly with the decision situation and clarifying its relationships to that step which precedes it and follows it, and the innumerable times it reappears in all the steps of Systems Analysis, are characteristics which should now be addressed.

THE DECISION SITUATION

Within any system or subsystem structure, a condition must exist that presents a decision maker with the opportunity to make a decision. Additionally, the situation should offer alternative courses of action to resolve the decision situation. Again, it is appropriate to repeat an earlier observation: if there is no decision-making situation there can be no decision, no alternatives. Strange as it may sound, some practitioners either forget this fact or even attempt to *create* a decision situation for which no problem or opportunity exists. Often there are the individuals who are so proud of a model that they are overanxious to find a problem to fit the model instead of vice versa, as it should be! At the other extreme, it is good to remember that a decision *not* to make a decision even where a decision situation exists *is* a decision in itself. The same observation holds true for alternative choices. If there are no alternatives, there is no choice. Only one outcome is possible. Choice has been eliminated. Likewise, a short-sighted decision maker or analyst may choose not to be concerned with any alternatives. He is the type who says, "don't bother me with the facts, my mind's made up."

A decision situation is the natural result of the discovery of a current problem, or of a foreseeable problem, or of a foreseeable opportunity to take advantage of or pursue. On balance, the record seems to favor the opportunity to take advantage of a situation more than is suspected. Of course, some opportunities are not always win-win or even win-lose ones. Recently, some interesting lose-lose situations have been appearing more frequently. These usually require a decision on the lesser of two important undesirable outcomes; in effect, the lesser of two losses.[2] As resources in the world continue to diminish and the demands on them continue to increase, one can speculate about the increasing number of trade-off decisions involving the question of who or what will be chosen to lose the least or the most.

The decision situation step in the formulation phase does not require much elaboration. It is either present or not, and if not, further efforts cease. However, if as in the preponderance of cases, a decision situation does exist, it is the signal to put further analysis into action.

[2] An example of the hard kind of lose-lose decision was the Allies' decision *not* to evacuate Coventry, England, in World War II, despite their having cracked the German code and learned of the coming devastating attack. The loss of Coventry was decided to be worth other future losses and the possible future advantages of not revealing that they knew the code.

Referring again to the case study, the decision situation is clear. The city does have an *opportunity* to decide on using an area for something new and different. As is usual in most cases, the *opportunity* is welcome but presents a *problem* of deciding which use will be the most beneficial or desirable. This leads to the next crucial step, determination of the objective.

The decision situation in the case now makes possible a broad spectrum of objectives. Hopefully, the chosen one will be the optimum one as circumscribed by the decision makers. It can range from the broadest area of regional welfare to all the subsystems examined thus far.

Quite often, as in this case, the decision situation itself also sheds further light on the possible alternatives, just as did the analysis of the system. Apart from the specific objectives Dick Stockton was given, the decision situation is truly a plural one with many alternatives to serve as backdrops for developing other objectives. The city does have a unique opportunity which requires very basic decisions concerned with economic gains, social gains, community gains, citizen welfare, ecological progress; all of these mentioned earlier. In making decisions, the city is forced into the most important step in the formulation phase, that of determining the objective(s).

THE OBJECTIVE OR PROBLEM

With the system and decision situation as background, the next step is to determine the objective(s) or problem(s). It may well turn out that the objective and the problem are two separate things, though usually they are one and the same. The statement of the objective is an attempt to come up with a solid, definitive one which sets forth exactly *what* the decision maker (with the analyst's help) desires to achieve. Note the emphasis on the *what* rather than the *how*, at this stage. We are still concerned with what is wanted and later will analyze how to get there.

THE OBJECTIVE DEFINED

The Glossary defines the objective as, "the purpose to be achieved, or the problem to be solved, or the position or opportunity to be obtained." Other substitutes for the word *achievement* can be *goal, mission,* or *task.* The objective also can be (1) a positive statement of the problem, (2) a mirror image of the problem (stating it backwards), or (3) a solution to a problem which turns out to be a symptom of a real problem. It is sometimes easier to define the objective if the word *"problem"* is considered more of a decision situation or even easier to look upon the objective as being the *question* asked.

At any rate, whichever definition is easiest, from this point on the objective serves as the focal point of the decision-making process.

In analysis there are usually two specific types of objectives relative to decision making:

1. *The System Objective.* The function or mission that the system containing the decision situation performs. For example, take the system involved in the effective delivery of air cargo from one place to another, or the system of handling the cargo within an airport.
2. *The Planning or Analytical Objective.* The goal or task identified by the decision maker as needing to be accomplished. An example would be alternative methods of delivering cargo from one city to another other than by air, or alternative methods of handling cargo within an airport (manual, mechanized, or both).

A final general note, objectives are frequently *not* agreed on. The choices that first come to mind, ostensibly between alternatives, are really choices of objectives. Again, more often than not, nonanalytical (judgmental) methods must be resorted to for a final reconciliation of views.

OBJECTIVES—SOME GROUND RULES

In order to come up with any of the above four objectives in the definition, i.e., purpose, problem, position, or opportunity, a period of intelligent and thorough probing—and continued probing—must be carried out by the decision maker and the analyst to strive for the *real* objective. This is the time for imagination, for probing depths, for searching upward, inward, outward, in all directions, to isolate *the* all-important objective. It is the time for creativity and objectivity. It is a time to become both listener and speaker, both critic and criticized. It is a time to "pull out all the stops" in good reasoning and open-mindedness. It is also the time for decision, or else the analysis stops here.

The analyst's responsibilities are again pointed out here. The analyst (or the decision maker if he or she or the group are one and the same) must keep the ground rules always uppermost in mind:

1. Continually *question* the objective. Never accept an objective or problem as initally stated by anyone (unless, of course, your job may depend upon such a situation!). An analysis without the correct objective becomes an exercise in futility.
2. Realize that developing the correct objective or problem almost always involves an *iterative* process. Plan on it being so. Let it happen. Better yet, insist upon it, whether you are the decision maker or analyst or both.
3. Above all, make certain that the final, stated objective is *consistent* with the higher level objectives it supports or will affect in attempting a suboptimized level.

Like all systems, in reality all objectives are subobjectives, suboptimizations of higher level ones. Suboptimization and the development and solution of subobjectives are not bad things. In fact, they are usually necessary objectives to be resolved before the major one can be approached. They can and do feed into decisions at higher levels. They can and do help break down objectives into manageable portions. A caveat to keep in mind is that the lower level solution to an objective does little good if it does not support the main problem solution. Quade and Boucher have singled out these points quite succinctly with their admonition that "it is more important to choose the 'right' objective than it is to make the 'right' choice among *alternatives*."[3]

Another caveat to keep in mind is that if objectives, once decided upon, are changed in any way, the alternatives may also be changed. Change may simply involve modifying the objective or showing preference for the alternatives as the objective changes, or the objectives may cease to be applicable altogether.

Having taken aboard those caveats, it is well to mention more *positive* payoffs of a good objective. Usually, a good objective will *suggest* an appropriate measure of effectiveness (MOE) and even an appropriate measure of cost (MOC), both used to measure the cost/benefit/effectiveness of alternative ways to attain the objective. These are explored in chapter 4.

To sum up, in identifying the correct objective, it cannot be overemphasized that it is far more important to discover the *right* one than it is to find perfect optimization techniques and processes. It is more important than all that follows. Subobjectives and suboptimization of the problem are often necessary and natural, but they should be recognized for what they are—pieces of the whole. They must be

[3] *E. S. Quade and W. I. Boucher, eds., Systems Analysis and Policy Planning: Applications in Defense* (New York, Elsevier, 1968), p. 39. (Italics mine.)

contributing pieces and not pursued in other than the right direction. Alternatives and their calculations must contribute to the objective. Interrelatedness of parts and mutual supporting parts of the whole are useful only if they do just that.

SOME OBJECTIVES IN THE CASE STUDY

These points of interrelatedness and support are good lead-ins to our case study objectives. As in the preceding steps, an intelligent search in all directions will identify such interrelatedness and support. Let us apply this approach to the process of identifying the objective in the case study, the objective that may or may not be the one given to the analyst.

A system, the city, exists. A subsystem of the city, a transportation system, also exists. As a matter of fact, two subsystems exist according to the scenario—the automobile and the subway. A subsystem of the automobile system exists in the parking system. Subsystems of the parking system exist in the form of (1) whether to continue a reliance on automobiles and thereby contribute to that system by building and operating a parking system, or (2) whether to rely on the same system but have private enterprise do it. In turn, subsystems of the parking facility are those of revenue, traffic congestion, or investment in land values.

What are the possible objectives for the city? Here are several, but others may occur to you or to other analysts:

1. To enhance business in the Central Business District (CBD) of downtown by providing parking for shoppers.
2. To provide offices for downtown workers by building an office building.
3. To provide the same as number two, but have the building accomplished by private enterprise.
4. To provide parking for downtown workers.
5. To increase the city's revenue through taxes on a commercially built and operated office and/or garage.
6. To build, lease, or sell the resources which would realize the greatest tax revenues.
7. To protect and enhance the beauty and ecology of the city by creating a public park and associated citizen attractions.
8. To revitalize downtown.
9. To gain more use of the music center by providing adequate parking for patrons.
10. To increase profits for downtown retailers for sales tax purposes.
11. To increase business for downtown businesses so that their property will provide jobs, profits, taxes, revitalization, etc.

12. To create more job opportunities downtown for office workers and businesses.
13. To divert businesses and retail outlets from the suburbs to the city.
14. To enhance land values by adequate parking which would increase the property tax base.
15. To hold, build upon, lease, or rent the property but not to relinquish it, as the objective for holding is to create an asset promising considerable future value for the city.
16. To relieve parking congestion and improper parking in the CBD.
17. To get the mayor reelected by pursuing the most popular objective!

These objectives are in addition to those given the planners by the mayor.

Thus, even at first without too much deliberation, it is possible to arrive at a list of objectives by employing a little imagination and insight. Objectives may be broad enough to identify a much larger objective like making Oakton the most desirable city in the state or region, which "plain reason" would rule out at this point in time. Perhaps another larger objective might be that of providing Oakton with more parking facilities for automobiles than any city of its size, or the objective of making the CBD an inner city of pedestrians by keeping private vehicles out, or its corollary objective of providing complete subway systems to reach the CBD and other parts of the city—all are more examples of *different* objectives even though they appear to be much too ambitious or undesirable.

A list of objectives such as the above is usually the product of many sources. For one, Dick Stockton must not only commence work on the objectives already deduced from the above but should be developing others to be submitted. Objectives could come from the city fathers, including the mayor, because they are the decision makers. If left to a group of businessmen or retailers, the objective(s) would no doubt reflect their interests. If left to ecological proponents, obviously different objective(s) could be expected. Even the taxpayers would have one or more objectives if solicited. All these sources are important to have in addition to the initial objective(s) which came from the mayor without consideration of other possible objectives. The broader and deeper the inputs, the greater the chance for the right objective(s) to surface.

OBJECTIVES—SOME CAVEATS

Proceeding carefully through the first two steps of the formulation phase, systems involved and decision situation(s) involved are essential in actually determining the objectives. When an analyst strives to do these steps correctly and thoroughly, an improved focus on the all-important objective(s) is almost automatic. However, the third step of objective definitions must be approached, with the realization that the first two steps may not have yielded the desired signs of what may be *the* objective.

Objectives from another source not to be overlooked are those which might be called idealized ones. Usually, these are the least quantifiable and should be split into several subgoals. An ecological improvement objective is a good example. There are many obvious subgoals inherent in such a broad but laudable objective. Ecological improvement could be a strong runner in the case study, especially if further investigation showed Oakton to be the most air-polluted city in the state, region, or nation.

Also, it is well to remember that an objective may only approximate the real objective, especially when multiple ones are developed. Objectives may be so dissimilar that they cannot be measured by a common denominator or measured with the main objective. They can and do conflict as they proliferate.

The best defense in avoiding these problems is a good offense. Question the source as well as the objectives. Keep the door open to revision of objectives. Insist on the test that lesser objectives, or for that matter, alternative major objectives, are in keeping with the major decision situation and major objective. Also, any objective should be considered in the light of its ability to relate to MOEs or MOCs or a criterion already in mind. These are the measuring tools and techniques which must be applied to an objective, and vice versa. Finally, to return for a moment to the case, having considered all these constraints and the long list of possible objectives, the question is, what *should be* the objective? Remember, the case directed two of these objectives: the first, to carry out the city's wishes and study the economic feasibility of building a downtown parking facility and its related costs compared to its benefits (costs/benefits) and the second, to experiment with rate structure. We have also mentioned a somewhat broader one, but one within the capability of the city to analyze, specifically, the objective of making the best use of the Elm Street site. The analysis of the first objective which Dick Stockton must perform will undoubtedly open up the broader one, as will be seen in the next chapter.

At this point in the formulation phase, the reader should be thinking about which objective he or she would choose. Perhaps it may be one different than any of those suggested. Also, it is well to remember that the entire formulation phase is highly judgmental from start to finish. Objectives can and often do change as more insight is gained in the thoroughness and iteration inherent in the Systems Analysis Approach.

ASSUMPTIONS

Before we leave the formulation phase, its fourth and final step must be considered. It, too, is the highly judgmental step of making assumptions. Assumptions are not only embodied in the formulation phase, they are necessary throughout the entire analytic study. The first thing to realize about them is that they are inevitable. The second is that sound judgment should be used to ensure they are reasonable assumptions. The third is to make them explicit. State them openly and give reasons for including them, and then examine the assumptions closely to have them accepted by those concerned, especially by the decision maker, because they are reasonable.

Assumptions are necessary to treat the nebulous area of *uncertainty* and the inevitable lack of sufficient information to reduce or remove uncertainty. Assumptions are first used in choosing the appropriate *system* and next in assuming the correct *decision situation* to be defined. Assumptions are as much a base for choosing *objectives* as they are a means of tackling *alternative methods* of reaching those objectives. They provide a way of explaining unknowns, of explaining away not only qualitative elements but quantitative ones as well. Even in performing calculations, assumptions are made about constants and variables. They remain a part of an analysis to the very end, even until the study report is presented in its final form.

Assumptions are used to limit the scope of a problem or opportunity, and to limit the scope of objectives and alternatives. Care must be exercised in this last application, for unduly restrictive assumptions will rule out some potentially significant objectives or alternatives. They can become so restrictive that the results of a study can produce conclusions which are actually erroneous. The best guide is to try to limit assumptions to those areas in which it simply is not possible to obtain facts. This last problem is greatly affected by resources and the time to gather information. Every day, managers and leaders of all kinds are faced with making decisions about which they want additional information more than anything else. Additional information seldom is available, primarily because of time pressures. Life is a series of decisions made on limited information and with the risks involved usually quite clear to those who must make them.

An additional point regarding assumptions is that once they are used to define the scope of the analysis, they should be maintained throughout unless the iterative process reveals an improper start or better objectives. The adage that horses should not be changed in midstream applies to assumptions, for one should not change them without going back to where they were first introduced and without examining their continued applicability. This is not to say that assumptions, once made, cannot be changed. They should be if they erroneously affect the course of the inquiry. To be factual, many assumptions are deliberately temporary until they can be reexamined. Using temporary or variable assumptions has a double purpose. To do so permits focusing on only one subproblem or set of subproblems at a time, or on one variable at a time in the search phase (while assuming the other variables are constant).

ASSUMPTIONS IN THE CASE STUDY

At first reading, the number and kind of assumptions made throughout the case may not be readily apparent. It is by another reading, concentrating only on assumptions, openly stated or implied, that we find the case replete with them. To identify and make certain they are recognized and made explicit, here are some examples from the case:

1. The assumption that a cost/benefit analysis is correct and adequate and that it can *readily* predict a profit or loss.
2. The assumption that parking is inadequate at present.
3. The assumption that a parking facility will increase retail sales.
4. The assumption that sales tax revenue of $19 per person ($8 million) sales will be obtained.
5. The assumption that a city-owned parking lot would realize the same percentage of use as existing commercial lots.
6. The assumption that the city can contract for $270,000, plus 10 percent above a certain income.
7. The assumption that current land values will continue and that the tax rate will continue.
8. The assumption of the opportunity cost at which the land could be sold ($1 million).
9. The assumption of a loss to the subway system.
10. The assumption that ground floor spaces would be fully rented.
11. The assumption that Dick Stockton will have the answers by the next meeting, including a recommended rate structure!

There are other assumptions, but the above should suffice to start. As for their relative force or effect on the outcome of the problem, i.e., their sensitivity and reasonableness—these will be examined in the search phase and the evaluation phase. However, they all have one thing in common at this point, the fact that they *are* assumptions and should *not* be ignored!

SUMMARY

This chapter on the formulation phase may leave the reader with an impression that almost *every* step is crucial. If so, this is the intention, since the primary, diagnostic determinations affect all that follows. A wrong start means a wrong ending and wrong conclusions. In Systems Analysis, if one were to rank the five major phases in order of relative importance, it is fairly certain that practitioners and professionals would agree that the steps in the formulation phase rank first. The diagnostic effort that must go into proper identification of the system or subsystems involved, the determination that a decision situation does in fact exist and is capable of solution—these are extremely important. But the third step is even more so: to arrive at a definitive statement of the right *objective(s)* or that which, if achieved, will be the optimum solution for the purpose, is paramount. Finally, the need to fully recognize assumptions, and the uncertainties they spring from, and then be entirely honest about their inclusion in every step are all requirements which have a profound affect on good analysis.

SUGGESTED FURTHER READINGS

COVENTRY, W.F., and BURSTINER, IRVING. *Management: A Basic Handbook*. Englewood Cliffs, N.J.: Prentice-Hall, 1977, Chapter 8.

HINRICHS, HARLEY H., and TAYLOR, GRAEME M. *Program Budgeting and Benefit Cost Analysis: Cases, Text and Readings*. Pacific Palisades, Calif.: Goodyear, 1969. Introduction and Parts II and III.

HINRICHS, HARLEY H., and TAYLOR, GRAEME M. *Systematic Analysis: A Primer on Benefit-Cost Analysis and Program Evaluation*. Pacific Palisades, Calif.: Goodyear, 1972. Parts I and IV.

QUADE, E.S., and BOUCHER, W.I., eds. *Systems Analysis and Policy Planning: Applications in Defense.* New York: Elsevier, 1968. Chapter 3.

SCHMALTZ, ROBERT E. "Semantics." In *A Compendium of Systems Analysis/Operations Research Methodology,* Vol. I. Washington, D.C.: U.S. Air Force, Asst. Chief of Staff, Studies, and Analysis, 15 July 1968.

4

The Search Phase

Once the system encompassing a decision situation has been decided upon and the objective or problem defined (the solution of which will solve that decision situation), and the assumptions made clear, it is time to move from the formulation phase to the search phase. Search is completely dependent upon a definition of the *right* problem or the *correct* opportunity, else all steps which follow will obviously be in pursuit of the *wrong* ends.

This chapter will explore the search phase, its interrelationships with the formulation phase which preceded it and the evaluation phase which follows. It will examine the concept of and search for alternatives, which in turn embody measures of effectiveness, measures of costs, and models, the very heart of the quantitative aspects of Systems Analysis. However, even the evaluation phase is not without qualitative considerations as well as quantitative ones; this will be seen as the solution unfolds.

The first goal is to formulate the best objective(s) possible and then to develop as many alternatives as are feasible to attain it(them). These alternatives will then undergo not only the test of competition with each other in regard to costs and benefits but also the test of accomplishing exactly what is desired, or meeting the criterion of what is best for the purpose.

When we obtain the raw data with which to begin, alertness and perception can provide useful insights into the cost/benefit areas immediately. It is a known fact that organizational patterns and meaningful relationships occur in intelligent thinking while information is being gathered and arranged in some structural fashion. On the other hand, too much data can obfuscate many a good alternative because of its complexity or the disorganized way it is presented. The lesson here is one of recognizing the difference between meaningful data, applicable to the problem, and a plethora of data irrelevant to the problem. It is also the problem of using that somewhat indescribable, initial conceptual *insight* that we may well have.

THE ALTERNATIVES

As the inquiry into the fascinating subject of alternatives begins, the *first* alternatives to consider are the *alternative sources* of *advice* and *expertise*. The most common source is someone with intuition—and that could include any of us. Intuition is not analytic. On the other hand, it is not mere guesswork. Deliberate consideration is first given consciously to the structure of a decision situation and its ramifications, and the best intuitive guess is then offered. Additionally, the intuitive person often has at least experience on his or her side, or has lived with the problem, and has a sincere desire to solve the objective. But there is no effort to deliberately structure a problem or to search methodically for cause and effect relationships. Unfortunately, too, the strictly intuitive decision maker often really believes in his or her solution above all others and has few qualms about stating that his or her intuitive opinion is enough.

At the other end of the continuum of decision-making processes is Systems Analysis. Between intuition and thorough analysis are various gradations of advice and analytic structure, many of which we explored in chapter 2. In addition to the procedures compared in chapter 2, mention should be made of one other source or alternative to a problem—the expert. Not to be confused with the intuitive individual, the expert is presumably trained, experienced, and impartial in approaching a problem. Experts have their place and often are the graduates of systematic methods which have taught them to cut many corners and to come up with fairly good solutions. An expert who also believes in Systems Analysis has my full endorsement. An expert who bases his decisions on intuition and perhaps reputation is a different problem.

Using two or more intuitive individuals, or groups of experts, can increase the chances of an acceptable solution. The same observation may be made of group methods in general. For example, the *Delphi method* described briefly in the Glossary is a good example of a group-think approach. It has proved to have value (even amazing results) in specific instances that defy quantification, analysis, or for which there is no other approach but a judgmental one. It is a method of pooling the intelligence and experience of qualified participants in an anonymous but systematic way of parlaying their collective knowledge into solutions that are surprisingly appropriate.

Still another way to choose an alternative among individuals is to turn the problem over to a committee. A committee could decide upon sound analytic techniques, since there is nothing to prevent them but their own charter or ground rules. However, the committee does not usually do so, but instead explores more vocal members' ideas and often arrives at either a consensus, a majority vote, an average answer, or a stalemate as their product. None of these comes from methodical analysis. Each depends upon the realities or constraints of individuals, time, group norms, status, interests, values, and a host of other variables.

Before proceeding, it is in order to state that subjective judgments, either by an individual or a group, can result from Systems Analysis. It has never been proposed that judgment can be supplanted by analysis. On the contrary, Systems Analysis practitioners have been very careful to emphasize this point. But they do hold that an analytical approach, *unlike* pure intuition or expertness, can provide solutions that are more explicit, that permit iteration, and that are always open to critical reexamination. It is about as scientific as is practicable in that its steps can be retraced by others and its decisions subjected to trial and replication in the proof or disproof of its solutions. Yet the Systems Analysis Approach lays no claim to being purely scientific. The very problems it addresses often preclude the use of a pure scientific method. They are problems of *real* magnitude and *real* life that transcend absolutes and "knowns." But Systems Analysis does lend itself as much or more than any other approach toward a conscious attempt to extend the standards and techniques of sound logic and hard-core sciences into areas where controlled experimentation has not been possible.

Whatever the alternative means, whether an intuitive individual, expert, group, or committee, it is fitting to conlude that in problem solving, although the same basic steps are followed, all choices are susceptible to the acid test of whether those concerned have done a good job or not.

ALTERNATIVES AND THE CASE STUDY

Referring now to the case study, the need to consider all alternative uses of the resource, a potentially valuable downtown site, becomes our next step. True, one alternative already has been directed from above, that of using it for a city-owned downtown parking facility.

This alternative will be subjected to the trials of costs and benefits before the same is done with other alternatives. It is because we hold to a broader systems view that more than the one alternative will be considered. If we remember that alternatives are, by definition, competitive, we will seek the one which not only attains the objective but can win in an analysis. Recall that the broader objective suggested in the last chapter would lead to far more alternatives than the one directed from above in the case. The suggested optimum objective which allowed for an adequate scope of inquiry was, "what is the best use for the Elm Street site?" Some of the other alternatives listed in chapter 3 exemplified how changing objectives can change alternatives. To expand on the list of possible alternatives inherent in the broader objective, these are offered:

1. Build a city-owned, multilevel garage.[1]
2. Build an office building and rent offices with garages beneath it for rentors.
3. Build either a garage or office building and sell it.
4. Increase revenues to the city by rents and parking receipts.
5. Lease, rent, or sell the site for business development.
6. Enhance the beauty of the city by creating a public park.
7. Strive for ecological progress by not building anything that would cause congestion, pollution, and so on.
8. Revitalize the central business district by providing more stores, retailers, businesses, and jobs; by building, renting, leasing, or selling the site for that purpose.
9. Provide for increased use of the new music center.
10. Bring new business to the city from outside by making the site available to outside interests.
11. Enhance land values with a garage or office building, which will increase the value of the site over the years, and/or will result in increased property tax revenues.
12. Hold the property for later profit. Use for open lot parking meanwhile.
13. Do nothing.

Although some of these may seem more attractive to us at the moment, let us first proceed with an analysis of the prescribed project. It is actually a two-part project as directed. First, to determine whether the city of Oakton should construct the proposed garage and second, to investigate the effects of rate changes.

---

[1] "Build," of course, implies contractor building, as most cities are not in the actual business of constructing parking facilities.

Assuming the city felt that the attainment of their first objective would carry with it a solution which would (1) reveal increased revenues, (2) relieve parking congestion, and (3) dispose of the site in consonance with the objective they had chosen, the first answer to be sought is one of a cost/benefit comparison. That it would prove profitable is also assumed to be part of their objective. In the arsenal of tools and techniques listed in the Glossary, one of the most appropriate here, as it is in most analyses, is that of a cost/benefit calculation to quantify the search phase. The solution in Appendix I is divided into three basic calculations necessary to such a calculation, Investment Costs, Annual Costs and Revenues, and the Cost/Benefit computation based upon them. We will use the same steps in *describing* how each is arrived at:

COMPUTATIONS OF COST
AND OF EFFECTIVENESS

I. INVESTMENT COSTS

This is a relatively easy set of costs since it involves only three numbers, which are fairly reliable:

1.	Demolition of the Embassy Theater	$ 40,000
2.	Garage Construction	2,000,000
3.	Opportunity cost-price at which site could be sold to private developers	1,000,000
	Total investment costs	$3,040,000

As is evident, Dick Stockton has appropriately included an *opportunity cost* of $1 million. It may not be the *best* opportunity cost, but that remains to be seen as other opportunity costs (opportunities lost) are developed. It is possible that some other opportunity such as building an apartment/office building complex might have returned more than $1 million to the city if it had been pursued. In fact, any project for which the city could expect to have received more, thus adding to the opportunity cost figure, might have been preferable. (There will be a further discussion of this matter in chapter 5.) Later, as we look more closely at all numbers and assumptions, another review of these investment costs will be made, but for now the demolition estimate could be considered the actual bid by a demolition company and the cost of constructing a garage could be verified by contractors. We will accept them as reflecting a fairly good capital investment cost picture for the present.

II. ANNUAL REVENUES AND COSTS

These are the continuing costs and revenues. Annual operating costs should be separated from capital costs, as in our case study. Revenues, also continuing, will be covered first in our solution.

A. Annual Revenues

Even before we begin the calculation of costs and benefits (including revenues), the first assumption becomes apparent, specifically, that the city will apply the same *rate schedule* now in effect at the private garage. By the time the objective is met, rates could be changed but for now, the assumption is made they will be the same as the prevailing rates of the private garage.

A second assumption also appears, that the *use* of the city-owned garage will follow the same pattern now being experienced by the private one. Both of these assumed variables have unknowns within them, but in view of the fact that both can be changed later in our calculations and that they are quite explicit, it seems reasonable to proceed despite the absence of other data at this time.

Revenues can now be calculated according to plans. The planned size of the city parking facility is to be twice the capacity of the private garage or 800 spaces. This number is important in all that follows.

1. Receipts from parking fees

a. *Weekdays*
   Any analysis should recognize the different parking patterns for different periods of a typical week.
   The first calculation for weekdays:
   75% (3/4 utilization by "all-day" parkers) × 800 (spaces) × $2.00 × 260, plus 800 × $1.50 (3-hour rate) × 260 = $624,000
   Annually for weekdays: $624,000
b. *Saturdays*
   Based on a 75% utilization from (Daytime) 7 a.m. to 6 p.m., with average stay of 2 hours.

75% (3/4 utilization) × 11 (hours of daytime use) × 800
(spaces), divided by 2 (average number of hours) = 3,300
cars @ $1.25 (2-hour rate)
Saturdays
(Evenings) Based on an average of four hours for moviegoers
3,300 (cars) × $1.25 (2-hour rate) × 52 (Saturdays) + 800
(cars) × 1.75 (4-hour rate) × 52 = $287,300
Annually for Saturdays: $287,300

  c. *Sundays*
Based on a 60% utilization from 6 p.m. to 12 a.m., with
average stay of 3 hours (dinner or movie) @ $1.50 (3-hour
Sunday rate).
Annually for Sundays:
60% (utilization) × 800 (spaces) × 6 (hours of use) × $1.50
(3-hour rate) × 52 (Sundays) divided by 3 hours=$74,880
Annually for Sundays: $74,880
Total Estimated Annual Parking Revenue $986,180
Since the above estimates are approximate, it would be
practical to use the following: *Estimated annual revenue, $1
million*

2. *Receipts from retail store rents*
This is given in the problem as $50,000
It should be noted that this figure assumes *all* stores are rented
annually.

3. *Increased sales tax revenue*
Based on the mayor's statement that *each* new parking space
would generate an additional $10,000 per year in retail sales,
the proposed facility would generate 800 (spaces) × $10,000
(per space in sales), which equals $8 million in retail sales.
Since the city sales tax is 3% this yields annual tax revenues of
$240,000

Now is an appropriate time to investigate the validity of important
assumptions inherent in the mayor's statement. We will calculate the
number of users by days of the week.

Weekdays. Assuming all the "all-day" parkers are workers and will not
make any retail purchases of significance then:

1. The 800 users of the garage on an hourly basis will be primarily (a)
businessmen making calls, (b) shoppers, and (c) entertainment seekers
in the evening.
2. Although there is no real evidence in the case to support this part of

the assumption, let's assume that one-third of the 800 cars fall in each of the above categories.
3. Therefore, about 267 cars are "shopper-parkers." We are given the average number of persons per car, one and three-quarter persons. Thus, we may estimate the total number of shoppers using the garage on weekdays as follows: 260 (weekdays) × 1.75 (persons per car) × 267 (shopper-parkers) = 121,485

Saturdays. It seems safe to assume that on Saturdays all the daytime parkers are shoppers. Earlier, we estimated 3,300 cars would use the garage on Saturdays during the daytime. The calculation for daytime would be as follows:
52 (Saturdays) × 1.75 (persons per car) × 3300 (cars) = *300,300*. For Saturday nights we assume the stores are closed (a rapidly changing assumption) = 0
Sundays. We can assume no shoppers on Sundays (another changing assumption but consistent with the Saturday night one). If either the Saturday night or Sunday assumption is incorrect, the error is on the positive side; that is, additional shoppers would increase the mayor's estimate.
Using this assumption, the calculation of purchases by each shopper is as follows:

$$121,485 \text{ (weekday)} + 300,300 \text{ (Saturday)} = 421,785$$

$$\frac{\$8,000,000 \text{ (estimated)}}{421,785 \text{ (number of shoppers)}} = \$19 \text{ per shopper.}$$

It now appears that the mayor's estimate of sales tax revenues, based on $8 million worth of sales is a reasonable one, perhaps even *too* low. Serious shoppers in today's world of inflated prices can obviously unburden themselves very easily of $19 on a shopping trip!

However, before we include the $240,000 sales tax revenues which would result from $8 million worth of sales, another caution from the finance director is in order. He has stated that he read a report claiming that two-thirds of all persons entering the central business district by car *would still* have made the trip by subway had they not been able to use their cars (apparently for lack of parking facilities). Additionally, the case tells us that "60% of all auto passengers entering the CBD on a weekday were on the way to work; 20% were shoppers; and 20% were businessmen making calls."

Thus, it appears that the "two-thirds" figure quoted by the finance director is *probably* composed primarily of people who *work* downtown. Our adoption of the $240,000 figure is therefore based on an

assumption that it represents additional sales tax revenues from purchases made by shoppers who would otherwise *not* have come downtown to shop.

Finally, we must take into account that the sales tax revenue, as
computed, does not include receipts from restaurants, theaters, and
various events. Presumably these, too, would benefit and constitute
additional tax revenues simply because more parking, more shoppers,
more likelihood of people eating downtown or attending a theater or
other event.

Next, let's turn to the calculations of annual costs, the second step
in an annual revenues and costs calculation.

B. Annual Costs

1. *Garage Operating Costs* (given) $270,000
2. *Loss of Property Tax Revenue*
   At present rates, this is estimated
   by the finance director as $200,000
3. *Loss of Revenue to the Mass Transit System*
   To determine this loss (cost) the number of cars each year
   which would use the facility must be determined.
   Number of cars:
   Weekdays 75% (3/4 utilization) × 800 (spaces)
   + 800 (non-full time parkers)   × 260 (weekdays) = 364,000
   Saturday 3300 (cars) + 800 (cars) × 52 (Saturdays) =
   213,200
   Sundays 60% (utilization) × 800 (spaces) × 6 (open hours) ×
   52 (Sundays) ÷ 3 (average hour stay) =   49,920
                                                                         ———————

Total cars annually   627,120

Applying the given figure of 1.75 persons per car times 627,120
(the number of cars) equals approximately 1,100,000 persons.If
two-thirds would have made the trip by subway if parking
were not available, presumably the garage would take away
from the subway a business of 2/3 × 1,100,000, or about
733,000 persons. At 50¢ per round trip this could be a loss to
the subway system (already operating at a deficit) of 50¢ ×
733,000 = annual loss of about $367,000.

Loss due to property tax revenue $200,000
Loss due to subway use $367,000
                                                                     ———————

Total losses: $567,000

Next, the step of comparing the costs (both investment and annual) with the annual revenues in a cost/benefit calculation.

III. Cost/Benefit Calculation

A. *Total Investment Cost* (from step I) $3,040,000
B. *Annual Income Attributable to the Garage*
   Parking receipts (from step II
   above) $1,000,000
   Less: Management fee $ 30,000
   (given)
        Operating costs $ 240,000
   (given)
   Net receipts: $ 730,000
   City's share (90%) $ 657,000
   Rent of Ground Floor Spaces $ 50,000
   Increase in Sales Tax Revenue $ 240,000
   Less:
   Property tax revenue   200,000
   Loss of revenue to
   subway system   367,000

                                                                 −$ 567,000
Total
   Net Annual Income to City Attributable to
   the Parking Facility $ 380,000

Now that we have a figure on the probable net annual income to the city if the city fathers built and had operated for them a parking facility, a cost/benefit calculation should also take into consideration the *cost of using resources* for the project. This calls for using tools such as choosing an acceptable discount rate and calculating the present value of the annual income expected to see the results of a *stream* of annual income of $380,000 over the expected life of the parking facility. The main purpose is to find out if the percentage of return on the investment is acceptable in light of the value of resources (money, in this instance) now, as compared to the future value, if we choose the designated project.

C. Choice of a Discount Rate.

In the case, the city's cost of capital is 5 percent. That is, the percentage the finance director has determined it will cost to float an issue of 20-year, tax exempt municipal securities. Note the assumption here that the bonds would require only 5 percent interest, but in view of their tax exempt status they may well be appropriate to a certain clientele. The implication in the case is that any percentage of return that exceeds the 5 percent cost would be acceptable. It should be noted that the federal government expects a 10 percent return on investments and the opportunity cost given by many economists is around 7 percent or 8 percent, although instances of 25 percent are not uncommon.

In finding the present value of a stream of income of $380,000 each year for 40 years (the expected life of the parking facility), Table 4.1, a chart of the present value at rates of 4 percent, 6 percent, 8 percent, and 10 percent from 20 years to 50 years, should suffice as a base for a decision. Present Value Charts for $1.00 for certain percentages for certain years, as well as Present Value Annuity Charts for $1.00 can be found in almost any accounting or finance book. A sample page of the latter is included at the end of Appendix I.

Following is an example of how the amounts are computed: The present value of $1 received annually for 20 years at 10 percent is 8.514. Multiplying 8.514 by $380,000 equals $3.24 million. The 8.514 is found in the Present Value Annuity chart by simply going across to the desired percentage and then down that column to the desired number of years. Present value is comparable to the reverse of compounding and gives the value of tomorrow's dollars today, which illustrates that a dollar today is worth more than one tomorrow, based on whatever expected return one desires.

To return to the case, Table 4.1 shows that *regardless* of the time period chosen from 20 to 40 years, the internal rate of return is roughly between 10 percent plus and 12 percent plus. The percentage return on investment is the net income figure divided by the investment.

If the garage facility had only an estimated life of 10 years at 10 percent, the internal rate of return still would be above 5 percent. But we are reasonably sure the life of the facility will be more likely 30 or 40 years. So any project that shows such a positive net present value

TABLE 4.1 Present Value of an Annuity of $380,000

	4%	6%	8%	10%
20 years	$5.16 million	$4.36 million	$3.73 million	$3.24 million
30 years	$6.57 million	$5.23 million	$4.29 million	$3.58 million
40 years	$7.52 million	$5.72 million	$4.53 million	$3.72 million
50 years	$8.16 million	$5.99 million	$4.65 million	$3.77 million

is considered profitable to undertake. Of course, the variant with the highest net present value is the most profitable. Thus, if the city were to arbitrarily set a required 10 percent rate of return, the following detailed calculations show that the target is exceeded at the end of various time periods:

$$10\% \ @ \ 40 \ \text{yrs.} = 9.779 \times \$380,000 = \frac{\$3,716,020}{3,040,000} = 12\% \ \text{plus}$$

$$10\% \ @ \ 30 \ \text{yrs.} = 9.427 \times \$380,000 = \frac{\$3,582,260}{3,040,000} = 11\% \ \text{plus}$$

$$10\% \ @ \ 20 \ \text{yrs.} = 8.514 \times \$380,000 = \frac{\$3,235,320}{3,040,000} = 10\% \ \text{plus}$$

Since the investment cost is $3.04 million, the calculations indicate a *positive net present value*, no matter which of the time periods is chosen. The variant of 40 years has the highest return of the three examples.

It would appear, therefore, that based on all the assumptions, the municipal parking facility is an economically desirable project. Having arrived at this point, however, we need other analytical considerations for a thorough analysis to further reduce the uncertainty of some of the assumptions, or to emphasize the effects of changing some of the key variables such as the rate schedule.

IV. SOME OTHER ANALYTICAL CONSIDERATIONS

Among the several other factors to consider are at least three separate additional paths to explore:

I. What is the accuracy of the estimates?
II. What rate structure should be employed?
III. What weight or importance should be placed on other costs and benefits not included in the calculations?

I. Accuracy of the Estimates

a. **Investment Costs** of $3,040,000
This has already been considered and the demolition costs, the building costs, and the opportunity cost seem fairly reliable.

b. Parking Receipts of $1,000,000

This is clearly an approximate figure despite the detailed calculation and explicit assumptions made to support it. It is based on two fundamental assumptions which bear reexamining at this step in the search phase. The first assumption is that the city uses the same rate structure in effect at the nearby private garage, and the second is that the city-owned facility will experience the same utilization pattern as the private garage. The first can be controlled, but the second needs exploration in addition to what was considered earlier:

1. It is more *likely* than not the city will experience the estimated demand for several reasons:

   The new music center will probably increase parking demand. Experience in other cities with civic or music centers bears this out.

   The new freeway will encourage more traffic to come downtown.

   There presently exists a "parking space deficit" in the central business district.

2. As for the utilization pattern, it should also be noted that the private garage is presently not being used to capacity. Dick Stockton's appropriate analysis of the utilization rate for the private garage contains a calculation using an approach similar to the earlier one for the city-proposed facility. Again, the different weekdays are calculated separately:

a. *Weekdays*

First assume that all-day parkers remain for a maximum of 9 hours on average. 75% (utilization) × 400 (spaces) × 9 (hours) = 2,700 "space hours" used. Add 400 cars that park for an average of 3 hours equal 1200 "space hours" used.

Total per weekday:	3,900

Total per week = 5 × 3,900   = 19,500 space hours

b. *Saturdays*

75% utilization from 7 a.m. to 6 p.m. =

75% × 400 spaces × 11   = 3,300 space hours
(hours open)

Add 400 cars assumed to park an average of 4 hrs.	=	1,600 space hours
Total for Saturdays		4,900 space hours

c. *Sundays*
60% utilization from 6 p.m. to 12 a.m. =

60% × 400 spaces × 6 (hours of use)	=	1,440 space hours
Total "space hours" per week	=	25,840

Capacity = 400 spaces × 17 hours daily × 7 days a week or

47,600 space hours

Therefore, the *present utilization rate of the private garage* is:

$$\frac{25,840}{47,600} = 54\%$$

Realizing that the question remains as to whether or not the city would achieve the anticipated demand for its city garage, and further realizing that the rate can be much higher during peak periods of the day or evening, Dick's solution proceeded with a break-even analysis.

BREAK-EVEN ANALYSIS

Choosing a 40-year life period of the investment and a discount rate of 6 percent, the question is, what parking receipts would be necessary in order to equate the present value of a given stream of income to an investment cost of a little over $3 million?

The first calculation is to find the total net income required to equal $3 million at 6 percent for 40 years. The total required annually would be about $200,000; the present value of $200,000 per year for 40 years at 6 percent equals $3,009,200, actual.

Next, there are some *fixed* components of the case which do not vary with the number of cars using the garage. These are:

1. Loss of property tax revenue	$200,000
2. Gain of ground floor rented spaces	50,000
3. Management fee	30,000
4. Operating costs	240,000

There are also *variable* components to single out:

1. Parking receipts $1,000,000
2. Increase sales tax revenue   240,000
3. Loss of subway revenue   367,000

(some *might* see a gain if the CBD is attractive and accessible; for example, *if* an increase of businessmen driving in and using the garage were offset by more shoppers and others using the subway).

Assuming that the rate structure stays the same and that demand for use of the garage will follow the same pattern of utilization set forth in step II (Annual Revenues and Costs), then the increase in sales tax revenue and the loss of subway revenue can be assumed to be approximately proportioned to gross receipts. That is, they should bear the same relationship to gross receipts as before.

Thus, annual receipts, or R, equals gross receipts from the *increase* in sales tax revenue, or

$$\frac{\$240{,}000 \text{ (increase in sales tax revenue)}}{\$1{,}000{,}000 \text{ (parking revenue)}} \times R = 0.24R$$

(and) The *loss* of revenue to the subway system would be:

$$\frac{\$367{,}000 \text{ (decrease in subway receipts)}}{\$1{,}000{,}000} \times R = 0.367R$$

If we recall that the net receipts are to be split 90/10 between the city and the operations firm, a break-even equation for R would be on an *annual* basis:

$200,000 (*net* income per year) = 90% × (R − 270,000 (operating costs) + 50,000 (rents) + 0.24R (sales tax increase) − $200,000 (loss of property tax) − 0.367R (loss of revenues to subway). Solving for R results in an approximate figure of *$767,000*.

Solving for R

Solving for R

$200,000 = 90% × ($R$ − 270,000) + 50,000 + 0.24R − 200,000 − 0.367R

(Reverse the equation. Move the unknowns to the left.)

0.90 × (R − 270,000) + 50,000 + 0.24R − 200,000 − 0.367R = $200,000

0.90R − 243,000 + 50,000 + 0.24R − 200,000 − 0.367R = $200,000

0.90R + 0.24R − 0.367R = 243,000 + 200,000 − 50,000 + 200,000

0.773R = 593,000

R = 767,141

Proof

$200,000 = 0.90 \ (767,141 - 270,000) + 50,000 - 184,114 - 200,000 - 281,541$

$200,000 = 0.90 \ (497,141) + 50,000 + 184,114 - 200,000 - 281,541$

$200,000 = 447,427 + 50,000 + 184,114 - 200,000 - 281,541$

$200,000 = \$200,000$

This is to show our demand could *fall* to about 77 percent of the estimated $1 million gross revenue before the project would cease to be attractive under the conditons and assumptions.

That is, the garage would have to have gross receipts of $767,000 per year in order to pay for itself or break even in 40 years at a discount rate of 6 *percent*. Such a calculation is only approximate, as other parking revenues and subway costs may enter the picture; on the other hand, the same two areas may also err in our favor. The numbers would change, of course, if we changed the life or the percentage expected. Now to return to a review of the accuracy of the other estimates, which we began on page 68.

c. Operating Costs of $270,000

This figure includes both the operating and management fees. It is probably as reliable as we need for the analysis. Naturally, it would depend on negotiations between the city and a potential operating firm. A contract of two to three years could be expected, subject to renegotiation or new bids at the end of a reasonable time. Operating costs, too, are prone to increase over a 40-year period. But in most of this analysis, it should be clear that we are ignoring inflation and price increases and working with constant dollars. An assumption could be made in defense of this in that if operating prices inflate, so too will parking costs and rentals. The consumer will be the ultimate source of keeping prices in balance at higher levels!

d. Rent of the Ground Floor Retail Spaces for $50,000

This is a fairly reliable estimate, based upon knowledge of prevailing rental costs in the central business district.

e. Increase in Sales Tax Revenues of $240,000

This has already been dealt with and rests on several assumptions, but it still appears quite conservative and likely that:

- A sales tax will continue (even increase).
- 422,000 "shopper-trips" will park and each shopper-trip will produce a purchase of $19—purchases that would not have been made if there were no garage.

f. Loss of Property Tax Revenue of $200,000

This clearly depends on (1) the assessed value of a building that could have been erected if the garage had not been built and (2) the prevailing tax rate. Like sales taxes, property taxes have seldom gone down, so the future loss of this property tax revenue may be understated over the long run. However, in the absence of any knowledge to the contrary, it may be assumed that this is Dick Stockton's best estimate of the annual loss of tax revenue for the immediate future. There is little choice but to accept it as a constant in the calculations.

On the plus side, the property tax loss trend of the future is offset by the likelihood that the value of the *site* will continue to rise, *and* the city will still own it after 40 years.

g. Loss of Revenue to the Subway System of $367,000

This is indeed an estimate, as it assumes that *if* a garage is built, 733,000 "person-trips" will be lost to the subway system each year. This is about 2,000 person-trips per day and was calculated earlier. The whole estimate is based on the following:

- A projected utilization pattern.
- That 1.75 persons per auto is a good average.
- That two-thirds would have made the trip by subway if adequate parking were not available.

Looking back over these calculations, it appears that three especially should be of concern:

- Parking receipts.
- Increase in sales tax revenue.
- Loss of revenue to the subway.

As long as we recognize their shortcomings, it is best to move forward in view of time constraints. We could, if we wished, continue on to refine these estimates by several means, all of which require more data. Surveys, samplings, and market-research investigations would be appropriate if time and money permit. These, too, are the tools of good Systems Analysis. One survey that would be most desirable would be to obtain additional data and experiences from *other* garages in the CBD. Also, helpful would be to know what *kinds* of parkers use those garages at various times of the day. Additionally, a survey or sampling of subway riders would be appropriate to enquire whether they would have driven if adequate parking were available. Or, a variation of the question, would they have taken the subway even if adequate parking were available? Finally, but by no means exhausting the possible information we would like, a marketing research or sales survey of how much shoppers actually *do* spend, and what the trends are in buying habits and places. Armed with such data, we would feel more comfortable in making basic determinations and forecasts about the future. Next, let's examine the possibilities and effects of rate structures.

II. What Rate Structure Should Be Used?

After a second look at Accuracy of Estimates, the second of three areas we should consider is the parking rate structure for the garage. It is perhaps the one variable which can affect calculations more than any other, if it were to be manipulated. Obviously, knowing more about *all* the key variables would be useful if time permitted, but for the moment, let us limit ourselves to this one variable and consider the effects of its manipulation. One of the first questions to be asked is that of a rate structure which would *discourage* all-day parkers. It would be fine if the all-day workers used the subway and helped that ailing system. It would be fine if a large turnover by shopper-parkers and others would develop, as there is profit in turnover, assuming the garage is used as projected. It would also be fine if *more* shopper-parkers came to the city to buy, instead of shopping in the suburbs. Their presence and turnover, as well as that of others such as visitors and business-callers, would surely help in a "revitalization of downtown."

To initiate a new pattern of uses, questionnaires could be used to gain an idea of the various rates at which various types of parkers would switch from the subway and vice versa. Data on the effects of rate changes obtained from other cities owning garages, as well as from other garages in Oakton, may be available.

Then, a series of alternative projections could be made based upon different rate structures, each associated with a projected utilization pattern. Or, the city might ignore rate changes and look for profit and changes in pattern by operating a self-parking facility instead of the attendant-parking facility envisioned in the case.

One of these hypothetical structures is offered in Table 4.2. Its impact on our total calculations becomes quite apparent as it is presented.

This extreme example is given to illustrate how a rate structure could be changed to really *penalize* all-day parkers, to make it *attractive* to short-time shopper-parkers, to obtain more utilization evenings and weekends, and in general, to change the pattern of clientele, their

TABLE 4.2 A Hypothetical Rate Structure

Day	Time	Rates
Monday–Friday	7 a.m.–6 p.m.	25 cents for first three hours $1.00 per hour for every hour in excess of three
	6 p.m.–10 p.m.	flat rate of $1.00
Saturdays	7 a.m.–6 p.m.	25 cents per hour
	6 p.m.–12 a.m.	flat rate of $1.75
Sundays	7 a.m.–7 p.m.	10 cents per hour
	6 p.m.–12 a.m.	flat rate of $1.00

habits, and the city's income not only from the garage but as a result of more business and buying in the city.

Next, the city could derive more reliable relationships between parking costs and demand for parking at various times of the day and for various purposes. These could easily be constructed into a model and computerized so that the calculations could be done easily, quickly and tried out for each change in each variable. A full analysis would employ such manipulation of rate changes, as well as a break-even analysis at each set of rates to produce several alternative outcomes. The possibilities are almost without limit except for time and reasonableness.

This brings us to the end of basic costs and benefits (effectiveness) considerations, i.e., the economic considerations. An attempt has been made to first choose the most reasonble costs and benefits, whether they be quantitative or qualitative. They have been reexamined in light of their assumptions, which were necessary before we could accept them. The assumptions have been made as explicit as possible, though time and effort could yield more data and more certainty in the resulting numbers.

One more caution before leaving cost/benefit considerations. If *cost* is defined to mean only dollar expenditures and if *revenues* are defined to mean only dollar receipts, many other costs and revenues (benefits) are left out simply because they defy using dollars as a criterion. Truly rational choices cannot be made by comparing costs and benefits in the restricted sense of dollars. Determining the non-dollar costs and the nondollar benefits requires judgment, experience, and intelligent intuition and foresight. Several of these choices were inherent in the list of opportunity costs (benefits lost) we were forced to give up by choosing the garage project. It is time to include them.

III. Other Costs and Benefits

Many other factors which have not been included in the evaluation thus far are of extreme importance and cannot be ignored. If they are overlooked, almost certainly someone or some group with an interest in the opportunity afforded in the case will be heard from.

Some of these factors are listed in Table 4.3 according to their probable effect on the decision to be made, i.e., either in favor of or not in favor of the garage choice. Accepting or rejecting these factors is up to the reader.

Indeed, the ramifications and interests concerned are many, especially if each were attempted as a calculation backed up by each new choice, each new assumption. However, by being explicit about them, the analyst has done his job and the decision maker must weigh the real costs and benefits, both measurable and unmeasurable. Next, a look at the model used in the case which embodied the cost/benefit considerations.

TABLE 4.3 Benefit-Cost Considerations

Benefits (Pros)	*Costs (Cons)*
1. Revitalization of downtown	1. Increased auto congestion in the city streets
2. More use of the new music center by suburbanites	2. Increased traffic control costs
3. Increased profit to downtown retailers	3. Delays and waste of time and energy
4. More downtown jobs	4. Frustration, both business and individual
5. More downtown business firms	5. Wear and tear on streets and highway
6. More downtown retail outlets	6. Increased air pollution; health considerations
7. Enhanced land values nearby the garage; increased property tax base	7. Increased noise, discomfort, irritation; reduced work efficiency
	8. An office building might mean more jobs and revenue than a garage
8. Increased value of the Elm Street site in the future with considerable residual value to the city.	9. More city services must be provided for new businesses, employers, employees, etc.
	10. Effects on city and suburban homes, rentals, home building, and so forth.

MODELS

Two writers on the subject of models have described the common idea of models as follows: "The layman's idea of the word 'model' probably concentrates on that sort which are commonly found in *Playboy* magazine and in fashion shows. However, if pressed to consider other varieties, most of us would probably react to the idea by describing a model airplane. In doing so we would have brought to light the most important characteristic of models as they are used in management, in decision analysis, and in this book."[2]

Whether it be the "ideal" female measurements alluded to in the quotation above or an airplane model which is considered a miniature replica of the real aircraft, the essential idea of a model is correct in both instances, in that both are *representations* of something else in the real world. One of the simplest and most effective examples of a model is a road map which portrays an area and places far too large to illustrate in reality.

The degrees of abstraction which models may take vary from a simple photograph of an object to a highly sophisticated, computerized, mathematical model of the probability of success in war. Without attempting a complete treatise on models, perhaps a brief taxonomy of models is appropriate to set the background before looking at the case models and also to gain an appreciation of their variety and classification. Fortunately, this task has been made easy by the work of Churchman, Ackoff, and Arnoff on the subject. They categorize models as either "iconic," "analog" or "symbolic."[3] Summarizing their more complete treatment, the following basic information about models is offered:

- *Iconic Models* are simple-scale transformations of the real-world system. Iconic models and the real systems or objects they represent are "look-alikes." The model airplane is an example, as is a model of the layout of a new plant.
- *Analog Models* are more abstract than iconic in that certain properties are transformed, or something altogether different is used to represent a real-world system or object. For example, a graph is used to represent historical sales.
- *Symbolic Models* are the most abstract variety of models. Symbols are substituted for properties. An algebraic equation is an example. So are mathematical and accounting models symbolic.

[2] David I. Cleland and William R. King, *Management: A Systems Approach* (Hightstown, N.J.: McGraw-Hill, 1972), p. 1.

[3] C. W. Churchman, R. L. Ackoff, and E. L. Arnoff, *Introduction to Operations Research* (New York: John Wiley and Sons, 1957), pp. 159–161.

Within these three categories one can construct mathematical models, word models, symbolic models, organizational models, terrain models, war-game models—models almost without limit except the imagination. In the case, a symbolic model can be used by a representation of costs and benefits in the form of an equation (break-even) or through the use of an analog model using words to represent costs and benefits and their impact on the interested parties.

Models portray infinitely complex production problems in the form of charts, graphs, progress, program evaluation, goal and critical path models. Computer programs use models to visualize the highly complex system of inputs, processing, and outputs, and others, the "black box" model to symbolize controls or processes beyond most human knowledge.

MODELS AND THE CASE STUDY

1. To return to the case, in order to represent costs, revenues, and return on investment, one feasible model is along simple accounting lines, a form of symbolic model. Costs are calculated separately and reduced to dollar amounts, and the same for revenues. Costs were divided into Investment (capital) plus Continuing Costs (variable and other), all of which could be done in words as shown in Figure 4.1.

At a glance, one can grasp the total cost and revenue picture except for the unmeasurable and judgmental aspects.

2. The case problem could be modeled slightly differently, depending on one's preference in accounting structure, as in Figure 4.2.

Notice how even simple models, such as the two illustrated, can

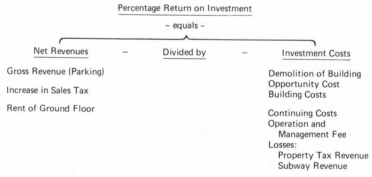

FIGURE 4.1 Percentage Return on Investment

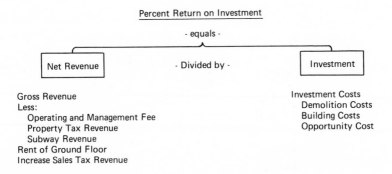

FIGURE 4.2 Percentage Return on Investment

be helpful in setting down on paper all of the main areas of cost and revenue one should not overlook in approaching the problem.

Both of these can also be made into equations, as was done for calculating the actual return on investment earlier in this chapter.

3. Another useful model to represent or at least make explicit the total cost and effectiveness of the case could be the one which highlights the two sides of the picture (Figure 4.3).

4. Figure 4.4 is another model which depicts the costs and revenues affecting the benefits, which in turn flow to recipients.

5. Another model, or rather supporting model, used was that of the calculation based on the present value of an annuity which yielded simple arithmetical returns for various percentages and years. This allowed us still another model, a simple chart ranking the various percentage and time yields, enabling the choice of whichever fit our criteria. We could have chosen the variant with the *highest* net present value had we desired it.

6. Sometimes a simple representation of inputs–comparison (processing)–outputs (pros and cons) is useful as a model. This is usually used to highlight performance, but it can also be used for characteristics or consequences. It is a good way to manipulate a variable (such as parking rates) while holding all other variables constant. As mentioned before, a thorough analysis of the case would include changing and manipulating *all* the *key* variables in turn to see their effects. This is a form of sensitivity calculation to determine which one or ones are really sensitive and affect the outcome most. Some variables could even be *deliberately* favored, though one other appears dominant; and if that one *still* survives after such deliberate favoritism, it stands as the *dominant variable*.

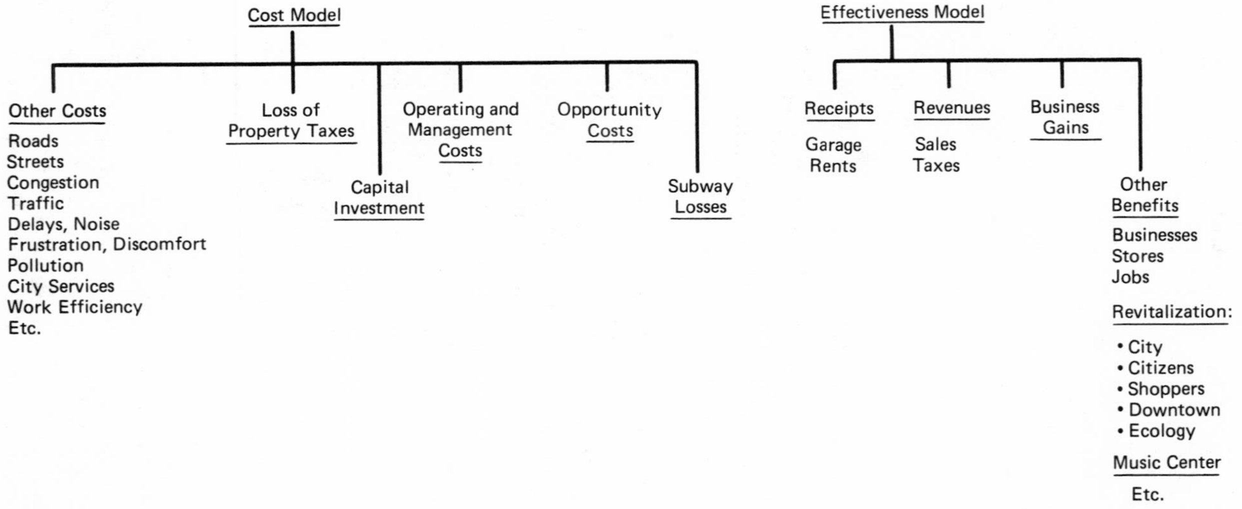

Cost Model

Other Costs
Roads
Streets
Congestion
Traffic
Delays, Noise
Frustration, Discomfort
Pollution
City Services
Work Efficiency
Etc.

Loss of
Property Taxes

Capital
Investment

Operating and
Management
Costs

Opportunity
Costs

Subway
Losses

Effectiveness Model

Receipts
Garage
Rents

Revenues
Sales
Taxes

Business
Gains

Other
Benefits
Businesses
Stores
Jobs

Revitalization:

 • City
 • Citizens
 • Shoppers
 • Downtown
 • Ecology

Music Center

Etc.

FIGURE 4.3 Cost-Effective Determinants

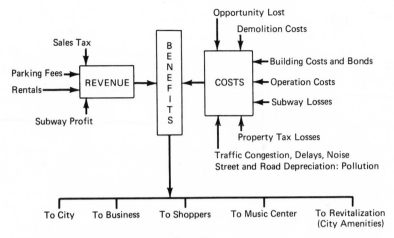

FIGURE 4.4 Model of Costs and Benefits

7. Last, after the possible models are exhausted, several alternatives could be calculated for their cost/benefit of the Elm Street site and compared on a *graph* model. Let us suppose that the benefit agreed to be the most important was the preservation of the city at all costs. Admittedly, this would be a departure from ranking according to economic return. If the need for more office space had been the criterion, it would have been selected regardless of the fact that a comparison might reveal a cost and effectiveness position quite different from the deliberate choice of a more costly enterprise.

Figure 4.5 clearly shows the park and garden as the most *costly* for solving the city's economic situation, yet it is the most *effective* alternative in the eyes of the decision makers because *that* is the criterion they may have selected.

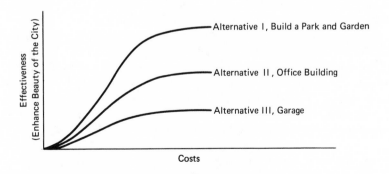

FIGURE 4.5 Cost-Effectivess Alternatives

SUMMARY

The search phase has taken us into the very heart of the Systems Analysis Approach. It has been the phase in which alternatives, costs, effectiveness, benefits, and models have all been directed toward quantifying and illuminating the problem as much as possible. Its foundation rests squarely on the formulation phase which preceded it. The objective dictated alternatives which would complete and achieve that objective. Now is a good time to emphasize this point in the succinct words of Quade and Boucher, "It is more important to choose the 'right' objective than it is to make the 'right' choice between alternatives."[4]

If the objective is a valid one and there is agreement that it is the opportunity or problem which, if resolved, will best satisfy the criterion, then the search for both quantitative and qualitative (judgmental again) variables and the full consideration of every alternative, every cost, and every benefit become a series of important steps which can provide the feeling of security that comes from valid numbers and relationships, and their rigorous reviews. If alternatives are dropped, replaced, or modified in the search phase, a change will result in costs, benefits, calculations, and the quantitative tools selected, as well as in the qualitative judgments made. Care should be taken to recognize that the direction may have changed and the process must be started again.

As in the formulation phase, assumptions and uncertainties are everywhere to be found in the search phase. Again, if they are recognized, faced up to, made explicit, and put to the tests of rationality and reasonableness, they are not insurmountable problems. The idea is to *do* something constructive, to look *forward* to a productive solution in spite of uncertainties which may be reasonably "assumed." This is no different from life itself.

Since we did use several quantitative tools and calculations in the case to measure costs and benefits, it is necessary to realize that many of the measurements are really *ad hoc*. That is, there is rarely a *single* measure of effectiveness or a benefit which is completely adequate. There is rarely one which pleases everybody. The MOE really measures *exactly* how well an objective has been achieved, and the preferred one will more likely be one based upon a criterion selected in advance or which becomes apparent as the MOE and MOC

---

[4] E. S. Quade and W. I. Boucher, eds., *Systems Analysis and Policy Planning: Applications in Defense* (New York, Elsevier, 1968), p.39.

are developed. Effectiveness lies within the final purview of decision makers who must apply judgment. This is acceptable as long as it is clear to all that it is impossible to satisfy all entrusted parties involved in complex problems.

Models often take form in the mind without deliberate thought. Some of the simplest are the best. $P = R - C$, Profit equals Revenues minus Costs, is still a model everyone can grasp, and yet its ramifications can be exceedingly complex. As an abstraction, the value of models lies in their ability to represent things we could never hope to manipulate in reality (if we could, the costs would be staggering). Models bridge the way to evaluation and as such, could be part of the evaluation phase which comes next. The models for the directed alternatives were included in this chapter to round out the calculations and portray the features. In the following chapter, a look at one or two *other* alternatives will also include the models involved. If we may want a better economic return, chapter 5 will reveal several.

Management models interest us the most in systems analysis because they often *represent* the heart of management—*decision situations*. Their use permits managers to assess and predict alternatives without the cost of actually carrying them out.

To understand the value of all the effort expended in the search phase is to be aware of the *payoffs* of such effort—better management decisions, based on better information, and the increased likelihood of being *right* about the way to reach one's goals.

SUGGESTED FURTHER READING

CHURCHMAN, C.W.; ACKOFF, R.L.; and ARNOFF, E.L. *Introduction to Operations Research*. New York: John Wiley and Sons, 1957.

CLELAND, DAVID I., and KING, WILLIAM R. *Management: A Systems Approach*. New York: McGraw-Hill, 1973.

Department of Defense Instruction. *Economic Analysis and Program Evaluation for Resource Management*. Secretary of the Navy Instruction 7000.14A, No. 7041.3, 1973.

FISHER, GENE H. *Cost Considerations in Systems Analysis*. Santa Monica, Calif.: Rand Corporation, 1971.

HITCH, CHARLES J. *Decision-Making for Defense*. Los Angeles: University of California Regents, 1965. Chapter III.

KASSOUF, SHEEN. *Normative Decision Making.* Englewood Cliffs, N.J.: Prentice-Hall, 1970. Chapters I and VI.

QUADE, E.S., and BOUCHER, W.I. *Systems Analysis and Policy Planning: Applications in Defense.* New York: Elsevier, 1968. Chapter III.

5

The Evaluation Phase

In the case study, the alternative of constructing a parking facility was directed by the city fathers. In actuality, the fathers would no doubt have had a better appreciation of the breadth and depth of possible alternatives—in this case, if not before, certainly *after* Dick Stockton's report. But for the sake of the example, the feasibility of a garage became the objective and its economic return the criterion, and it is with that criterion we must first be concerned. But first, a few pertinent thoughts are in order regarding the criterion in general.

THE CRITERION

Unfortunately, the word *criterion* has a conventional meaning in English. So much so that everyone seems certain of its meaning. But to an analyst it has two parts. First, as mentioned earlier, it is a way of relating effectiveness and cost. Second, it is a *decision rule.* Why the dichotomy? Here's a simple illustration.

Suppose you have a headache and want to buy a bottle of aspirin. You have two choices at the drugstore: a bottle of brand X with 100 tablets that costs $1.00 and a bottle of brand Y with 250 tablets that costs $2.00. Both are equally effective and you know the cost of each. Which would you pick? One has more, one is cheaper; yet both are as effective. Normally, you would choose the "most for the money." By dividing effectiveness by cost, the one with the maximum ratio is the bottle of 250. This illustrates how a criterion is put together, a way of relating cost to effectiveness by dividing effectiveness by cost and choosing the alternative which gives the highest value of that ratio. Or you could simply divide cost by effectiveness to get unit cost and choose the lower unit cost (4/5¢ as compared to 1¢). The "most for the money" makes sense in dealing with something as inexpensive, small, and lasting as a bottle of aspirin.

But what if these were *eggs?* Most families could not store 250 eggs even if they could eat them before they spoiled. Or suppose the same relative deal existed for *watermelons?* The criterion used above is still valid, given ratio and cost, but not very *sensible* if it is eggs or watermelons one is buying. More reasonably, a decision would be made to buy two dozen eggs or two watermelons and take *whatever alternative* lets you get *that* amount for the least money. Another way might be to allocate a *certain* amount of money from the food budget and buy the *maximum* number of eggs you can with that amount of money.

The point is that common decision rules used in the formulation of a criterion are not fixed. They can range from fixed cost, maximum effectiveness; to fixed effectiveness, minimal cost; to some ratio between them; to profit (where units are compatible); to the constraints of the decision environment, such as politics or social constraints; to several factors which are appropriate, such as best estimate, worst case, *a fortiori* analysis, and dominance. (See the Glossary for these and more contingency choices.)

The *usual* form of a criterion is a statement about both effectiveness and cost; however, it does not always say *what* effectiveness to maximize and *what* cost to minimize. It is likely that some types of effectivness are more critical than others; for example *kinds* of supplies in warfare, such as fuel and troops. Simply to state a requirement for the maximum flow of supplies might exclude the most critical types. Also, in addition to an accurate statement of the *kind* of effectiveness desired, it is necessary to define what *types* of cost are going to be included in the criterion. Although dollar costs are popular, they are only approximate in a situation in which dollars can be exchanged for goods. Since exchanging dollars for resources which are *needed* but *lacking* is not possible in a situation in which all the money in the world could not, at that time, get the resources, it is necessary to state the criterion in other terms. For example, suppose a specific number of cargo ships is all we have at a given time during a war with an overseas enemy. Supplies must be transported to our allies and for our own troops. If the enemy is equipped with the likely weapons of submarines and aircraft and is capable of sinking a high percentage of our ships, it becomes quite apparent that an exchange of dollars for ships which *don't exist* is not possible in the short-range period. In time, we may be able to replace them faster than they are sunk, just like any other fixed cost or capital equipment in business. So the costs that might be proposed in this situation could be stated in terms of actual supplies lost; specific, key supplies lost; the loss of supplies sunk by submarines; the number of ships of various types lost during operations; the number of antisubmarine warfare escorts (destroyers and others) lost to submarines; the level of effort used by the escorts in conducting their protection mission; or even the ambitious goal of trying to define a cost related to the effectiveness of the entire operation of the war abroad.

Each of the measures of effectiveness we started with above might be combined with each of the costs to provide a large number of criteria. Some of the possible criteria are, for instance, submarines sunk per escort ship lost, with the decision rule being that of maximizing the ratio; another could be supplies delivered minus supplies lost, and the associated decision rule would be to maximize that difference. Still another might be *certain quantities* of supplies delivered, with the rule being to minimize one of the costs identified. And so on. The term *decision rule* used above is generally called the *criterion*.

RELATIONSHIP OF THE CRITERION AND OBJECTIVE

No matter which criterion or criteria are chosen, the point is to examine it or them closely to see exactly what objectives are really being adressed. This can be done by examining what effects the single purpose criterion used would have on the operation. For example, using submarines sunk per escort ship lost, an operation conducted to maximize that ratio would probably save some escorts but would not be very well designed to carry out the *real* mission of protecting convoy merchantmen on their way across the ocean. In fact, it would have the effect of taking escort ships *away* from convoys to go after submarines. This tactic would not coincide with the objective of delivering x tons of supplies abroad.

In the case of supplies delivered minus supplies lost as the criterion, it, too, can be criticized in that the *least* supplies lost to submarines could probably be achieved by carrying *insufficient* supplies in *too few* ships and under heavy escort. The unbounded use of such criteria as the above and the tendency to strive for a maximized or minimized ratio usually lead to absurd results. What's the answer to this illustration? Well, it probably will emerge near the actual specification of a *certain* minimum level of *certain* supplies to be transferred at minimum cost.

In real life, recognizing which alternatives are *not* feasible due to

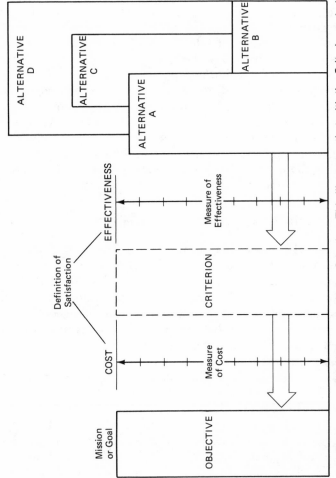

FIGURE 5.1 Cost, Effectiveness, and the Criterion. This illustrates that with the Criterion set at an acceptable point or measure on the effectiveness scale, Alternative A comes closest to satisfying the Objective. The other alternatives are below or exceed the acceptable Criterion.

constraints, applicability, and the pursuit of objectives which do not solve the problem as illustrated above, is just as important as discovering those alternatives which are feasible. All decisions are made within some constraints. Or at least almost all. The closest example to the contrary was the Manhattan Project (the atomic bomb) or perhaps the Polaris Project (nuclear propelled submarines carrying Polaris guided missiles). Even technical constraints were overcome with sheer resources. But normally, constraints such as physical or administrative ones, budget size, legal blocs, technological limits (of the moment), and even political ones, may exclude many alternatives.

SOME MODELS AND CALCULATIONS
OF OTHER CASE STUDY ALTERNATIVES

Of the baker's dozen of alternatives listed in chapter 4, a brief foray into two or three may be interesting at this juncture. The first alternative to analyze is that of building an office building/parking garage unit and renting both office space and garage space to the tenants. After all, we can usually go up if we can't go outward! Analyzing this alternative will be easier now that we have done one and also have some numbers acceptable for other alternatives. The second alternative will be an even more ambitious one of an apartment building/office building/parking garage in one unit.

A third will be at the other end of the scale, that of simply razing the theater, building a park, and holding the property for future profit.

I. CONSTRUCTING AND OPERATING AN OFFICE BUILDING AND PARKING FACILITY AND RENTING BOTH.

a. Investment Costs
We already know these for the garage:

Demolish theater	$ 40,000
Opportunity cost	1,000,000
Construct garage	2,000,000
Total	$3,040,000

b. Continuing Costs
Operation and management of garage $ 100,000
(Reduced greatly because of self-parking of office tenants weekdays)

Operation and management of office building	$ 250,000
(Interior office cleaning by tenants)	
(Includes administration offices for staff)	
Property tax loss	$ 200,000
Total Continuing Costs	$ 550,000

c. *Revenues*

Rent of ground floor shops (none)	0
Rent of garage spaces	
Weekdays (800 × $2.00) × 260 =	$ 416,000
Saturdays (same as alternative #1)	287,300
Sundays (same as alternative # 1)	75,000
Rent of Offices	
$300 per office × 600 × 12 months =	$2,160,000

(Average rental for first class office in city at present)

It is quite possible to park 200 cars per floor in a one-acre square size facility. Thus, it would require four floors of parking for 800 cars. One floor could be below street level. The stores in the first level would be eliminated. All four floors would be for office tenant parking exclusively, with spaces available for visiting business persons.

The size of the office structure erected on top of the garage also would be a square acre in size, and let's assume it to have enough floors for offices to accommodate each office tenant.

Recalling the 1.75 persons per car figure established earlier, 800 cars could carry 1400 office building individuals. With such a convenience it is assumed all 800 spaces will be filled. (Yes, the author is aware of the "American way" of one car-one person, but the survey shows 1.75 is the average.)

Next, assuming an average of 10 persons per modern *business* office, requiring a suite of 3 spaces, and 4 persons per professional office, also using 3 spaces, an average of 7 per 3 spaces may be reasonable, even low. The combination envisaged is about half and half. Thus, if there are 3 office spaces for every 7 people and we have parking for 1400 tenants, there will be a need for a building of about 600 office and service spaces. It is reasonable to assume at least 12 spaces per outside side of the building per floor, and 8 spaces per inside side. Thus, $(12 \times 4) + (8 \times 4) = 80$ spaces per floor. An 8-story building would yield 640 spaces, sufficient for offices, service rooms and perhaps other attractions. As an 11-story structure, it would be a relative dwarf among modern city buildings.

Returning to investment costs, the most recent construction the author has been aware of was the building of two 5-story, very deluxe, long-lived edifices with garages beneath them (actually 7 floors). The cost of each was about $4.5 million. They were of granite facade with superb foundations, carpeted, fireproof, air-conditioned, steel, concrete, and glass structures befitting a prestigious government building. The cost was about $900,000 per floor, leaving the garages out of the picture. Hence it seems reasonable to expect that $750,000 per floor for the usual commercial building is an acceptable figure.

$$8 \text{ floors} \times 750,000 = \underline{\$6,000,000}$$
$$\text{Total Investment Costs } \$9,040,000$$

Thus, ignoring the highly probable other revenues due to more business persons downtown, restaurants, retailers, workers, and city revenues, the approximate annual net income could be

$$\$2,388,300 \text{ or about } \$2.4 \text{ million}$$

II. COST/BENEFIT COMPARISON

Investment costs of $9 million divided by $2.4 million equal a return on investment of less than four years, a remarkable return for real estate.

If the project life is still considered as 40 years, approximately $96,000,000 gross return will be realized for an investment of $9,000,000. This is a remarkable *gross* return on the investment. However, *before computing present value* of the investment, which is, of course, the only valid projection, let's compare alternatives.

The garage-alone project, with no office building, provided a gross return of only $15.2 million or 51 percent. The comparison is already self-evident. Next, as we look at the discount (present value), the comparison is as follows:

- Alternative #1 (garage)
  Present value of $380,000 per year for 40 years at 10 percent equals $3.72 million. (Investment of $3 million; annuity multiplier of 9.779). $3.72 million ÷ $3 million = 12 percent return
- Alternative #2 (garage and offices)
  Present value of $2.4 million per year for 40 years at 10 percent equals 23.5 million (Investment of $9,000,000; annuity multiplier of 9.779) $23.5 million ÷ $9 million = 26 percent return

Admittedly, our second alternative does not consider a loss to the subway or sales tax revenues, both of which are subject to modification under alternative #2. Some pluses and some minuses could offset one another here. Also, we have not helped the parking situation for shoppers, but we may have forced them into making more use of the subway. The "equalizers" are up for analysis!

To summarize the economic return for alternative #1, the internal rate of return produced roughly 10 percent to 12 percent regardless of the time period chosen from 20 to 40 years. It was considered satisfactory. For a 10 percent rate the $3,720,000 (10 percent for 40 years of $380,000 × 9.779 multiplier) when divided by the investment of $3,040,000 yielded a 12 percent plus return.

In the second alternative, the discounted 40-year return at 10 percent yielded $23.5 million. When divided by $9 million investment, it yielded a 26 percent plus return.

Even if our assumptions were 50 percent *wrong* for alternative #2, the difference is acceptable.

As a timely afterthought to the above alternative to construct a combination garage/office building, an interesting example is being aired over the media. The New York Radio City Music Hall has just been saved for another year by a $2 million subsidy from the State of New York. Suddenly, no less than three authoritative sources claimed simultaneously to have been the first to think of the alternative for the future, that of constructing an office building atop the music hall which would return about $2 million annually. Sounds apropos to our case.

A MODEL FOR THE GARAGE/OFFICE BUILDING REPRESENTATION

A simple model similar to one of those for the garage-alone alternative could be represented as shown in Figure 5.2.

Granted, there is leeway in this brief calculation and model for questioning some assumptions, but the comparison between alterna-

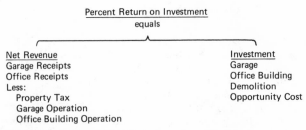

FIGURE 5.2 Percentage Return on Investment

tives #1 and #2 is enlightening. Let's do another alternative very briefly, again from the economic return objective, but one which has implications for a "future way of life" which is already upon us in some cities.

III. CONSTRUCTION AND OPERATION OF
A PARKING FACILITY, OFFICE BUILDING,
AND APARTMENT BUILDING AS A UNIT

The assumption here is that the entire unit would be for parking, working and living in by only the tenants; a rapidly developing possibility and actuality in some cities in view of several powerful factors—the energy crises and a crime rate coupled with a virtual state of siege on the horizon for law-abiding citizens,

a. Investment Costs
Demolition, opportunity and garage
construction costs $ 3,040,000
Office building costs   9,000,000
Apartment builing costs:
If we required 8 floors for 1400 office
workers, we should allow for double that
number in the proposed one, two, three
rooms and apartments or 2800 persons. This
requires a 16 floor apartment atop the offices,
or double the office building segment   18,000,000

Total Investment Costs $30,040,000

The edifice is now a 31-story building, still well within reasonable height in the modern city.

b. Continuing Costs
Same as alternative #2 $ 520,000
Plus maintenance and renting of apartments   250,000
(all three rental services and other services
to operate from a central office)

$ 770,000

It seems reasonable to assume that such a
consolidation of rental and service functions
could be done for half the individual costs or $ 380,000

Property tax loss	200,000
Total Continuing Costs	$ 580,000

c. *Revenues*

Rental of parking spaces	$ 778,300
Rental of office spaces	2,160,000
Rental of apartment spaces Average of $200 per space per month is "reasonable." 16 floors × 80 spaces × $200 × 12 months =	3,072,000

Again, let us ignore other highly probable benefits from increased population in the city with sales, retailers, workers, tax revenues, etc.

Total Revenues	$6,010,300
Less Continuing Costs	580,000
Annual Net Return	$5,430,300

d. *Cost/Benefit Comparison*

$30 million ÷ 5.5 million = about 5½-year payback.

If the project life remains at 40 years, the gross return, undiscounted, would be $217,212,000. However, applying present value annuity calculations, the return would be based on 10 percent × 40 years or a multiplier of 9.779 × annual net revenue of $5,430,300 equals $53,-102,903. On an investment of $30 million, this would be about an 18 percent return.

Thus it appears that comparing alternative #2 to #3, #2 offers a higher return of 26 percent after discounting compared to 18 percent for #3. However, the *amount* of money generated by #3 is $53 million, compared to $23.5 million for #2. And there may be *no other* opportunity to get the same *amount* from another alternative. On the other hand, the city would be investing only $9 million for #2, compared to the risk of $30 million for #3. To put the question squarely: $9 million gets you $23.5 million, $30 million gets you $53 million. Which would you take, a plus $14 million or a plus $23 million, assuming you had the investment *capability* of $9 million and $30 million respectively? This is where *real* decision making comes in, not only determining criteria, and the economic needs of the city, but also in *risk taking* for *more* return; and in making the nonquantifiable decisions concerning the city's long-range objectives, revitalization, business growth, amenities, and so forth, indeed, a whole way of life is at stake. Let's conclude this foray into alternatives with a brief consideration of one which does *not* have as its objective economic return, but the comfort of city dwellers, beautification, and ecological goals.

IV. DEMOLISH THEATER, BUILD PARK, AND HOLD PROPERTY FOR FUTURE BENEFITS.

a. *Investment Costs*
Demolition	40,000
Opportunity cost	1,000,000
Construct park	250,000
Total	$1,290,000

b. *Continuing Costs*
Repairs & Maintenance $60,000 per year × 40 years	$2,400,000
Total	$2,400,000

c. *Revenues*

d. *Property Appreciation*
After 40 years at 10 percent per year (no compounding)	$4,000,000

e. *Return on Investment*
   $3.69 million ÷ $4.0 million = 9 percent

However, there is *no stream of income* available during the 40 years, and the discounted dollar becomes less and less. In this alternative, the actual original investment of $1.2 million is be coupled with the continuing costs. Hence, the return of less than 10 percent after 40 years, with no continuous stream of income for use by the city during the years the dollar is worth more, appears to be a washout, unless public demand and the city's economy are such that a meaningful return is unimportant.

EVALUATION AND RANKING OF THE ALTERNATIVES

The alternatives used in this handbook were deliberately chosen to emphasize the need to question and pursue objectives other than the one first directed. If the decision maker is wise, he or she will insist upon a *range* of alternatives and even criteria. In the case, economic feasibility of a garage was directed, but as has been suggested, what may be the *best use of the site* is more appropriate.

Ranking the ones we did investigate relative to their economic return, based on the *best use* objective as well as simply the garage objective, they appear as follows:

1. The Garage/Office Building—most return for the investment.
2. The Garage/Office/Apartment Building—next best (or best?).
3. The Garage—next best.
4. A Park—last.

Looking at the consequences, that is, evaluating the alternatives against the decision rule, is another consideration. The first is the feasibility of building and operating a downtown parking facility. There are some evaluations to be concerned with in addition to the implied economic return consequence. A garage would bring with it added noise, pollution, traffic costs, road and street wear, decreasing amenities to the downtown area, and other problems. The same costs would occur in the choice of the other two, a garage/office and a garage/office/ apartment, except that both offer a greater return for the investment. Both also offer other economic returns in the wake of an office building filled with people who would certainly buy downtown, if only many of their meals. The apartment dwellers added in alternative #3 would become *downtown* shoppers and help revitalize the whole area and the city.

The park, on the other hand, may not have the consequences of pollution, noise, and traffic and street wear, but it might cost extra police protection, vandalism, noise of a different kind, and so on. The city dwellers may be willing to pay the price and loss of income, but that could only result if they or the city fathers, as the decision makers, decided upon that objective.

The whole future pattern of life in the inner city is a consequence. Is progress a matter of garages and cars accommodated, with its commercial benefits, or is it to be measured in beauty and keeping cars *out* of the city? The subway system may be fine for those who can use it, but what of the accessibility for businessmen, out-of-towners, and visitors and the competition with suburbia? It all rests upon the choice of objectives. If those in a position to decide choose the economic route, then several alternatives apply and can be ranked according to their effectiveness.

An economically oriented analysis will provide the most cost-effective alternative, whether we look for the *least cost for maximum benefit*, or *fixed effectiveness* for *least cost*; or even *unequal benefits* and *unequal costs* may be deliberately chosen. A satisfaction-oriented analysis will produce another kind of alternative whereby the outputs are measured by how satisfied people are with that alternative, while economic alternatives are ignored. In either case, systematic examination of all the possibilities will yield the data upon which decision makers can make more rational decisions.

This leads to a final discussion of the criterion (or criteria), which is the key to how the decision rule is applied.

THE CRITERION: APPLICATIONS

The criterion is *one's own* determination of the test one wishes to apply in selecting an alternative. It is anticipatory, in that decision makers determine in advance the rule or test which, when applied, will help them select the preferred solution or their idea of an optimum course of action. It is the *standard* by which judgment is made about the relative merits of a choice. It is the standard for ranking alternatives in order of desirability, *provided* they achieve *the* objective determined earlier.

Normally, the criterion or decision rule is expressed in one of the following ways, briefly mentioned in the earlier outline and until now touched upon but not categorized completely:

1. Provide the *same level of effectiveness* for all alternatives, and select the one with the least cost. This is the discounted or present value cost, if investment and returns are concerned, which is the situation in the greatest number of cases. This is called the *least cost* alternative or, to reverse it, the fixed effectiveness, minimized cost rule.
2. Provide the *same cost* for all alternatives and select the one with the *most effectiveness*. As a rule, in cases where benefits or outputs are the determining factor, it is usual to prefer that alternative which yields the greatest effectiveness for a given level of cost, again discounted where applicable. In situations where quantifying benefits or outputs is difficult, it still pays to provide as much useful information as possible to enable a good decision based upon knowledge and sound reasoning. This is called the alternative of *maximum benefits*, or fixed cost, maximum benefits.
3. Determine a *ratio* between cost and effectiveness. Care should be exercised here, as a favorable ratio must be a feasible one. Remember our aspirin, eggs, and watermelons.

4. When *both* *benefits* and *costs* are *unequal*, there is no all-purpose criterion for ranking alternatives. However, if the benefits of a higher cost alternative are judged greater than a lesser cost alternative, a choice must still be made. In such a case, if analysis can show the *extent* to which benefits would have to increase to *justify* the choice of the added cost alternative, it will have served its purpose. This is called the *unequal cost* and *unequal benefits* alternative. It is one which occurs more often than imagined.
5. Where all units are compatible and comparable, *profit* is usually the criterion, as it is in most business situations.
6. If special considerations require the selection of something other than a cost/benefit alternative and criterion, the situation requires a decision, but one that is *compelling* and *defensible*. These kinds of criteria include those relating to choices between contingencies such as the best estimate, the worse case, a priori analysis, or dominance.

It is interesting to note that in any decision theory one may use, little guidance is provided as to *how to really select decision rules*, other than the guidelines given above. The selection is pretty much up to the analyst and decision maker.

Applying the guidelines to the case illustrates the criteria:

1. Build and operate a garage—an alternative with an implied criterion of *maximum benefits*.
2. Build and operate a garage and office building—another alternative with the same *maximum benefits* as the criterion, except the benefits are greater than those in alternative #1.
3. Build and maintain a public park—an illustration of a *special consideration* criterion, believed to be compelling and defensible.
4. Leave the site vacant—an alternative of *least cost* of a special kind. The fixed effectiveness is simply to provide a park.
5. Build and own a "self-parking" garage—the alternative of *least cost* with, one hopes, the same benefits as a managed and operated garage.
6. Any of the alternatives which call for such objectives as greater business activity or more city amenities, where costs may be incapable of being clearly defined and may be unequal, or benefits may be unequal (as judged by decision makers), could be classified as *unequal costs* and *unequal benefits*. The passage of time and events usually proves or disproves the reasonableness of such choices.

In selecting any alternative, one of the greatest difficulties is that of providing the same level of benefits for all alternatives and then selecting the one with the least cost, or vice versa. Ideally, to have the benefits clearly defined and the same for *all* alternatives is the best situation. But, as can be imagined, the sheer numbers of *different cost* levels or *different effectiveness* levels usually prevail and different results are obtained at each level. To make it easier to decide when presented with such an array of choices, it is best right from the start to set a minimum or a maximum standard for costs and/or effectiveness to help reduce the scope of the problem. Good judgment (or a fixed budget) may reveal quite clearly when the cost of *additional* effectiveness becomes simply prohibitive. When reasonable limits are set this way, it is another illustration of the necessity for subjective judgment as the deciding factor.

SUMMARY

In the evaluation phase, the primary task is to choose from among alternatives, using an appropriate criterion selected as a decision rule. The alternative chosen must agree with the objective and it must be predictable; that is, the alternative must illuminate what the consequences would be if it were selected. Evaluation may rest in the hands of any authority ranging from a single expert to the obvious results of good cost and effectiveness models. Evaluation is mostly the result of ranking alternatives according to the criterion decided upon by the decision-maker. There was only rudimentary use of models in the case study because of its nature, but in complex problems of greater magnitude, considerable "working" of a model to try out many and varied strategies is perhaps the closest that Systems Analysis comes to being scientific experimentation. This, when added to its demanding, thorough, quantitative, and systematic steps, makes it a most useful approach to modern problem solving.

It is equally important to look *outside* the model, to contemplate other alternatives which fit the objective. These alternatives may appear when assumptions are questioned. To put much of what has been set forth about alternatives and evaluation in the form of some useful self-questions, perhaps these will serve to remind the user of questions to be asked about the analysis and of the key decisions:

1. Should alternative A, B, or C or more be chosen?
2. Why?
3. Is there a better, different, or less costly way to reach the objective, not included in A, B, or C?
4. Will the benefits exceed the costs?
5. Why and what needs to be done to ensure they do?
6. Will A, B, or C accomplish more for a given cost, or cost less for a given effectiveness?
7. Are there factors common to each alternative, identifiable and equal? If so, can they be accepted?

8. Are the specified or unspecified *different* factors identifiable in each alternative? If so, they become dominant ones and require the most attention. The challenge is to rank them in some way as to importance and effect on the solution.

Delineating the whole range of alternatives and making a list of similar and different factors can yield insight, meaning, and comprehensiveness. The next test of a good analysis comes in the interpretation phase and then the acid test of the verification phase.

SUGGESTED FURTHER READING

CLELAND, DAVID I., and KING, WILLIAM R. *Management: A Systems Approach.* New York: McGraw-Hill, 1973.

FISHER, GENE H. *The Analytical Bases of Systems Analysis.* P-3363 (DDC No. AD 634512). Santa Monica, Calif.: RAND Corporation, 1966.

HARRISON, E.F. *The Managerial Decision-Making Process.* Boston: Houghton Mifflin, 1975.

6

The Interpretation Phase

The interpretation phase may be summed up as the phase of *using* the predictions obtained from the calculations and models, and the costs and effectiveness information derived from the predictions. This phase also uses whatever other information or *insight* is relevant to further compare alternatives, then derives conclusions about them, and then decides upon a course of action. The key phrase is "decides upon a course of action."

The players are the decision maker and the analysts. The decision is promulgated in the form of a recommendation for action by the players. This may sound like a bit of heresy to allow the analyst to participate, especially to Systems Analysis "purists," but the fact is, he or she does participate.

Let's pause for a moment to contemplate the enormous importance of the process and act of decision. One of the greatest living scholars of management today, Herbert A. Simon, opens his often quoted classic, *The New Science of Management Decision*, with these words:

What part does decision making play in managing? I shall find it convenient to take mild liberties with the English language by using "decision making" as though it were synonymous with "managing." ... All of these images [of a decision maker] have a significant point in common. In them, the decision maker is a man at the moment of choice, ready to plant his foot on one or another of the routes that lead from the crossroads. All the images falsify decision by focusing on its final moment. All of them ignore the whole lengthy, complex process of alerting, exploring, and analyzing that precede that final moment. In treating decision making as synonymous with managing, I shall be referring not merely to the final act of choice among alternatives, but rather to the whole process of decision.[1]

Although this quotation might well have been appropriate to open this handbook, it was deliberately reserved for this chapter to reemphasize how central the process is to all managerial actions, as well as to emphasize its particular rise to well-defined prominence in the interpretation phase of Systems Analysis.

THE DECISION

Earlier, I defined the decision in several ways, but the key words were inherent in this definition—the act of making a choice from among alternatives that satisfies the objective of the decision maker. The importance of this "act" is self-evident. It carries with it a determination to implement and to verify and perhaps to either confirm the solution or go back and start over again.

Ideally, decisions are made from an array of alternative results. Ideally, too, the array is made up of "same level" effectiveness results, and thus the least cost one can be selected. Usually, however, there are both maximum and minimum standards not only for effectiveness but of costs. The requirement for incremental analysis techniques and judgments are then used to reduce the scope and set reasonable (acceptable) limits in the *range* of choice.

However, after using these aids in developing reasonable *quantitative* measures of effectiveness, which in themselves require judgment, there remain the *qualitative* factors or the truly subjective considerations emphasized throughout the handbook. These often become *the* deciding factors. It is interesting to see how such subjective considerations even become *subjective probabilities.*

Some scholars of analysis have gone to great lengths *quantitatively* to prove that the most prevalent and interesting decision situations do *not* involve certainty or objective probabilities. Kassouf, for example, in his *Normative Decision Making* deals in some depth with what he calls "subjective probability." He notes that,

political strategy is based on the likelihood of war and peace, and throughout history different policy makers have held very different

---

[1] Herbert A. Simon, *The New Science of Management Decision* (New York: Harper & Row, 1960), p. 1.

estimates. In the stock market an individual who believes the likelihood of falling prices to be greater than the likelihood of rising prices makes a decision to sell a security to an individual whose expectations are more sanguine. Bankers and businessmen often view quite differently the chances for success of an enterprise, bettors at a horse race often have different "favorites." . . . if an individual has clear-cut preferences over a specified set of strategies he will act as if he assigned probabilities of various outcomes. These probabilities, called subjective probabilities, have all the mathematical properties of objective probabilities except they are unique to the individual.[2]

THE ROLE OF ITERATION

Decision makers should keep in mind that decisions are rarely irrevocable except in certain extreme circumstances. Warfare conditions, for example, are such an exception. It is more usual to find that if the decision needs to be revoked, the Systems Analysis Approach not only allows for another round of analysis by restricting the trial to something far less than an all-out implementation but also *insists* upon another such round if the decision is distrusted, does not solve the problem, or is simply not the best one. The process is called *iteration* and Figures 6.1 and 6.2 illustrate it, showing what should take place, following the interpretation phase during verification.[3]

Figure 6.2 may be helpful to show the functional steps in their iterative relationship.

Figure 6.3, which is found on page 105, is a combination of two of Hinrichs and Taylor's schematics dealing with iterations. It is also useful in visualizing the process.[4]

The point is that if the first analysis is not correct, a second, third, or more rounds of iteration may be necessary to ensure correctness. Hence, virtually nothing in analysis is irrevocable. Time, pressure, and resources may be the key factors which determine the practicability of iterations.

[2]Sheen Kassouf, *Normative Decision Making,* Prentice-Hall Foundation of Administration Series, (Englewood Cliffs, N.J.:, Prentice-Hall 1970), p. 40.

[3]E. S. Quade and W. I. Boucher, eds, *Systems Analysis and Policy Planning: Applications in Defense* (New York, Elsevier, 1968), pp. 14, 35.

[4]Harley H. Hinrichs and Graeme M. Taylor, *Systematic Analysis:* A Primer on Benefit-Cost Analysis and Program Evaluation (Pacific Palisades, Calif.: Goodyear, 1972), pp. 145, 148.

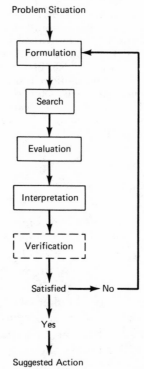

FIGURE 6.1 Phases of Systems Analysis

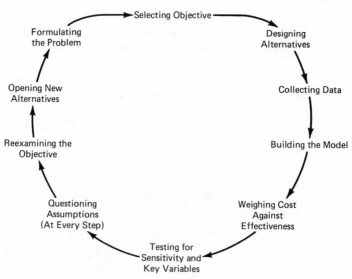

FIGURE 6.2 Iteration

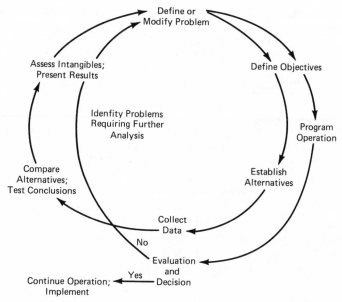

FIGURE 6.3 Analysis and Iteration

THE ROLE OF THE DECISION MAKER

In the interpretation phase, the sponsor or decision maker is primarily responsible for interpreting the analyst's work, but he should be assisted by the analyst in such interpretation. The decision maker is probably the best one to inject the real world back into the problem, which may lead to an iterative cycle. If he does, it is usually because the model was imperfect in representing the real world, or because he simply needs a better answer. Some practical questions the decision maker (or manager) should ask are these:

1. Is the problem stated the *real* problem?
2. Are the assumptions too restrictive or too optimistic?
3. Are any feasible and significant alternatives omitted?
4. Is the study adequately documented? (The documentation and report form will be covered later in this chapter.)
5. Are the facts stated correctly?
6. Are the cost estimates relevant?
7. Are incremental costs considered?
8. Is an amortization cost appropriate or used?

9. Is the model adequately identified and its representation of reality explained?
10. Is the model intuitively acceptable?
11. Is the effectiveness measure appropriate to the functions to be performed (the mission)?
12. If quantitative measures of effectiveness are unattainable, is a qualitative comparison feasible?
13. Are the criteria consistent with higher echelon objectives? Remember the *systems* concept.
14. Have all the significant ramifications been considered in arriving at the conclusions and recommendations?
15. Are the conclusions and recommendations intuitively satisfying?

Now, these questions are by no means meant to replace the need to question every phase and step, but they are among the more popular and productive ones to be asked by decision makers.

Alain C. Enthoven, in his efforts to introduce the Systems Analysis Approach in the Department of Defense, was always extremely careful to define the roles of the decision maker and the analyst. He wrote:

By using Systems Analysis and taking it seriously, I do not mean that the decision-makers must accept the results of the analyses uncritically or that they must rely exclusively on the Systems Analysis input. Far from it. Every analysis must be based on many assumptions, and a responsible decision-maker may not choose to accept the assumptions that his analysts have made. What *is* important is that the analyses be given a fair hearing and be acted upon if they successfully stand up under reasonable debate or criticism; or, if they are not acted upon, that the analysts are told why so that they can correct their work in the future.[5]

Good criteria and good answers can best be found by working with a problem, as the analyst does. They cannot be developed a priori. Ends and means will always interact and their consequences must be clearly borne in mind.

THE ROLE OF THE ANALYST

A good analyst will have anticipated the above questions and be prepared to answer them as *he* or *she* sees the problem, but that is not necessarily the same as the decision maker's personal preferences and

---

[5]"A Modern Design for Defense Decision—A McNamara–Hitch–Enthoven Anthology," ed. Samuel A. Tucker, (Washington D.C.: Industrial College of the Armed Forces, 1966).

opinions. Nevertheless, to be as prepared as possible is just good common sense for any analyst. How far should the analyst go in persuasion, or in "selling" the solution? Some say he should have no part in any final decision. This seems not only impractical and unreal but absurd as well. To cut off the best source of information, assuming the analyst is honest and unbiased, is to cut off interpretation born of close association and actual working with the problem. I side with those who feel that an analyst should arrive at conclusions which, by their obvious appropriateness, become recommendations toward a decision. When the analyst and decision maker are one and the same, the propitiousness of the argument simply evaporates. This is often a necessity when the decision maker must, for various reasons of size, resources, or the nature of the organization, be his *own* systems analyst. That, incidentally, is one of the main purposes of this handbook, to assist the manager who has the determination and foresight, but not the resources, to perform his own analysis of a problem or an opportunity.

Decision making is the final province of the authority who sets forth the objective. This was spelled out as a given in the outline of Systems Analysis in chapter 2. That outline also concluded the decision section by stating that the analyst, having done all he can and clarified all alternatives, must leave the final choice to the authority. As a matter of principle, the statement is true as it stands, yet common sense dictates that the authority is going to and often does query the *analyst's* recommendations.

Having served on several "general staffs" in the military and on boards of directors in civilian life, the author can vouch for the fact that the authority will *actively* seek staff (analyst) recommendations and indeed would have little confidence in the analyst if he or she did not have such recommendations ready to submit. The trick is to have an analyst or staff person who is honest, unbiased, and objective. That is a situation which is not as easy to come by as one would expect. Oxes and axes are gored and ground, respectively, by many sources, and the same is true from within. All that can be done is to recruit the best person and rely on managerial intuition or prior evidence and, until proven otherwise, to rely on one's team members.

Indeed, various categories and various combinations of decision makers exist in real life. (1) There is the single decision maker of a dictatorial nature with purely passive followers. (2) There is a more democratic decision maker who shares the decision among those whose interests are at stake. (3) There are gradations in between these two, and even further, the laissez-faire decision maker who lets the followers make the decision. (4) There is the original type versus the traditional type, i.e., the situational decision maker. (5) There is the high-risk taker versus the low-risk taker; the short-term versus the long-term decision maker; and the successful versus the unsuccessful (who nevertheless continues to hold on to his or her prerogatives). Behavioralists give several names to all these: autocratic, democratic, laissez-faire, participative, situational, human skills or traits oriented, and other categories. Each style implies a range of from one and only one decision maker all the way through and including the lowest participant *capable* of making a decision. Hence, we should not be alarmed at the idea of the analyst or staff person also having an input to the final decision. The real question is, does the decision-maker's choice, made with or without others, produce the best decisions? If it does, if it works, then so be it!

THE RECOMMENDATIONS

Some thoughts on the subject of the propriety of the recommendations have already been set forth, but because of their impact if *implemented,* a few other observations are in order. Also appropriate at this point is a brief treatment of the kind of report recommended to back up an analysis, and more importantly, any conclusions or recommendations.

It is important for the analyst to distinguish carefully between what a study actually shows and the recommendations he or she may make on the basis of what he or she thinks the study implies. But, having clarified that point, the analyst should *not* be prevented from making recommendations or, at the very least, from drawing some conclusions.

An analysis is often far from over when it is presented to the decision maker. There will always be unanswered questions, new problems, new areas for investigation. But everything has to have some cutoff point and an initial report must be rendered. Extension of the study can come later.

THE REPORT

Before leaping ahead, let's examine what some experts have used as guidance in the matter of reporting practices.

One who has had experience in controllership includes this list of elements of a final report and summary:

ELEMENTS OF THE FINAL REPORT AND THE REPORT SUMMARY

1. General Objectives
2. Specific Requirements
3. Background Information
4. The Environment and Mission Mix
5. Facts
6. Assumptions
7. Reasons for Assumptions
8. Decision Criteria
9. Analytical Techniques
10. Conditions Under Which These Analytical Techniques Can Be Used
11. The Alternatives
12. Results of the Study Effort
13. Recommendations (Optional)
14. Documentation[6]

The author has no quarrel with any of the parts of a good report, as listed. However, one or two may need clarification for the reader. The breakdown of "General Objective" into "Specific Requirements" is, of course, suboptimization. It permits the broad objective to be handled in practical contributing parts, but each must be clearly reported upon as a contribution to the main objective. "Background Information" is always helpful to orient the user. "The Environment and Mission Mix" means that, for a product to be profitable, the proper market structure must be determined. Systems Analysis cannot be performed in a vacuum. Conditions under which the solution will operate must be defined. If the objectives are to be realized, the mission mix must be clearly defined. That is, the type of application and frequency must be determined. For example, one hears of "real time" on a computer being very important these days, However, how often is an *immediate* printout needed, say, on the background of each employee, as compared to an immediate printout of an enemy attack? In brief, the mission must be realistic and the solution geared to the needs. When one "mixes" the mission with two or more goals, additional care must be taken. In short, the question to keep in mind is, what is the right mission, its timing, and its importance vis-a-vis related missions?

"Facts" means facts and needs no elaboration, as does "Assumptions," which has been repeatedly emphasized in the handbook. Make

[6]Paul L. Peck, Jr., "Management and the Systems Analysis Mystique," extract from *Economic Analysis and Military Resource Allocation*, ed. T. Arthur Smith, Washington, D.C.: Office of Comptroller, Dept. of Defense, 1968), p. 5, Figure 1.

the assumptions explicit and explain the reasons for the assumptions or *why* they were chosen. "Decision Criteria" means exactly that—what criterion or criteria did the decision maker set? Have they been met? "Analytical Techniques" and the "Conditions Under Which These Can Be Used" are always a welcome clarification to a decision maker. He or she should not have to guess at what tools, techniques or calculations were made. His or her job (your job?) is tough enough! "Alternatives" speaks for itself—a crucial part of the report. "Results and Recommendations (Optional)" also is strongly urged. The manager must be given the benefit of the analyst's knowledge; he deserves it! "Documentation" is essential. If numbers are arrived at or critical sources used, then by all means document the work already laboriously done. The time spent in having numbers, equations, models, or judgments which have been omitted from a report explained fully to a manager is one of the most wasteful kind of "drills," about which I know only too well. Endless hours of discussion and clarification can be avoided by including them.

Another, more flexible reportorial set of formats has been successfully used by Hinrichs and Taylor and appears throughout the wide range of reports tailored to unusual problems in their cost study reports in *Program Budgeting and Benefit Cost Analysis.*[7] The authors include whatever is appropriate for each analysis from the following parts:

1. The Problem
2. Goal and Objective
3. Data Gathered
4. The Analysis
5. Input and Output Measures
6. Cost Measures
7. Effectiveness/Benefit Measures
8. Criterion
9. Control Data (Constraints and Other Factors)
10. Alternatives (Costs and Benefits of Each)
11. Suggestions as a Result of the Study (or) Comments on the Analysis
12. Calculations

Still another, shown in Figure 6.4, is a highly formalized but practical format for costing out government decisions, used by the Comptroller's Office of the Department of Defense.[8]

[7]Harley H. Hinrichs and Graeme M. Taylor, *Program Budgeting and Benefit Cost Analysis: Cases, Text, and Readings* (Pacific Palisades, Calif.: Goodyear 1969), *Passim.*

[8]U.S. Department of Defense Instruction, "Economic Analysis and Program Evaluation for Resource Managers" (Washington, D.C., 18 October 1972), No. 7041.3, Enclosure (1).

SUMMARY OF COSTS FOR ECONOMIC ANALYSIS/
PROGRAM EVALUATION STUDIES
FORMAT A

1. Submitting DoD Component: _____

2. Date of Submission: _____

3. Project Title: _____

4. Description of Project Objective: _____

5. Alternative: _____   6. Economic Life: _____

8. Program/Project Costs						
7.	a. Non-Recurring		b. Recurring	c.	d.	e. Discounted
Project Year	R&D	Investment	Operations	Annual Cost	Discount Factor	Annual Cost
1.						
2.						
3.						
.						
.						
.						
.						
25.						
9. TOTALS						

10a. Total Project Cost (discounted)
10b. Uniform Annual Cost (without terminal value)
11.   Less Terminal Value (discounted)
12a. Net Total Project Cost (discounted)
12b. Uniform Annual Cost (with terminal value)

FIGURE 6.4

SUMMARY OF COSTS FOR ECONOMIC ANALYSIS/
PROGRAM EVALUATION STUDIES
FORMAT A

13. Source/Derivation of Cost Estimates: (Use as much space as required)

    a. Non-Recurring Costs:

        1.) Research & Development:

        2.) Investment:

    b. Recurring Cost:

    c. Net Terminal Value:

    d. Other Considerations:

14. Name & Title of Principal Action Officer   Date

FIGURE 6.4 (continued)

Although the method is called economic analysis, one must keep in mind the purpose for which the requirement was meant, namely, the *economic soundness* of decisions affecting the taxpayer's dollar.

This reprint of a basic reporting form helps the Department of Defense to compare and to arrange in order of priority the thousands of component (resource) requests received by the largest single enterprise in the United States—the U.S. military establishment.

Other similar formats are acceptable, designed for various components, but the example given is basic and typical. Note the emphases on the alternative, on economic life and total costs, ranging from nonrecurring to recurring, and on the discount factor and discounted annual cost. Projects really are in competition with each other in the Defense Department. Moreover, they are subjected to analysis at unit levels, fleet and force levels, major command levels, indeed at all levels, prior to review and choice by the Pentagon. In effect, this means that, today, every command is an analysis center and must be competent to perform economic analysis *and* Systems Analysis to apply for and defend expenditures. This practice may come as some consolation to taxpayers. The required reports are but part of a complete description of the tools of analysis and the steps taken in justifying new outlays of resources for anything important, whether it be a new or improved military installation, a weapons system, or even a new warehouse at a supply depot. Needless to say, the task required some assistance by analysts; however, it has worked. Of course, it would be naive to rule out the constraints of subsequent political reactions, scarce resources, human personalities, and so forth, but it is an improvement.

Lastly, a kind of report used in local governments, in nonprofit organizations, or in businesses of any kind is well illustrated by the case study solution. This report lacks only specific recommendations, which are left to the reader as the various alternatives unfold. Again, it is here that economic, social, political, ecological, or other objectives may influence the recommendations.

IMPLEMENTATION

Now that we are aware that the act of decision may possibly be presented in the form of a recommendation to the decision-making authority, it is well to remember that the same route upwards can apply as well to the decision maker who must, in turn, recommend the decision to a higher authority. There are times when one may wonder where "the buck stops," but it does; it must.

What is equally important to remember is that the decision maker may *not* be the one who must *implement* the decision. It may hinge on the approval of a corporate or political or other body. Hence, the recommendation must be convincing enough to result in implementation of the trial solution.

Recommendations, if used, should be supported by the kind of full reports outlined in this chapter. They should be explicit about all the assumptions, uncertainties, and sensitive variables which went into the analysis. Above all, they should not be a "sales job," but the step in which explicitness and honesty are the keynotes.

Implementation is a tough job. Most analysts and planners and some decision makers avoid it like the plague. It is a difficult task for many reasons. First, it requires a special kind of manager, a committed, hard-driving person with a high frustration threshold. It requires finding scarce resources. It requires selling the decision (and change) to those in entrenched positions or programs. It requires a whole set of action-oriented individuals: planners, operators, controllers, and administrators of a special breed. It requires "doers" who meet the challenge of change and all its difficulties. It is they who must give life to the model, the decision, even though they know it may be a one-shot deal or the creation of a whole new enterprise. Since the decision *is* based on another decision not to go all out until the first trial is verified, theirs is a peculiar and rare position of commitment to have to champion.

Implementation is replete with exasperating experiences, especially if some other authority is determined not to have the test carried out. What is worse, it is impossible if the implementors are not sold on the solution.

Also, implementors face a variety of personalities, attitudes, selfishness, entrenchment, ambition, individual and group values and beliefs—all of these and more. As a former analyst, decision maker *and* implementor, the author can vouche for the implementation phase as deserving of far more study and understanding than it has received.

Implementation means, to a large extent, commitment. Commitment means the expenditure of resources. Implementation means the acid test—was the decision correct or must we go back to the drawing board of analysis? That is why it is under the scrutiny of all the other participants of the management game, such as labor and the tax-paying public.

Fortunately, however, there are implementors and they do their job. Otherwise, we would be observing a stagnant state of affairs. Luckily, the Systems Analysis Approach encourages a trial implementation, subject to verification, during the next phase in the approach.

THE INTERPRETATION PHASE AND
THE CASE STUDY

Returning to our case study, the decision step of the interpretation phase is left open to the city fathers and to the reader. Dick Stockton's report was thorough and obviously fair in his analysis of the objective given him. In his initial report (the solution) he went further than the objective and offered an impressive list of other considerations which could not be quantified. His solution was also a good attempt to quantify all that could be short of deeper investigation, surveys, and other methods. Had he gone further in the economic area, he would have investigated the next alternatives, which were discussed in chapter 5. Or, he would have investigated other objective paths such as the creation of a park, also as described in chapter 5. In short, with adequate assistance and more time, Dick had several alternatives open for further analyses.

The format of his report was quite like that of the illustrations in this chapter, but mostly like the Hinrichs-Taylor of the Systems Analysis Approach phases and steps. Starting with the opportunity and problem in the case study, on through the systems evaluation, the subobjectives or suboptimizations, the analysis in terms of cost, benefits, model, and criterion, then on to reexamination of assumptions and uncertainties, and final determination that the project was *economically* feasible, all fit the format of a good report. He did not delve into other alternatives, but he did examine *externalities* and other side effects and suggested other objectives and alternatives. The detail into which he went for all calculations is the secret to success. No decision maker wants to go back to the mathematical or statistical "work bench" to prove what the analyst should do; hence, the analyst's detailed computations are welcome to busy managers who are frustrated and "turned off" by having to search for unexplained numbers. If the computations are such that they can be contained in the body of the report, that is where they belong. If the study produces longer, more complex source information, the calcualtions should be placed at the end as appendices or attachments and so designated in the body of the report. All this may seem elementary, but it is surprising to know of the number of fine studies and reports which have lost their effect on the reader due to too lengthy, unorganized, or simply unexplained final data.

In our case study it is clearly the role of the decision makers, the city fathers, to make the decision. But Dick has left the door open to encourage their consideration of other alternatives, for the analyst in this case is also a member of the decision-making group.

Implementation in the case study could well be assigned to the engineer with the city's planner and finance director as members to plan for and carry out the decision. They could either serve in person or assign their designates to serve. Perhaps a separate group of second echelon city professionals could be used. Or, the "project" arrangement, whereby one official is given the task with *full authority* to call on and use appropriate individuals from any department, is feasible.

In the case study, the actual erection of a garage would be irrevocable; however, to erect it with plans for enlargement to a garage/office or garage/office/apartment complex would still be possible. Implementation might even be restricted to an in-depth study of two or three similar projects, in the city or in other cities, before carrying out the construction of the parking facility. This, of course, would require time and effort, but in view of the project would appear to be in order.

SUMMARY

The interpretation phase is broader than its name implies. Commencing with the important act of making a decision to go ahead with an alternative (at least a prototype or single product) the next step is implementation, the phase which requires *commitment* of resources.

The recommendation which flows from a good report or study can be the result of single or joint actions. Fortunately, Systems Analysis has even one more phase, that of verification, before proceeding to full implementation, or returning to the problem and objective in order to carry out the iterative process. The verification phase is usually short but the crucial point is to decide whether to "go" or "no go." This phase will be described briefly in the next chapter.

SUGGESTED FURTHER READING

HINRICHS, HARLEY H., and TAYLOR, GRAEME M. *Program Budgeting and Benefit Cost Analysis: Cases, Text and Readings.* Pacific Palisades, Calif.: Goodyear, 1969.

KASSOUF, SHEEN. *Normative Decision Making.* Prentice-Hall Foundations of Administration Series, Englewood Cliffs, New Jersey: Prentice-Hall, 1970.

PECK, PAUL L., JR. "Management and the Systems Analysis Mystique." In *Economic Analysis and Military Resource Allocation.*

Edited by T. Arthur Smith. Washington, D.C.: U.S. Department of Defense, 1968.

QUADE, E.S., and BOUCHER, W.I., eds. *Systems Analysis and Policy Planning: Applications in Defense*. New York: Elsevier, 1968. Chapter 3.

SIMON, HERBERT A. *The New Science of Management Decision*. New York: Harper & Row, 1960.

TUCKER, SAMUEL A., "A Modern Design for Defense Decision—A McNamara-Hitch-Enthoven Anthology." Washington, D.C.: Industrial College of the Armed Forces, 1966.

U.S. Department of Defense Instruction. "Economic Analysis and Program Evaluation for Resource Managers." No. 7041.3, Enclosure (1). Washington, D.C.: 18 October 1972.

7

The Verification Phase

VERIFICATION OF INITIAL
IMPLEMENTATION

The verification phase is shorter and more decisive than the preceding phases. Simply put, it is an evaluation of the initial (trial) implementation followed by a "go" or "no go" decision for full implementation. When the alternative decided upon is built, simulated, or produced in any form, a host of strange events can follow. Significant omissions and unforeseen relationships and side effects suddenly manifest themselves and must be taken into consideration. After all, if the Systems Analysis Approach is to be true to its precepts, its effects upon other systems and subsystems are important. The worst thing to do is to ignore them. The best thing is to face them and consider those which may "drive" the problem to an entirely different solution or to those which may be acceptable as trade-offs.

UNFORESEEN CONSTRAINTS

The first of such unforeseen factors may be labeled constraints, that is, constraints which are in addition to those initially recognized and which were dealt with in the analysis.

Many decisions in business may well be part of a political or social process as well as an economic one. It may become obvious that to achieve the most efficient and effective objective, considerations greater than cost and effectiveness are at stake. Some of these constraints may be such unmeasured facts as the morale of those affected, their possible adverse behavior, unforeseen political ramifications, traditions, fairness, humaneness, the need for *quid pro quos*, or the need for trade-offs before the decision can be implemented. All these and more surface during the verification phase. Sources of problems or objectives never dreamed of during analysis are quick to show up if it appears that something is *really* going to be done about something!

This leads to a few pertinent remarks about the first appearance of a study report and the act of reporting during and after the presentation of findings. For years the social psychologists have known that a bad idea can be peddled in a fancy box. On the other hand, a great innovative solution may be ignored because it is not properly presented. The lesson here is self-evident.

But more important, complete studies often trigger an "adversary process." It can range from a counteranalysis to a detailed critique of the original analysis. The latter attack forces the original analyst(s) to defend the *analysis* and not necessarily the solution. The best defense is to stick to the system being analyzed and the *objective* for which it was intended. If the analysis as a *process* becomes the focus of attention, if it has not been properly done (and here is where the Systems Analysis Approach, with its rigor and thoroughness, is strongest), the finding may well be destroyed by antagonists. This is an agonizing experience for one who has dedicated much time and considerable effort to a problem.

To return to constraints, Hinrichs and Taylor, who have worked with Systems Analysis in perhaps a broader range of problem areas than most others, emphasize their extreme importance.[1] To paraphrase some of their observations, they first list limited resources as the prime constraints that might be expected in the real world of scarcities. However, these are generally discovered in the course of analysis. They "drive" the solution to remain within such limited resources from the beginning. But the additional constraints, which may be acknowledged in the course of analysis but left to be dealt with later, now become just as important. There are *physical constraints*, the constraints of the state of technology and knowledge at a given time, for example. There are *legal constraints*, the laws, property rights, international conventions, agency rulings, and so on, which can further reduce the field of feasible solutions. There are *administrative constraints*, because programs to be implemented require people to be hired, trained, and put to the task. As an example, a newly devised tax

---

[1]Harley H. Hinrichs and Graeme M. Taylor, *Systematic Analysis: A Primer on Benefit-cost Analysis and Program Evaluation:* (Pacific Palisades, Calif.: Goodyear, 1972) pp. 15–16.

system for a less-developed country may be unrealistic without the administrative processes and personnel to administer it. Indeed, this is often the most limiting set of constraints upon good economic analyses in the federal government. There are *distributional constraints,* i.e., the kind which affect the equality of economic or other kinds of distributions to certain income groups or age groups. Patterns of income distribution do exist. If disturbed by implementation of a decision, they can be potent constraints. There are *political constraints* which reveal that optimal decisions may not be realizable because of the practical politics of the moment. This is especially true if some short-term real income or group welfare may have been sacrificed to preserve political consensus. There are purely *financial constraints,* real budgetary problems which are discovered later in the analysis during implementation and verification. Finally, there are *traditional, social, and religious constraints.* Mores, values, and customs all have the power to preclude possible actions.

To ignore constraints is to depart from the real world. Conversely, to regard all solutions *except one* as being blocked by some constraint is to remove the problem from *any* analysis. Constraints, if treated as variables, can lead to choices as to which might be overcome or relaxed. A practical approach to dealing with them is to look on them as trade-offs and bargaining factors.

It is often difficult to draw the line between experimentation and all-out implementation. The verification phase is often described as that of testing the conclusions by experiment. According to this definition, it could be included in the interpretation phase. But the author would emphasize *testing* and offer the opinion that real testing more often requires commitment to full implementation of most business decisions. This was certainly true in the case study.

Applying constraints to the case study, it is clear that the decision to build and operate a parking facility could well have been negated by (1) the *distributional constraint* of private enterprise wanting to keep the city *out* of private enterprise; (2) the *political constraint* of practical politics of which the Mayor may be well aware, e.g., the objection of the public to go into private business or to change downtown; (3) the *physical constraint* of finding out the land would not support a structure as planned, or the lack of builders willing to take on a complex structure of garage/offices/and apartments; (4) the *administrative constraint* of not having the personnel to spare to implement and remain with the project until completion; (5) the *budgetary constraint* which may prevent the city from investing even $3 million; and finally, (6) the *traditional constraint* of having the garage perhaps flanked by churches or a historical burial ground or historical landmarks whose beauty would be affected, is not beyond imagination as a real impediment.

MEASURABLES AND UNMEASURABLES

The quantitative emphasis in Systems Analysis and decision making is generally concerned with countable and measurable features. But there are unmeasurables like convenience to parkers and shoppers, amenities to the city, ecological improvement, and political factors that are intangible and not normally subject to systematic quantitative analysis. Such unmeasurables are too important to be ignored, yet they defy analyzing. In such cases, the best thing is to present them systematically and in words. If the analyst attempts to put a quantitative and subjective numerical value on unmeasurable factors, it is something like the bathing-beauty contest in which each judge puts numerical scores on each of the features of human appearance—on human flesh and bone! The analyst should take care not to present the decision maker with such subjective numbers unless fully explained. Otherwise, the analyst is indeed making the decision.

In everyday use, the assignment of numbers to unmeasurable factors is an everyday occurrence, but in analysis, one must always precisely define any *interpretation* given to nonmeasurables. In the case study, one or two factors bordered on the unmeasurable, but most were measurable. It is in the "other considerations" part of a solution that unmeasurables are commonly found.

The decision-making sequence is heavily grounded in cost and benefit comparisons, as we have been in the case study. The crux of comparison is having the same yardstick, the same unit of account. Unfortunately, the problem of assigning values to inputs and outputs is tougher for public programs than it is for business or private decisions. As public programs and the public sector in general continue to grow, the problems of measurement become more critical to our economy. The question will be put to the public more and more, "how *much* is enough?" And it will usually be answered with "more." Fortunately, when a businessman contemplates a decision, the main worry is about revenues and costs and comparisons (though this too is changing as the social role and responsibility of business is being emphasized more and more). Also, for private decision makers the value problem is less difficult. At least the public need not be introduced into the picture unless the decision is an unusual one with far-reaching ramifications.

COMMENSURABLES AND INCOMMENSURABLES

Hopefully, any incommensurables, as well as unmeasurables, spill overs, side effects and sheer unknowns, are found during the analysis. These incommensurables are at least treated subjectively as they arise and are fully illuminated for the decision maker. But, like the "proof of the pudding" they may not all be revealed until the verification phase. Another of these difficult factors is called *incommensurables*. This means there are aspects of the system under study which cannot be treated in common terms. If they can be measured together they are called *commensurable*. It is well established that some factors in a decision situation can be measured while others cannot. It is the issue of what measurements can or can't be combined with other measurements that is important. One cannot add apples and alligators. Morale cannot be subtracted from mobility. Even though the first pair is countable, and *each* of the pair is measurable, they are not commensurable. The second pair cannot be measured even separately (except in a judgmental way such as "more" or "less" morale or mobility) let alone being commensurable with each other. Thus, these are spoken of as being incommensurable, i.e., not being in the same *kind* of units. Commensurability and its negative form, incommensurability, is a matter of common pairs or sets of qualities. Another commensurable pair is miles per gallon and kilometers per gallon. A single measurable factor is mail received, but it cannot be really measured with, say, morale. In the case study, dollars (costs) enabled us to comeasure factors, but even there, it was impossible to measure dollars with something like public opinion.

To deal with the "common denominator" problems, one can only recognize them, make them explicit and rely on reasonableness. It is when they are deliberately "paired" erroneously that they become dangerous to the decision, nor can they be substantiated.

UNKNOWNS: RISKS AND UNCERTAINTIES REVISITED

Unknowns, still another of the troublesome factors lurking in analysis, refer to those elements of the problem which are not and cannot be known or predicted with *any* degree of certainty.

One of the most difficult unknowns is the amount of risk involved in a decision. Even the use of present value and the concept of *streams of dollar benefits and costs* projected by an analyst are really probability assumptions. No one knows what time will bring about. In the case study the whole economic feasibility of the project rests on the uncertainty of the future or, to view it another way, the efficacy of income projections and discounting effects.

Where sheer unknowns exist, there are a few possibilities to pursue. One of them is to inject an adjustment factor into the forecast and subject the costs and benefits to more sensitivity analysis. How far off can one be and still have an acceptable solution? In the case study we allowed for 77 percent of the projected income to which receipts could fall and we could still "break even." Also, the basic philosophy underlying an objective could be changed by setting ranges of maximum and minimum values. The range could be from one of simple maximization, to a strategy of maximum (the maximum return on a minimum, set cost), or to maximax (the maximum in each case and the choice of the maximum of all of them). These tactics could help the knowledge of limitations, but not the probabilities within them.

The simple alteration of a discount rate, which is merely the compounding function of time, could also be used—but cautiously. Or, the "time horizon" could be altered to be more limited and hence *less* unknown in its long-term effects. These all presume that uncertainty is something undesirable and, "that people are willing to pay something to avoid it."[2] As Hinrichs and Taylor point out, however, some recent analysts argue that uncertainty is not an "undesirable" for the public sector as a whole, that because of the very *number* of undertakings and *variety* of outputs, the uncertainty in any one investment can be removed from the *total* decision process.

Nevertheless, the treatment of a future known to contain unknowns is largely unresolved. Thus, in practice, it is necessary to "make allowance for the presence of risk, and uncertainty is usually observed in the breach."[3]

Most of the above remedial measures have to do with economic costs and benefits, but what of the other unknowns and their consequences? These are usually called *side effects* and *spillovers* and will be discussed next.

[2]Hinrichs and Taylor, *Systematic Analysis*, p. 24.
[3]*Ibid.*

SIDE EFFECTS AND SPILLOVERS

The best categorization of side effects and spillovers is that found in Hinrichs and Taylor's *Systematic Analysis*.[4] Of the few works on the subject, it alone seems to treat them with the respect and attention they deserve. To paraphrase their treatment, it rests upon the very nature of analysis and model building to include some things and exclude others—that is, to abstract. Because of this, the test of an analysis rests on two main questions. (1) Are the variables in the model grouped together in order not to distort the analysis, and (2) Are the variables deliberately left out of a kind that would not seriously alter the results? The variables which are internally relevant to the analysis are called *internalities*. The variables determined to be *not* relevant to the analysis but *very much so* outside the problem are called *externalities*. They are also called *spillovers* and *side effects*, and they often have considerable impact, if not on the problem at hand, then certainly on the environment without. Four kinds of external effects which the analyst should be sensitive to are the following:

1. *Production-to-production spillovers:* activities by one producer which can affect the output of other producers. As examples, the water pumped from one mine can affect the production of others; heated water from an energy plant can affect the fishing industry. If these things happen, the analyst as well as the decision maker must account for the externality.
2. *Production-to-consumption spillovers:* activities by a producer which affect the environment or goods of consumers. The creation of noise, air, and water pollution as the result of production are well known examples.
3. *Consumption-to-consumption spillovers:* activities by a consumer or group which affect other consumers. Loud noises in the park on a quiet afternoon or the imposition of delays by a slow driver on other drivers on a thruway are examples.
4. *Consumption-to-production spillovers:* the reverse of number two, activities by which a consumer affects the environment or goods produced. A hunter destroying crops or causing a fire which burns out woodland is an example.

In the case study, each of these is a possibility. The city's entrance into the parking business may well adversely affect private garage owners. The creation of added noise and pollution downtown by more automobiles affects consumers (city dwellers). A parker may be careless and an accident delay entrance or egress of other parkers. A parker

---

[4]*Ibid.*, pp. 16–20.

may drive an unsafe car which burns and puts the garage out of commission for a while.

All of these illustrate both "real" externalities and not just "money" externalities. Indeed, it would be difficult to come up with a decision that does not impose some adverse effects on others. But, by the same reasoning, good side effects or spillovers are possible. The number of retailers who spring up to sell to the parkers in the case study, the gas stations that can benefit, the snack shops to provide services, the repercussions that reach back into suburbia with more people, more homes—all are possible beneficial spillovers. If the pecuniary spillovers are real, that is, *new* sources, and not merely "transfers" of existing income from one place or person to another, then they are truly countable.

Finally, on the subject of commensurables, incommensurables, measurables, unmeasurables, unknowns, spillovers and side effects, the best advice for handling all such factors which result from the analysis is simply, *do not ignore them.*

SUMMARY

Verification of the analysis is important because it can lead to full commitment. Commitment, while revocable in many cases, still carries with it the risk of using valuable resources which may *not* be replaceable and also the risk of affecting the rest of society with unforeseen and unexpected effects. It also means giving up something else; the opportunity cost takes effect.

Constraints surface in the Implementation Phase, constraints of a physical, administrative, distributional fairness and political nature, in addition to the ever-present financial and other resource constraints.

It is in this phase that the analysis is revealed to all concerned and to others who believe they are concerned. The "adversary process" is triggered and if care is not taken, a good analysis can be negated by those who attack it both as an analysis or with counteranalyses. This can be an agonizing period for one who may have devoted his or her very best to the problem, but it is the real world. Adequate preparation and a faultless report, *systematically* arrived at and unchallengeable in its rigor and thoroughness, are the best counterweapons.

Then too, it is during the phases of implementation and verification that other unforeseen effects appear. Things which were believed measureable may prove not to be so; things which seemed to be commensurable may prove not to be so; unknowns and uncertainties appear which require readjustments of forecasts, discount rates, sensitivity testing, time adjustments, etc.—all of which are designed to *reduce* the amount of uncertainty and to make known the unknown; to treat side effects and spillovers which may not have been foreseen, especially the important external ones.

But all these impediments must have occurred in the past and will again. And they have been successfully resolved. The progress and wealth of the world testify to a spirit of successful optimistic enterprise, and to the ingenuity of mankind.

SUGGESTED FURTHER READING

HINRICHS, HARLEY H., and TAYLOR, GRAEME M. *Systematic Analysis: A Primer on Benefit Cost Analysis and Program Evaluation.* Pacific Palisades, Calif.: Goodyear, 1972. Part I.

TIBBETTS, LARRY N. "A Practitioner's Guide to Systems Analysis." An unpublished paper by Colonel Tibbetts as a student at the U.S. Naval War College, Newport, R.I., 1975.

8

The Future
of Systems Analysis
in Decision Making

SOME FINAL CAVEATS

Most authors on the subject of Systems Analysis seem almost as obsessed with explaining its pitfalls and limitations as they are with its positive uses and potentials. Perhaps this is because of the fear it will not be seen as *they* see it—a superb methodology that assures the best approach yet known to problem solving—perhaps a fear that it will be judged on its lack of theory, and that a fallacy or two may prejudice its acceptance by forward-looking management.

Fallacies are errors in reasoning, and Systems Analysis really strives to eliminate them. Blunders are likely in almost any unstructured approach, but fallacies can and should be avoided through systematic analysis. Unfortunately, we live in a working environment in which a single fallacy (which by no means invalidates the work) is blown up out of all proportion to its effect. A fairly safe generalization is that there will *always* be the "ten-percenters"—those who deliberately overlook the 90 percent of what is *right* with human accomplishments and make their living by exaggerating the 10 percent that may be questionable. Such people often get promoted by such tactics. They are in every work environment from the world of academe to the government to the business world.

To make sure the reader is aware of the more common pitfalls or sources of error (which are *not* restricted to Systems Analysis), the next annotated list will serve the purpose of a checkoff list to help prevent the errors discussed below:[1]

---

[1]E.S. Quade and W.I. Boucher, eds. *Systems Analysis and Policy Planning: Applications in Defense* (New York: Elsevier, 1968) pp. 345–63.

- *Underemphasis on Problem Formulation.* A major pitfall is failing to allocate the total time intelligently, and spending an *insufficient* share in deciding what the problem really is. The desire to "get going" is hard to overcome at the crucial phase. "Look before you leap."

- *Inflexibility in the Face of Evidence.* Early conclusions can occur to the trained analyst. To come to any early conclusion in itself is not a mistake; the iterative process will prove whether it is valid. The real pitfall here is an unwillingness to discard a conclusion made early *or* late, in the face of new evidence.

- *Adherence to Cherished Beliefs.* In the formulation phase, the most serious error is to look at an unduly *restricted* range of alternatives. Quade and Boucher call this the "attention bias," or an unconscious adherence to a "party line," "company policy," "cherished belief," or just plain politics.

  Kahn and Mann in their *Ten Common Pitfalls* call the party line "the most important single reason for the tremendous miscalculations that are made in foreseeing and preparing for technical advances or changes in the strategic situation."[2] The party line is real; it must be dealt with.

- *Parochialism.* Quite similar to the above pitfall is the expectation that any man or any organization creating a system should reveal its faults. This manifests itself in several ways, one of which is the N.I.H. (Not Invented Here) syndrome, which prevents one's seeing one's own faults. The author documented this on the part of the United States in a government publication on international weapons coproduction efforts.[3] Another manifestation is found in the competition between and among military services and other governmental agencies.

- *Communication Failure.* If the analyst fails to communicate effectively with other professionals on the combined efforts, he or she commits a communication failure. Having someone on the team who is an expert in all phases and factors will help a great deal to ensure correct communication of technical data and all other "need to know" information to and among the contributing team members.

- *Overconcentration on the Model.* There is an almost inexplicable and inevitable tendency for good model builders to become more interested in their model than in the solution. Technical experts naturally like to show their talents in model building and mathematical data handling. The advice to adhere to in this pitfall is to be aware especially of those who would "fit your problem to their model."

- *Excessive Attention to Detail.* Complicated formulas and relationships can become so involved that it is no longer possible to use them, let alone understand them. Many say, as does the author, that the most convincing analysis is one which a *nontechnician* can think through.

---

[2]H. Kahn and I. Mann, *Ten Common Pitfalls* (RAND Corporation, R.M. 1937, July 1957), p. 42.

[3]A.H. Cornell, *An Analysis of International Collaboration in the Organization and Management of Weapons Coproduction,* U.S. Government, National Technical Information Service, Publication 22151, (Springfield, Va., 1969). Approved for public release.

The pitfall to be avoided is that of becoming so engrossed in the means that they become the ends. Paradoxically, connected with the error of focusing on means as ends is the error of *not* considering a means as an end when it really is. Due process of law is an example, as is reaching group decisions through democratic processes which are more valuable than the outcome itself.

- *Neglect of the Question.* The message here is that it is the question being asked that determines the model, not a complicated proposition that treats every possible aspect of the problem.

- *Incorrect Use of the Model.* Incidental computations from a model are plentiful but not always useful. The question the model represents is the paramount product. (Another problem with models is a belief that there are universal models. There are none.)

- *Disregard of the Limitations.* It is an error to forget the limitations which were self-imposed on the ranges of relationships, costs, benefits, and so on.

- *Concentration on Statistical Uncertainty.* The essence of most problems is uncertainty, otherwise the problems would not be as tough as they are. Trying to reduce uncertainty to definitive probabilities can have disastrous effects. Again, the best advice is to keep simplicity in mind and be careful of excursions too far into the highly sophisticated realm of probabilities. If needed, experts can be found who are good at probability.

- *Inattention to Uncertainties.* This has been dealt with completely earlier. The lesson is to keep uncertainties in mind, not to ignore them, and to realize their effect on other problems and other people when a course of action is decided on.

- *Use of Side Issues as Criteria.* If, after analysis, there is uncertainty about which alternative is best, beware of accepting a "side issue" analysis as adequate. The point to stress is that the decision must be made with full recognition of the fundamental objective, and the side issues, principally uncertainty, should not drive one to a harder or easier decision which does not solve the main objective. Mention might be made here of the dilemma of *multiple objectives.* If the objective is, say, to increase per capita income, a series of objectives dealing with distribution of income, fairness, and many lesser objectives can make the problem difficult. For example, a high benefit-cost ratio on a bridge between two wealthy suburbs and financed by a general sales tax is not comparable to a lower benefit-cost ratio between two poor cities, financed by a progressive income tax. However, a range of assumptions can help so that even political judgments can rest on explicit costs and not political intuition alone.

- *Neglect of the Subjective Elements.* Because of the emphasis of Systems Analysis on quantitative processes where possible, one must never forget the subjective elements. Quantification can be overdone. The place of nonquantifiable judgments must be maintained. They exist, they will prevail, and they must be made known to be realistic.

- *Failure to Reappraise the Work.* Here the decision maker must give the analyst *time* to make basic changes. Deadlines play a tremendous part in decision making, but time for reappraisal and iteration pays handsome dividends in better quality decisions. Try to restrain the momentum of events sufficiently to reserve time for reappraisal.

Neglect of the "Soft" Factors in Systems Analysis. One final caveat which may or may not be of real importance to most businessmen but is of unquestionable importance in government are those factors which James R. Schlesinger calls the "soft factors" in systems studies. [4] He is referring to, first, the self-imposed limitation of playing down the broader *political* factors, a "political wisdom" which may well corrupt the analysis. Second, he observes that this corruption may cause a transition from the fundamentals to too much suboptimization. Third, an important system study, even when stated to be limited and suboptimized, inevitably incorporates a greater number of nontechnical assumptions. Without careful examination of the nontechnical factors, adoption of a highly specialized study may be detrimental instead of helpful, especially in national policy. He would have us consider the soft factors of politics: sociological effects, psychological effects, broad strategic criteria, even the bureaucratic organization itself, rather than fervently, if not secretly, hoping that these "soft" elements will go away, or have a minimum effect on the results. Translating these observations from the political scene to the business arena is not too difficult. There are bureaucratic, political, and psychological sides to almost every business that comes to mind. Mr. Schlesinger concludes, as does this author, that, happily, systems analysis is still in its infancy. There is yet time to grapple with the "soft" factors head on. If we don't, it is possible that we will hand over the final dependence to decision makers who *do* employ them in analysis at the end of the process. Perhaps, then, it is too late to remain objective.

One final word is in order on the subject of pitfalls and limitations before a more *positive* list of good precepts is offered. Systems Analysis never promised any user a rose garden. It promised fewer thorns and better quality roses, but not unlimited quality for management. It is still done by humans (or increasingly man-machine decisions today), and has the limitations of humans. Its proof still lies in implementation, as do all approaches to problem solving. It is always incomplete, just as is almost everything. Additional information will still be sought by decision makers. Its measures of effectiveness are man-made and approximate. There is yet to be discovered a satisfactory way to predict the future with complete accuracy, and pure scientific research is a hard taskmaster; thus, no analysis can become an *exact* science. So be it. Let us get on, then, with the job of sorting out correct paths to the future and make progress by the best analyses of which we are capable.

[4]James R. Schlesinger, "The 'Soft' Factors in Systems Studies," *The Bulletin of the Atomic Scientists*, The Educational Foundation for Nuclear Science, November 1968.

SOME PRECEPTS FOR GOOD ANALYSIS

The first precept to bear in mind is that Systems Analysis, while it is becoming more and more scientific because of more widespread use and proficiency, and also because of the introduction of computers for complex problems, has permitted more complex models, calculations, and iterations only dreamed of in earlier days. However, Systems Analysis is still to some extent an *art*. This is good, because a combination of professionalism and art has proved its value in almost every important profession.

A few other precepts to bear in mind are these, which, like all the planning and review guidelines included in the handbook, can be used as a simple checklist:

1. Primary attention should be paid to problem formulation.
2. Keep the analysis systems-oriented.
3. Consider every alternative. Exclude them only if they do not stand the test of competition.
4. State assumptions from the beginning, even if a conclusion may be self-evident, yet not proven by analysis.
5. The problem should shape the model, not vice versa.
6. Try to avoid overemphasizing higher mathematics and computations but, if necessary, get expert advice and help. Keep unnecessary detail to a minimum, but cover the essentials.
7. Tackle a problem as if there were an *opponent* involved; competition keeps one sharp.
8. Be explicit about uncertainties. Repetitious yes, but *so* essential.
9. Watch out for a *suboptimized* objective, alternative, or decision becoming the *main* objective, alternative, or decision.
10. Do the best you can. Realize that what you are doing is far better than intuition or an undisciplined approach to the problem.

With a few good principles added, the preceding can serve as a list of pitfalls to be avoided, as well as a list of good precepts. It simply depends upon one's associations or point of view. Some final principles:

1. Use efficient expert judgment; use interdisciplinary teams if available.
2. The decision or alternative is as important as its analysis.
3. The broader the question, the more the need for added contingencies.
4. A partial answer to a good question is better than a perfect one for a poor question.
5. Cost estimates are the most essential ones in order to make a choice. (As if one needed reminding!)
6. New ideas are the lifeblood of analysis.[5]

---

[5]Paraphrased from Quade and Boucher, eds. *Systems Analysis and Policy Planning*, pp. 418–29.

THE CASE STUDY REVISITED

Before proceeding to a final appraisal of the future of Systems Analysis, a brief revisit to the case study to view its conformity to all the above precepts is in keeping with the theme of the handbook.

First, while there may have been fallacies in some of the city fathers' inputs of data, it does not appear they made outright blunders, nor did Dick Stockton.

Second, they did not underemphasize the problem of formulation, although more time could have been allocated to deciding what the opportunity really was and there could have been less of a tendency to "get going." Offsetting this last, however, was Dick's report, which left the door open to different objectives and different solutions. His treatment of "other factors" is especially indicative of his grasp of the size and effects of the opportunity.

Third, the analyst and decision makers were not guilty of complete "inflexibility." In the face of new ideas, new evidence, it can be assumed the study went on from where it had to be terminated for the sake of brevity. Moreover, the actions taken to verify and reverify assumptions and calculations were good analytic procedure. The same might be said for adherence to "cherished beliefs." None was evident.

"Parochialism" did not rear its head, as yet, in the problem and the competition of ideas between interested city departments or individuals was not in evidence.

As for any "communication failure," it would have been better to have allowed Dick more time to acquire data and carry out surveys, and to have more access to other professionals. But we can assume that this was the first analysis, simply to verify the economic feasibility, and that more investigation would follow.

There was no "overconcentration on the model" because of the simplicity of the cost/benefit factors which were easily depicted in the ways they were. Had the analyst pursued, say, the rate structure change variable, another model emphasizing its sensitivity would have been in order. On the other hand, if the rate changes became an objective which overrode the main objective, namely, the *best use of the downtown site*, then it could be criticized.

As for "excessive attention to detail," it is possible Dick included too much, but still its simplicity and direct effect on the objective does not appear to be excessive to the author or, one hopes, to the reader.

The question certainly was *not* "neglected." Nor was their "disregard of the limitations" under which the study was undertaken. The limitations of size, costs, benefits, and so on, could easily have been redirected and changed by the decision makers if alternatives two, three, or four were pursued.

"Statistical uncertainty" did exist. It was reduced to probabilities by assumptions and calculations and a second review. The saving factor here was the simplicity of the uncertainties and the fact that further study could well have reduced them even more. Certainly Dick can be lauded for his "attention to the uncertainties" and his explicitness in describing them.

"Side issues" as objectives, alternatives, or criteria were not present in any appreciable way to affect the initial study and so become the main issue. It was not until the end that the possibility of other objectives was introduced. This would probably not occur in a business problem study in which the decision makers *initially* are trained to think about the formulation phase thoroughly beforehand. Competition ensures this in real life.

As for "neglect of subjective elements," the case study is a good example of their inclusion rather than neglect.

Time prevented sufficient reappraisal of the work, but more experienced decision makers would normally allow the analyst (and themselves) adequate time. "Deadlines" are a necessary evil but a very limiting reality with which to cope. Do the best you can with this ever-present limitation.

Dick included the "soft factors" of politics, social effects, psychological effects, and ecological effects, in his final section of the report. It is almost a certainty they would play an important role in any decision in the case study. Given time, they could have been addressed *during* the analysis, not only after its presentation.

Thus, in summary, the case study as an analysis illustrates more pluses than minuses. Primary attention was paid to one opportunity formulation. There should have been more. The analysis was systems oriented even though the system under study may have been not as appropriate as the one that should have been attempted. The alternatives came in due time, following the completion of the first charge given to the analyst. Assumptions and uncertainties were closely stated from the start. Higher mathematics and computations were avoided. (Probability theory *could* have had a "field day.") Dick did the best he could and avoided intuition in coming up with an answer to the feasibility of building and operating a parking facility. It is well to remember that the decision on the *next* objectives and alternatives would be far more crucial than the first analysis. A good answer to a single question was obtained, however. Cost estimates were essential and adequate attention given to them, but in this case the benefit estimates proved to be more difficult. Dick's opening up new ideas in the study was in keeping with the fundamental precept that such new ideas are the lifeblood of good analyses, and good analyses of the right objectives mean not only right, but *quality* solutions.

THE FUTURE OF SYSTEMS ANALYSIS

And so we come to the close of this codification of a workable and successful means of decision making—the Systems Analysis Approach. The attempt has been to lay out a means of performing more correctly and comfortably the biggest job of management—decision making. There have been some changes in System Analysis since its beginnings. One of the biggest has been the complex analytical activities required to activate data processing, and the quantitative inputs of management science. These welcome analytical activities have taken place in the business of commerce, in the government, and in personal decision making. We now have the technical capacity to automate a great portion of decision making. We have also the human capacity to use the technical capacity to arrive at nonprogrammed decisions.

No one has a monopoly on decision making. Individuals, groups, clubs, boards of directors, citizens, parents, chairpersons, kings, queens, and presidents must choose from an available, feasible set of alternatives. How well they will do depends upon the method of arriving at the set of alternatives and a proper choice.

The Systems Analysis Approach is believed to be the best approach we have right now to produce the correct set of alternatives. Yet it, too, is still in its infancy according to some experts. If so, its successes to date (whether it is called by any other name such as the Planning, Programming and Budgeting System) outnumber its failures. Its failures, according to my knowledge, have occurred mostly in political or military "second-guessing." Despite early resistance in the government, it is now an accepted way of management. In business, it is becoming increasingly popular. New techniques are still being introduced, but the framework, the "boxes" into which intelligently arrived at factors can be sorted, is still the best means of arriving at the right decision. These techniques embody good sorting, "rather than supplying a mechanical adding up of the benefits and costs once they are sorted."[6]

Quade and Boucher sum up the worth of Systems Analysis as they close with:

[6]Hinrichs and Taylor, *Program Budgeting and Benefit Cost Analysis*, p. 20.

Systems Analysis strives to do more, however, than simply supply solutions that correctly follow from sets of arbitrarily chosen assumptions in narrow problems. It aspires to help the decision-maker find solutions that experience will confirm in the broadest of problems. The goal ... is still far from being attained. But a greater understanding of the nature and roles of systems analysis promises to bring it closer.[7]

Perhaps what we are all trying to say is that there is no substitute for a methodical, thoughtful, thorough approach to problem solving, at which almost *anyone* can be successful, *if* the analytic path is followed. Good analysis and good luck with your decisions—may they always be right!

SUGGESTED FURTHER READING

KAHN, H, and MANN, I. *The Common Pitfalls*. RAND Corporation, R.M. 1937, July 1957.

QUADE, E.S., and BOUCHER, W. I., eds. *Systems Analysis and Policy Planning: Applications in Defense*. New York: Elsevier, 1968. Chapters 19 and 22.

[7]Quade and Boucher, eds. *Systems Analysis and Policy Planning*, p. 429.

APPENDIX I

The Downtown
Parking Authority Case

PROPOSED MUNICIPAL PARKING
FACILITY

In January 1968, a meeting was held in the office of the Mayor of
Oakton to discuss a proposed municipal parking facility. The participants included the Mayor, the Traffic Commissioner, the Administrator
of Oakton's Downtown Parking Authority, the City Planner, and the
Finance Director. The purpose of the meeting was to consider a report
by Richard Stockton, executive assistant to the Parking Authority's
Administrator, concerning estimated costs and revenues for the proposed facility.

Mr. Stockton's opening statement was as follows:

"As you know, the Mayor proposed two months ago that we
construct a multilevel parking garage on the Elm Street site. At that
time, he asked the Parking Authority to assemble all pertinent information for consideration at our meeting today. I would like to summarize our findings briefly for you.

"The Elm Street site is owned by the city. It is presently occupied
by the remains of the old Embassy Cinema, which was gutted by fire
last June. The proprietors of the Cinema have since used the insurance
proceeds to open a new theatre in the suburbs; their lease of the city-
owned land on which the Embassy was built expired on December
31st.

"We estimate that it would cost approximately $40,000 to demol-

"The Downtown Parking Authority Case" is used by permission of Graeme M.
Taylor, Management Analysis Center, Inc., Washington, D.C.

ish the old Embassy. A building contractor has estimated that a multilevel structure, with space for 800 cars, could be built on the site at a cost of about $2 million. The useful life of the garage would probably be around forty years.

"The city could finance construction of the garage through the sale of bonds. The Finance Director has informed me that we could probably float an issue of 20-year tax-exempts at 5% interest. Redemption would commence after three years, with one seventeenth of the original number of bonds being recalled in each succeeding year.

"A parking management firm has already contacted us with a proposal to operate the garage for the city. They would require a management fee of $30,000 per year. Their proposal involves attendant parking and they estimate that their costs, exclusive of the fee, would amount to $240,000 per year. Of this amount, $175,000 would be personnel costs; the remainder would include utilities, mechanical maintenance, insurance, etc. Any gross revenues in excess of $270,000 per year would be shared 90% by the city and 10% by the management firm. If total annual revenues are *less* than $270,000 the city would have to pay the difference.

"I suggest we offer a management contract for bid, with renegotiations every three years.

"The city would derive additional income of around $50,000 per year by renting the ground floor of the structure as retail space.

"It's rather difficult for the Parking Authority to estimate revenues from the garage for, as you know, our operations to date have been confined to fringe area parking lots. However, we conducted a survey at a private parking garage only three blocks from the Elm Street site; perhaps that information will be helpful.

"This private garage is open every day from 7 a.m. until midnight. Their rate schedule is as follows: 75¢ for the first hour; 50¢ for the second hour; and 25¢ for each subsequent hour, with a maximum rate of $2.00. Their capacity is 400 spaces. Our survey indicated that, during business hours, 75% of their spaces were occupied by 'all-day parkers'—cars whose drivers and passengers work downtown. In addition, roughly 400 cars use the garage each weekday with an average stay of three hours. We did not take a survey on Saturday or Sunday, but the proprietor indicated that the garage is usually about 75% utilized by short-term parkers on Saturdays until 6 p.m., when the department stores close; the average stay is about two hours. There's a lull until about 7 p.m., when the moviegoers start coming in; he says the garage is almost full from 8 p.m. until closing time at midnight. Sundays are usually very quiet until the evening, when he estimates that his garage is 60% utilized from 6 p.m. until midnight.

"In addition to this survey, we studied a report issued by the City College Economics Department last year. This report estimated that we now have approximately 50,000 cars entering the central business district (CBD) every day from Monday through Saturday. Based on correlations with other cities of comparable size, the economists calculated that we need 30,000 parking spaces in the CBD. This agrees quite well with a block-by-block estimate made by the Traffic Commissioner's office last year, which indicated a total parking need in the CBD of 29,000 spaces. Right now we have 22,000 spaces in the CBD. Of these, 5% are curb spaces (half of which are metered, with a 2-hour maximum limit for 20 cents), 65% are in open lots, and 30% are in privately owned and operated garages.

"Another study indicated that 60% of all auto passengers entering the CBD on a weekday were on their way to work; 20% were shoppers, and 20% were businessmen making calls. The average number of people per car was 1.75.

"Unfortunately, we have not yet had time to use the data mentioned thus far to work up estimates of the revenues to be expected from the proposed garage.

"The Elm Street site is strategically located in the heart of the CBD, near the major department stores and office buildings. It is five blocks from one of the access ramps to the new crosstown freeway which we expect will be open to traffic next year, and only three blocks from the Music Center which the Mayor dedicated last week.

"As we all know, the parking situation in that section of town has steadily worsened over the last few years, with no immediate prospect of improvement. The demand for parking is clearly there, and the Parking Authority therefore recommends that we go ahead and build the garage."

The Mayor thanked Mr. Stockton for his report and asked for comments. The following discussion took place:

Finance Director: "I'm all in favor of relieving parking congestion downtown, but I think we have to consider alternative uses of the Elm Street site. For example, the city could sell that site to a private developer for at least $1 million. The site could support an office building from which the city would derive property taxes of around $200,000 per year at present rates. The office building would almost certainly incorporate an underground parking garage for the use of the tenants, and therefore we would not only improve our tax base and increase revenues but also increase the availability of parking at no cost to the city. Besides, an office building on that site would serve to improve the amenity of downtown. A multilevel garage built above ground, on the other hand, would reduce the amenity of the area."

Planning Director: "I'm not sure I agree completely with the Finance Director. Within a certain range we can increase the value of downtown land by judicious provision of parking. Adequate, efficient parking facilities will encourage more intensive use of downtown traffic generators such as shops, offices, and places of entertainment, thus enhancing land values. A garage contained within an office building might, as the Finance Director suggests, provide more spaces, but I suspect these would be occupied almost exclusively by workers in the building and thus would not increase the total available supply.

"I think long-term parking downtown should be discouraged by the city. We should attempt to encourage short-term parking—particularly among shoppers—in an effort to counteract the growth of business in the suburbs and the consequent stagnation of retail outlets downtown. The rate structure in effect at the privately operated garage quoted by Mr. Stockton clearly favors the long-term parker. I believe that, if the city constructs a garage on the Elm Street site, we should devise a rate structure which favors the short-term parker. People who work downtown should be encouraged to use our mass transit system."

Finance Director: "I'm glad you mentioned mass transit, because this raises another issue. As you know, our subways are presently not used to capacity and are running at a substantial annual deficit which is borne by the city. We have just spent millions of dollars on the new subway station under the Music Center. Why build a city garage only three blocks away which will still further increase the subway system's deficit? Each person who drives downtown instead of taking the subway represents a loss of 50 cents (the average round trip fare) to the subway system. I have read a report stating that approximately two-thirds of all persons entering the CBD by car would still have made the trip *by subway* if they had *not* been able to use their cars."

Mayor: "On the other hand, I think shoppers prefer to drive rather than take the subway, particularly if they intend to make substantial purchases. No one likes to take the subway burdened down by packages and shopping bags. You know, the Downtown Merchants Association has informed me that they estimate that each new parking space in the CBD generates on average an additional $10,000 in annual retail sales. That represents substantial extra profit to retailers; I think retailing after-tax profits average about 3%

of gross sales. Besides, the city treasury benefits directly from our 3% sales tax."

Traffic Commissioner: "But what about some of the other costs of increasing parking downtown and therefore, presumably, the number of cars entering the CBD? I'm thinking of such costs as the increased wear and tear on city streets, the additional congestion produced with consequent delays and frustration for the drivers, the impeding of the movement of city vehicles, noise, air pollution, and so on. How do we weigh these costs in coming to a decision?"

Parking Administrator: "I don't think we can make a decision at this meeting. I suggest that Dick Stockton be asked to prepare an analysis of the proposed garage along the lines of the following questions:

(1) Using the information presented at this discussion, should the city of Oakton construct the proposed garage?

(2) What rates should be charged?

(3) What additional information, if any, should be obtained before we make a final decision?"

Mayor: "I agree. Dick, can you let us have your answers to these questions in time for consideration at our meeting *next* month?"

THE DOWNTOWN PARKING AUTHORITY CASE: A SOLUTION

INTRODUCTION TO THE SOLUTION[1]

This brief but provocative case provides the opportunity for demonstration of a number of analytical techniques and the Systems Analysis Approach. It also raises a number of issues associated with the performance of any analysis and benefit-cost calculations. This solution is intended to be only suggestive. The reader may vary his approach and his selections of techniques and tools, which may be based in part upon the assumptions and calculations which have been offered. Among the many techniques, issues and analytic steps that can be found in this solution are the following:

- the need to take a systems view of what otherwise appears to be a simple problem.
- identification of the systems and subsystems involved.

[1] This Introduction was prepared by Dr. Alexander Cornell.

- identification of a decision situation(s).
- the importance of thorough diagnosis of a problem or opportunity.
- definition of an optimum objective.
- the continuing need for creativity and judgment in analysis.
- the need to question and reexamine objectives handed down from above.
- the identification and treatment of assumptions and uncertainties throughout the process of analysis.
- the need to make assumptions explicit and to reduce uncertainties as much as possible.
- the value of time and adequate information in analysis.
- the need to determine alternative means of accomplishing objectives.
- the need to determine alternate uses for resources.
- the need to recognize and deal with special interests involved.
- measures of effectiveness.
  —accuracy of data and estimates.
  —economic measures of effectiveness.
  —other measures of effectiveness; the range of measures.
  —validity of human created measures of effectiveness.
  —the place of judgment.
  —environmental measures.
  —spillover and other effects.
- measures of cost.
  —accuracy of data and estimates.
  —use of cost/benefit calculations and analysis.
  —use of break-even analysis.
  —use of sensitivity analysis.
  —use of present value calculations; choice of a discount rate.
  —the concept of opportunity costs.
  —other costs relevant to analysis; investment, relevant and continuing.
  —the accuracy of revenues.
- the calculation and use of the internal rate of return.
- the manipulation and interdependency of variables.
- the selection of a criterion.
  —limitations of ratios and averages.
  —the problem of disaggregation of data.
- the need for additional data; the inevitability of nonquantifiable factors.
- the roles of creativity and judgment in all analysis phases.
- the role of quantification.
- weighting quantifiable and nonquantifiable factors.
- changing rate schedules, the use of price as a rationing or change mechanism to serve policy and objectives.
- recognition of uncommensurables, unmeasurables, spin-offs, and spillovers.
- the initial findings; to recommend or not to recommend.
- the decision and trial.
- iteration.

This brief solution, which is developed step by step in the handbook, is repeated here for ease of reference. Its calculations are organized as follows:

I. Investment Costs
II. Annual Revenues and Costs
III. Benefit-Cost Calculations
IV. Other Analytic Considerations
     Accuracy of Estimates
     Break-Even Analysis
     Alternative Rate Structures
     Other Costs and Benefits

To appreciate the thoroughness of the Systems Analysis Approach, it must be recognized that the calculations are not the *only* considerations. Most of those are dealt with throughout the chapters.

THE SOLUTION ITSELF[2]

I. INVESTMENT COSTS

(1) Construction of garage	$2,000,000
(2) Demolition of Embassy [Cinema]	$ 40,000
(3) Opportunity cost price at which the site could be sold to a private developer	$1,000,000
	$3,040,000

II. ANNUAL REVENUES AND COSTS

A. REVENUES

(1) *Receipts from parking fees*
First, let us assume that the City applies the same parking rate schedule that is now in effect at the private garage. Let us also assume that the use of the municipal garage will follow the same pattern as then experienced by the private garage (described earlier in the case). Under these two assumptions, annual receipts would be as follows: (rounded off numbers)

(a) *Weekdays:*
$(75\% \times 800 \times \$2.00 \times 260) + (800 \times \$1.50 \times 260)$
$$= \$624,000$$

[2] Used by permission of Graeme M. Taylor, Management Analysis Center, Inc. Washington, D.C.

(b) *Saturdays:*
75% utilization from 7 a.m. to 6 p.m.; average stay is 2
hrs. Therefore, no. of cars $= \dfrac{75\% \times 11 \times 800}{2} = 3{,}300$ cars

@ \$1.25

Evenings: 800 cars —assume stay is 4 hours @ \$1.75
Annual receipts = (3300 × \$1.25) × 52 + (800 × \$1.75)
× 52 = \$287,300

(c) *Sundays:*
60% utilization from 6 p.m. until 12 a.m. Assume average
stay is 3 hours @ \$1.50/car

Annual receipts $= \dfrac{60\% \times 800 \times 6}{3\,\text{hrs.}} \times \$1.50 \times 52 =$

\$74,880

Total estimated annual receipts = \$986,180

(Since the above estimates are very approximate, we shall use: *estimated annual receipts = \$1 million*)

(2) *Retail rent:* \$50,000

(3) *Increased sales tax:*

The mayor stated that each new parking space would generate an additional \$10,000 per year in retail sales. Accepting this *estimate*, the proposed garage would generate an additional (800 × \$10,000), which equals \$8 million in retail sales.

Since the city sales tax [equals] 3 percent, this yields additional annual tax revenues of \$240,000.

Let us now consider the validity of this figure.

We must first estimate the number of shopper-parkers using the garage.

Weekdays

Assume all the all-day parkers are workers and will not make any retail purchases.

The 800 other cars using the garage will be primarily (a) business-men making calls, (b) shoppers, and (c) entertainment seekers (in the evening).

We have no real evidence in the case to support this assumption, but let us guess that one-third of the 800 cars fall into each of the above 3 categories.

Therefore, 267 cars are shopper-parkers. We are told that the average number of persons per car = 1.75. Thus, we estimate that the total number of shoppers using the garage each year on weekdays will be:

$$260 \times 1.75 \times 267 = 121{,}485$$

Saturdays

Let us assume that all the daytime parkers are shoppers, and that none of the evening parkers are shoppers. We estimated that 3300 cars would use the garage during the day. Thus, we estimate that the total number of shoppers using the garage each year on Saturdays will be:

$$52 \times 1.75 \times 3300 = 300{,}300$$

Sundays

We will assume no shoppers on Sundays. This implies that each shopper makes an average retail purchase, per trip, of

$$\frac{\$8{,}000{,}000}{421{,}785} = \$19$$

This estimate does not appear too unreasonable. In fact, it may be rather *low*, based on the assumption that most shoppers who make the effort to come downtown are probably serious shoppers and possibly interested in major purchases.

Before adopting the $240,000 figure as representing additional sales tax revenues due to the presence of the parking garage, we must consider one additional factor. The finance director stated that he had read a report claiming that two-thirds of all persons entering the CBD by car would still have made the trip by subway if they had not been able to use their cars. Elsewhere, the case tells us that "60% of all auto passengers entering the CBD on a weekday were on their way to work; 20% were shoppers, and 20% were businessmen making calls."

It would appear that the "two-thirds" figure quoted by the finance director is *probably* composed primarily of people who *work* downtown. Our assumption, then, in adopting the $240,000 figure is that it represents *additional* sales tax revenues from purchases made by shoppers who would otherwise *not* have come downtown to shop.

(Note: this figure does *not* include revenues from taxes on the receipts of restaurants, theaters, cinemas and other places of entertainment; presumably these places would also benefit, and constitute additional tax revenues, by having more parking spaces nearby.)

B. COSTS

(1) *Garage operating costs:* $270,000 per year

(2) *Loss of property tax revenue:*
    Estimated by the finance director to be (at present rate)
    [equal to] $200,000 per year (if fully rented)

(3) *Loss of revenue to the mass transit system:*
    We must first estimate the number of persons each year
    who would use the parking garage.
    No. of cars:
    Weekdays - (75% × 800) + 800) × 260   =   364,000

$$\text{Saturday - } (3300 + 800) \times 52 \qquad = \qquad 213{,}200$$
$$\text{Sundays - } 60\% \times 800 \times 6 \times 52 \div 3 \text{ hrs.} \quad = \qquad 49{,}920$$

Total: $\qquad = \qquad 627{,}120$

Assuming 1.75 persons per car, we have No. of persons using garage each year = $1.75 \times 627{,}120$ = approximately 1,100,000 persons

Two-thirds of these persons would have made the trip by subway if they had not been able to use their cars. Therefore, *presumably* the garage would take away from the subway $2/3 \times 1{,}100{,}000 = 733{,}000$ persons. At 50¢ per round trip, this represents a net loss to the subway system (since they are currently operating at a deficit) of 50¢ × 733,000 = about $367,000 per year

III. BENEFIT-COST CALCULATION

A. Total Investment Cost (From Step (I) above): $3,040,000
   Annual income to the city attributable in the garage:
   Parking receipts: $1,000,000
   less:

| | Management fee: | $ 30,000 |
| | Operating costs: | $240,000 |

Net receipts:	$ 730,000	
City's share equals 90 percent		$ 657,000
Rent of ground floor retail space:		50,000
Increase in sales tax revenue:		240,000

$ 947,000

Less:

Loss of property tax revenue:	$ 200,000	
Loss of revenue by subway system:	367,000	
		$ 567,000

B. *Net Annual Income to the City*
   Attributable to the Garage: $ 380,000

C. *Choice of Discount Rate:*
   The city's "cost of capital" in this instance is 5 percent. A

private developer would probably expect at least a 10 percent return on his investment. The figure for the "solid opportunity cost" of capital given by some economists is around 7 percent.

Let us therefore find the *present value* of a stream of income of $380,000 per year for 40 years (the expected life of the garage) at 6 percent, 8 percent and 10 percent. Let us also determine present value for periods of 20 years, 30 years, and 40 years, using a Table of Present Value of $1.00 Received Annually for "*N*" Years. (See Table [I.4] at the end of [Appendix] I.)

TABLE I.1 Present Value of an Annuity of $380,000

	4%	6%	8%	10%
20 years	$5.16 million	$4.36 million	$3.73 million	$3.24 million
30 years	$6.57 million	$5.23 million	$4.29 million	$3.58 million
40 years	$7.52 million	$5.72 million	$4.53 million	$3.72 million
50 years	$8.16 million	$5.99 million	$4.65 million	$3.77 million

Now, let us find the internal (present value) *rate of return* on the project for periods of 20, 30, 40 and 50 years:

Regardless of the time period chosen (from 20 to 50 years), the internal rate of return is between *10 percent and 12 percent* plus. (This is of course due to the very long time periods involved. If our garage had an estimated life of only 10 years at 10 percent, the internal rate of return would have been about 7 percent.) ("Payback" of 8 years can be expected - $\dfrac{3,040,000}{380,000} = 8$.)

Example: 10% @ 40 years $= 9.779 \times \$380,000 = \dfrac{3,716,020}{3,040,000} = 12.2\%$

10% @ 20 years $= 8.514 \times \$380,000 = \dfrac{3,235,320}{3,040,000} = 10.6\%$

Since our involvement is $3.04 million, Table I.1 indicates that the project results in *positive net present benefits*, no matter which of the three discount rates is used, for lives of 20 to 30 years. For a 40-year life at 10% the internal rate of return is just over 12 percent. It would appear, therefore, that *based on all our assumptions*, the municipal garage is a desirable project, *economically*.

IV. OTHER ANALYTIC CONSIDERATIONS

However, we must consider *other* factors. Our analysis must continue along three separate investigative paths:
(1) What is the accuracy of our estimates?
(2) What rate structure should be employed?
(3) What weight should be placed on other costs and benefits not included numerically in the above calculations?

(1) Accuracy of Estimates

> *Investment costs* (value of site, demolition of cinema, construction)–$3 million. This figure is probably fairly reliable.
> *Parking receipts*–$1 million.

This is clearly a very approximate figure. It is based on *two fundamental assumptions*, namely, (a) we use the same rate structure that is currently in effect at the nearby private garage, and that (b) we experience the same utilization pattern as the private garage.

It is quite likely that we would experience the estimate demand:

- The new music center will probably increase parking demand.
- The new freeway will encourage more traffic to come downtown.
- There presently exists a "parking space deficit" in the CBD.

However, we should note that the private garage is presently not being used to capacity. Let's explore that variable.

Weekdays
Assume "all-day" parkers park for a maximum of 9 hours on average, then 75% × 400 × 9 = 2,700 "space-hours" used. Plus, 400 cars that park for an average stay of 3 hours = 1200 space-hours.
Total per weekday = 3,900 space-hours
Total per week   = 5 × 3,900 =   19,500 space-hours
Saturdays
75% utilization from 7 a.m. until 6 p.m. =
75% × 400 × 11 =   3,300 space-hours
Plus, 400 cars assumed to park an average
of 4 hours =   1,600 space-hours
Sundays
60% utilization from 6 p.m. until 12 a.m.   1,440 space-hours

$$= 60\% \times 400 \times 6 = \frac{1{,}440 \text{ space-hours}}{25{,}840 \text{ space-hours}}$$
$$\text{[Total:]} \qquad \text{per week}$$

"Capacity" = (400 spaces × 17 hrs)
× 7 days per week,   TOTAL -   47,600 space-hours per week
Therefore, present utilization rate of *private* garage =
$$\frac{25{,}840}{47{,}600} = 54\%$$

It might be questioned, therefore, whether or not we would achieve the demand estimated for our garage. (Of course, the utilization rate is much higher during peak periods during the day and evening.)

(2) Break-Even Analysis

It might be useful to perform a *break-even* analysis as follows: (let us *choose* a 40-year period and a discount rate of 6 percent). What parking receipts would be necessary in order to equate the present value of the stream of income to the investment cost of $3 million?

First, the *total net* income required would have to be $200,000 per year (present value of $200,000 per year for 40 years discounted at 6 percent equals $3 million) (using the Table of Present Value of $1.00 Annuity).

Fixed components of this (i.e., which do not vary with the number of cars using the garage) are:

    (1) loss of property tax revenue   = $200,000
    (2) rent of ground floor retail space   =   50,000
    (3) management fee   =   30,000
    (4) operating costs   =   240,000

Variable components are:

    (1) Parking receipts   =   380,000
    (2) Increase in sales tax revenue   =   240,000
    (3) Loss of subway revenue (also a *possible* gain if the
         CBD is more attractive and accessible)   =   367,000

Let us assume that the rate structure remains as previously used, and that the demand for use of the parking garage will follow the same *pattern* of utilization used in (II), Annual Revenue and Costs. Then, the increase in sales tax revenue and the loss of subway revenue can be assumed to be *approximately* proportioned to gross receipts, bearing the same relationships to gross receipts as before.

Thus, yearly receipt R = gross receipts from the increase in *sales tax revenue*, or $\dfrac{240,000}{1,000,000} \times R = 0.24R$; and *loss of revenue* to the subway system =

$$\frac{367,000}{1,000,000} \times R = 0.367R$$

Remembering that net receipts are split 90/10 between the city and the management firm, our *break-even equation* for R is: $200,000 = 90\% \times (R-270,000) + 50,000 + 0.24R - 200,000 - 0.367R$. ($200,000$ = operating costs) ($50,000$ = rent) ($0.24R$ = gross receipts, increase in sales tax revenue) ($200,000$ = loss of taxes) ($0.367R$ = loss of revenue to subway). [solving for R =]   [about] $767,000
That is, our garage would have to have gross parking receipts of about $767,000 per year (assuming the same pattern of utilization at the same rate structure as previously assumed) in order for the garage to pay for itself in 40 years at a discount rate of 6 percent.

In other words, our demand could fall to about 77 percent of the $1 million estimate used before the project would cease to be attractive under the conditions and assumptions stated. Let us now continue to examine the probable accuracy of our individual estimates:

- *Operating costs:* $270,000, including the management fee. This is probably quite reliable. It would depend on negotiations between the potential management firm and the city, following which it would be contractually established (subject to renegotiation every three years). *(We are ignoring price increases, and are of course working in 1968 dollars throughout these calculations.)*
- *Rent of ground floor retail space:* $50,000. This is probably a fairly reliable estimate, based on Mr. Stockton's knowledge of prevailing rental costs in the CBD.
- *Increase in sales tax revenues:* $240,000. This is, of course, a very approximate figure. It clearly depends on several assumptions, particularly the following:
  —That a sales tax of 3 percent will continue indefinitely
  —That *422,000* shopper-trips will make use of the garage during the year, and that each shopper-trip will produce retail purchases of *$19* that would *not* have been made *without* the garage.
- *Loss of property tax revenue:* $200,000. This figure clearly depends on (1) the assessed value of the building that would have been erected on the Elm Street Site, and (2) the prevailing tax rate. In the absence of any knowledge to the contrary, we must assume that this figure represents Mr. Stockton's best estimate of the annual loss of revenue in the immediate future. Without knowing the trend of property tax rates and assessed values in Oakton, we have little choice but to accept the figure as constant in our calculations. In a sense, of course, this is offset by the likelihood that the value of the site will continue to rise, and the city will still own the site after 40 years.

• *Loss of revenue to subway system:* $367,000. This figure *is* an approx-
imate estimate. It assumes that the presence of the garage means that
733,000 person-trips would be lost to the subway system each year (or
2,000 person-trips per day). It is based on a series of assumptions:
—Our projected utilization pattern.
—1.75 persons per auto on average.
—Two-thirds would have made the trip by subway if they had not been
able to park.
In summary, we are *particularly* concerned about the accuracy of the
following figures used in the calculations:
—Parking receipts
—Increase in sales tax revenues
—Loss of revenue to the subway system.
We could refine our estimates by several means, all of which would, of
course, require more data obtained through surveys and "market-
research" investigations. We could also obtain data from other parking
garages in the CBD—What kinds of parkers use the garages at various
times of the day? Would they have taken the subway if they had not
been able to park? If shoppers, how much did they spend? What have
been the trends of overall utilization rates in these garages? etc.

(3) Alternative Rate Structures—What Should be Adopted?

In addition to the data suggested above, it would also be useful
to know what rate structure would discourage all-day parkers and
encourage shopper-parkers and others who might constitute the "revitalization of downtown." Questionnaires could be devised which
would give a rough idea of the rates at which various types of parkers
would switch from the subway to the auto and vice versa. Perhaps data
from other cities could be obtained. Mr. Stockton could then prepare
a series of alternate projections based on different rate structures, each
with its associated projected utilization pattern.

*He might also consider the costs of operating a self-parking
facility, instead of the attendant-parking facility envisioned in the
case.* For example, a hypothetical structure such as the following would
have a *significant* impact on the calculations:

Day	Time	Rates
Monday–Friday	7 a.m.–6 p.m.	25 cents for first three hours $1 per hour for every hour in excess of three
	6 p.m.–12 a.m.	Flat rate of $1.00

Saturdays	7a.m.–6 p.m.	25 cents per hour
	6 p.m.–12 a.m.	Flat rate of $1.75
Sundays	7 a.m.–7 p.m.	10 cents per hour
	6 p.m.–12 a.m.	Flat rate of $1.00

If Mr. Stockton could derive reliable *relationships* between parking costs and demand for parking at various times during the day for various purposes, he might be able to construct a simple computer model to assist him in performing the detailed calculations. He should constantly employ the techniques of *sensitivity analysis* and *break-even analysis* to assist him in evaluating the results.

[(4) Other Costs and Benefits]

Let us now consider other factors which have not been included in our evaluations to this point. We can only tabulate them according to their probable effect on our decision—i.e., as to whether they would favor or not favor the decision to build the garage.

[TABLE I.2]

PRO (Benefits)	*CON (Costs)*

• Revitalization of downtown
• More use of new music center by suburbanites
• Increased profits to downtown retailers (3 percent of $8 million)
• More jobs downtown
  - business firms
  - retail outlets
• Presence of garage might enhance land values nearby, thus increasing property tax base.
• The value of the Elm St. site would no doubt increase overtime, and so would have considerable "residual value" at the end of the period used in our calculations, etc.
	• Increased auto congestion in city streets
	- traffic control costs; delays, frustration; wear and tear on city streets, etc.
	
	• Increased air pollution
	- potential hazard to health; medical costs
	• Increased noise
	-discomfort, irritation, reduced work efficiency
	• Office building on Elm St. site would mean more jobs in Oakton (assuming it was built by a new employer—otherwise it would merely divert employment from other sections of the city)
	• More city services would have to be provided to the extent that these were new residents.
	- home building would be affected. etc.

TABLE I.3 Present Value of $1

Years Hence	1%	2%	4%	6%	8%	10%	12%	14%	15%	16%	18%	20%	22%	24%	25%	26%	28%	30%	35%	40%	45%	50%
1	0.990	0.980	0.962	0.943	0.926	0.909	0.893	0.877	0.870	0.862	0.847	0.833	0.820	0.806	0.800	0.794	0.781	0.769	0.741	0.714	0.690	0.667
2	0.980	0.961	0.925	0.890	0.857	0.826	0.797	0.769	0.756	0.743	0.718	0.694	0.672	0.650	0.640	0.630	0.610	0.592	0.549	0.510	0.476	0.444
3	0.971	0.942	0.889	0.840	0.794	0.751	0.712	0.675	0.658	0.641	0.609	0.579	0.551	0.524	0.512	0.500	0.477	0.455	0.406	0.364	0.328	0.296
4	0.961	0.924	0.855	0.792	0.735	0.683	0.636	0.592	0.572	0.552	0.516	0.482	0.451	0.423	0.410	0.397	0.373	0.350	0.301	0.260	0.226	0.198
5	0.951	0.906	0.822	0.747	0.681	0.621	0.567	0.519	0.497	0.476	0.437	0.402	0.370	0.341	0.328	0.315	0.291	0.269	0.223	0.186	0.156	0.132
6	0.942	0.888	0.790	0.705	0.630	0.564	0.507	0.456	0.432	0.410	0.370	0.335	0.303	0.275	0.262	0.250	0.227	0.207	0.165	0.133	0.108	0.088
7	0.933	0.871	0.760	0.665	0.583	0.513	0.452	0.400	0.376	0.354	0.314	0.279	0.249	0.222	0.210	0.198	0.178	0.159	0.122	0.095	0.074	0.059
8	0.923	0.853	0.731	0.627	0.540	0.467	0.404	0.351	0.327	0.305	0.266	0.233	0.204	0.179	0.168	0.157	0.139	0.123	0.091	0.068	0.051	0.039
9	0.914	0.837	0.703	0.592	0.500	0.424	0.361	0.308	0.284	0.263	0.225	0.194	0.167	0.144	0.134	0.125	0.108	0.094	0.067	0.048	0.035	0.026
10	0.905	0.820	0.676	0.558	0.463	0.386	0.322	0.270	0.247	0.227	0.191	0.162	0.137	0.116	0.107	0.099	0.085	0.073	0.050	0.035	0.024	0.017
11	0.896	0.804	0.650	0.527	0.429	0.350	0.287	0.237	0.215	0.195	0.162	0.135	0.112	0.094	0.086	0.079	0.066	0.056	0.037	0.025	0.017	0.012
12	0.887	0.788	0.625	0.497	0.397	0.319	0.257	0.208	0.187	0.168	0.137	0.112	0.092	0.076	0.069	0.062	0.052	0.043	0.027	0.018	0.012	0.008
13	0.879	0.773	0.601	0.469	0.368	0.290	0.229	0.182	0.163	0.145	0.116	0.093	0.075	0.061	0.055	0.050	0.040	0.033	0.020	0.013	0.008	0.005
14	0.870	0.758	0.577	0.442	0.340	0.263	0.205	0.160	0.141	0.125	0.099	0.078	0.062	0.049	0.044	0.039	0.032	0.025	0.015	0.009	0.006	0.003
15	0.861	0.743	0.555	0.417	0.315	0.239	0.183	0.140	0.123	0.108	0.084	0.065	0.051	0.040	0.035	0.031	0.025	0.020	0.011	0.006	0.004	0.002
16	0.853	0.728	0.534	0.394	0.292	0.218	0.163	0.123	0.107	0.093	0.071	0.054	0.042	0.032	0.028	0.025	0.019	0.015	0.008	0.005	0.003	0.002
17	0.844	0.714	0.513	0.371	0.270	0.198	0.146	0.108	0.093	0.080	0.060	0.045	0.034	0.026	0.023	0.020	0.015	0.012	0.006	0.003	0.002	0.001
18	0.836	0.700	0.494	0.350	0.250	0.180	0.130	0.095	0.081	0.069	0.051	0.038	0.028	0.021	0.018	0.016	0.012	0.009	0.005	0.002	0.001	0.001
19	0.828	0.686	0.475	0.331	0.232	0.164	0.116	0.083	0.070	0.060	0.043	0.031	0.023	0.017	0.014	0.012	0.009	0.007	0.003	0.002	0.001	
20	0.820	0.673	0.456	0.312	0.215	0.149	0.104	0.073	0.061	0.051	0.037	0.026	0.019	0.014	0.012	0.010	0.007	0.005	0.002	0.001	0.001	
21	0.811	0.660	0.439	0.294	0.199	0.135	0.093	0.064	0.053	0.044	0.031	0.022	0.015	0.011	0.009	0.008	0.006	0.004	0.002	0.001		
22	0.803	0.647	0.422	0.278	0.184	0.123	0.083	0.056	0.046	0.038	0.026	0.018	0.013	0.009	0.007	0.006	0.004	0.003	0.001	0.001		
23	0.795	0.634	0.406	0.262	0.170	0.112	0.074	0.049	0.040	0.033	0.022	0.015	0.010	0.007	0.006	0.005	0.003	0.002	0.001			
24	0.788	0.622	0.390	0.247	0.158	0.102	0.066	0.043	0.035	0.028	0.019	0.013	0.008	0.006	0.005	0.004	0.003	0.002	0.001			
25	0.780	0.610	0.375	0.233	0.146	0.092	0.059	0.038	0.030	0.024	0.016	0.010	0.007	0.005	0.004	0.003	0.002	0.001	0.001			
26	0.772	0.598	0.361	0.220	0.135	0.084	0.053	0.033	0.026	0.021	0.014	0.009	0.006	0.004	0.003	0.002	0.002	0.001				
27	0.764	0.586	0.347	0.207	0.125	0.076	0.047	0.029	0.023	0.018	0.011	0.007	0.005	0.003	0.002	0.002	0.001	0.001				
28	0.757	0.574	0.333	0.196	0.116	0.069	0.042	0.026	0.020	0.016	0.010	0.006	0.004	0.002	0.002	0.002	0.001	0.001				
29	0.749	0.563	0.321	0.185	0.107	0.063	0.037	0.022	0.017	0.014	0.008	0.005	0.003	0.002	0.002	0.001	0.001	0.001				
30	0.742	0.552	0.308	0.174	0.099	0.057	0.033	0.020	0.015	0.012	0.007	0.004	0.003	0.002	0.001	0.001	0.001					
40	0.672	0.453	0.208	0.097	0.046	0.022	0.011	0.005	0.004	0.003	0.001	0.001										
50	0.608	0.372	0.141	0.054	0.021	0.009	0.003	0.001	0.001	0.001												

Source: Robert N. Anthony, *Management Accounting Principles*, Homewood, Illinois: Richard D. Irwin, Inc., 1965.

152

TABLE I.4 Present Value of $1 Received Annually for N Years

Years (N)	1%	2%	4%	6%	8%	10%	12%	14%	15%	16%	18%	20%	22%	24%	25%	26%	28%	30%	35%	40%	45%	50%
1	0.990	0.980	0.962	0.943	0.926	0.909	0.893	0.877	0.870	0.862	0.847	0.833	0.820	0.806	0.800	0.794	0.781	0.769	0.741	0.714	0.690	0.667
2	1.970	1.942	1.886	1.833	1.783	1.736	1.690	1.647	1.626	1.605	1.566	1.528	1.492	1.457	1.440	1.424	1.392	1.361	1.289	1.224	1.165	1.111
3	2.941	2.884	2.775	2.673	2.577	2.487	2.402	2.322	2.283	2.246	2.174	2.106	2.042	1.981	1.952	1.923	1.868	1.816	1.696	1.589	1.493	1.407
4	3.902	3.808	3.630	3.465	3.312	3.170	3.037	2.914	2.855	2.798	2.690	2.589	2.494	2.404	2.362	2.320	2.241	2.166	1.997	1.849	1.720	1.605
5	4.853	4.713	4.452	4.212	3.993	3.791	3.605	3.433	3.352	3.274	3.127	2.991	2.864	2.745	2.689	2.635	2.532	2.436	2.220	2.035	1.876	1.737
6	5.795	5.601	5.242	4.917	4.623	4.355	4.111	3.889	3.784	3.685	3.498	3.326	3.167	3.020	2.951	2.885	2.759	2.643	2.385	2.168	1.983	1.824
7	6.728	6.472	6.002	5.582	5.206	4.868	4.564	4.288	4.160	4.039	3.812	3.605	3.416	3.242	3.161	3.083	2.937	2.802	2.508	2.263	2.057	1.883
8	7.652	7.325	6.733	6.210	5.747	5.335	4.968	4.639	4.487	4.344	4.078	3.837	3.619	3.421	3.329	3.241	3.076	2.925	2.598	2.331	2.108	1.922
9	8.566	8.162	7.435	6.802	6.247	5.759	5.328	4.946	4.772	4.607	4.303	4.031	3.786	3.566	3.463	3.366	3.184	3.019	2.665	2.379	2.144	1.948
10	9.471	8.983	8.111	7.360	6.710	6.145	5.650	5.216	5.019	4.833	4.494	4.192	3.923	3.682	3.571	3.465	3.269	3.092	2.715	2.414	2.168	1.965
11	10.368	9.787	8.760	7.887	7.139	6.495	5.937	5.453	5.234	5.029	4.656	4.327	4.035	3.776	3.656	3.544	3.335	3.147	2.752	2.438	2.185	1.977
12	11.255	10.575	9.385	8.384	7.536	6.814	6.194	5.660	5.421	5.197	4.793	4.439	4.127	3.851	3.725	3.606	3.387	3.190	2.779	2.456	2.196	1.985
13	12.134	11.343	9.986	8.853	7.904	7.103	6.424	5.842	5.583	5.342	4.910	4.533	4.203	3.912	3.780	3.656	3.427	3.223	2.799	2.468	2.204	1.990
14	13.004	12.106	10.563	9.295	8.244	7.367	6.628	6.002	5.724	5.468	5.008	4.611	4.265	3.962	3.824	3.695	3.459	3.249	2.814	2.477	2.210	1.993
15	13.865	12.849	11.118	9.712	8.559	7.606	6.811	6.142	5.847	5.575	5.092	4.675	4.315	4.001	3.859	3.726	3.483	3.268	2.825	2.484	2.214	1.995
16	14.718	13.578	11.652	10.106	8.851	7.824	6.974	6.265	5.954	5.669	5.162	4.730	4.357	4.033	3.887	3.751	3.503	3.283	2.834	2.489	2.216	1.997
17	15.562	14.292	12.166	10.477	9.122	8.022	7.120	6.373	6.047	5.749	5.222	4.775	4.391	4.059	3.910	3.771	3.518	3.295	2.840	2.492	2.218	1.998
18	16.398	14.992	12.659	10.828	9.372	8.201	7.250	6.467	6.128	5.818	5.273	4.812	4.419	4.080	3.928	3.786	3.529	3.304	2.844	2.494	2.219	1.999
19	17.226	15.678	13.134	11.158	9.604	8.365	7.366	6.550	6.198	5.877	5.316	4.844	4.442	4.097	3.942	3.799	3.539	3.311	2.848	2.496	2.220	1.999
20	18.046	16.351	13.590	11.470	9.818	8.514	7.469	6.623	6.259	5.929	5.353	4.870	4.460	4.110	3.954	3.808	3.546	3.316	2.850	2.497	2.221	1.999
21	18.857	17.011	14.029	11.764	10.017	8.649	7.562	6.687	6.312	5.973	5.384	4.891	4.476	4.121	3.963	3.816	3.551	3.320	2.852	2.498	2.221	2.000
22	19.660	17.658	14.451	12.042	10.201	8.772	7.645	6.743	6.359	6.011	5.410	4.909	4.488	4.130	3.970	3.822	3.556	3.323	2.853	2.498	2.222	2.000
23	20.456	18.292	14.857	12.303	10.371	8.883	7.718	6.792	6.399	6.044	5.432	4.925	4.499	4.137	3.976	3.827	3.559	3.325	2.854	2.499	2.222	2.000
24	21.243	18.914	15.247	12.550	10.529	8.985	7.784	6.835	6.434	6.073	5.451	4.937	4.507	4.143	3.981	3.831	3.562	3.327	2.855	2.499	2.222	2.000
25	22.023	19.523	15.622	12.783	10.675	9.077	7.843	6.873	6.464	6.097	5.467	4.948	4.514	4.147	3.985	3.834	3.564	3.329	2.856	2.499	2.222	2.000
26	22.795	20.121	15.983	13.003	10.810	9.161	7.896	6.906	6.491	6.118	5.480	4.956	4.520	4.151	3.988	3.837	3.566	3.330	2.856	2.500	2.222	2.000
27	23.560	20.707	16.330	13.211	10.935	9.237	7.943	6.935	6.514	6.136	5.492	4.964	4.524	4.154	3.990	3.839	3.567	3.331	2.856	2.500	2.222	2.000
28	24.316	21.281	16.663	13.406	11.051	9.307	7.984	6.961	6.534	6.152	5.502	4.970	4.528	4.157	3.992	3.840	3.568	3.331	2.857	2.500	2.222	2.000
29	25.066	21.844	16.984	13.591	11.158	9.370	8.022	6.983	6.551	6.166	5.510	4.975	4.531	4.159	3.994	3.841	3.569	3.332	2.857	2.500	2.222	2.000
30	25.808	22.396	17.292	13.765	11.258	9.427	8.055	7.003	6.566	6.177	5.517	4.979	4.534	4.160	3.995	3.842	3.569	3.332	2.857	2.500	2.222	2.000
40	32.835	27.355	19.793	15.046	11.925	9.779	8.244	7.105	6.642	6.234	5.548	4.997	4.544	4.166	3.999	3.846	3.571	3.333	2.857	2.500	2.222	2.000
50	39.196	31.424	21.482	15.762	12.234	9.915	8.304	7.133	6.661	6.246	5.554	4.999	4.545	4.167	4.000	3.846	3.571	3.333	2.857	2.500	2.222	2.000

Source: Robert N. Anthony, *Management Accounting Principles*, Homewood, Illinois: Richard D. Irwin, Inc., 1965.

APPENDIX II

Glossary
of Analytical and Associated Terms

This glossary endeavors to include most words and phrases used in decision-making and analytical reasoning processes, ranging from general management to economic, quantitative, and analytical reasoning. Another way to present these terms would have been to include them all under the single heading, Systems Analysis. However, their sequential grouping in this glossary may be helpful in moving from basic economic to complex quantitative terms and then to analytical reasoning, processes, and techniques. It should be recognized that words and phrases are often varied in meaning depending upon the users and authors. Here the intent is to provide a common starting point for all users to help achieve better communication. An asterisk alongside the term means it is a tool or technique explained more fully by illustration and use in Appendix III, *Some Popular Quantitative and Other Techniques and Tools Used in Analysis.*

ECONOMIC REASONING

Allocation. The process of choosing optimum uses for limited resources. In a free market system the price structure performs this function. In the productive organization the manager has this responsibility.

Alternative cost. See OPPORTUNITY COST.

Benefits. The degree of satisfaction of objectives achieved by selecting any one alternative. It is the net result of productive output

154

gained from a given resource utilization minus the opportunity costs incurred.

Balance of payments. A systematic record of the economic transactions between the residents of a country and the residents of the rest of the world during a given period.

Budget (budgeting). A proposed plan for a given period of time covering anticipated resources and their estimated expenditure in pursuing a program or objectives. A financial plan to attain planned programs. Budgeting is the process of determining allocation of resources to carry out plans and programs.

Capital. All economic goods existent at a particular time that yield realized or imputed income. In business, capital may refer to the investment in a business or to its net worth.

Comparative advantage. An economic concept that applies opportunity cost to the mix of more efficient and less efficient producers. It states that, even though weapon system *A* is more effective than *B* weapon system against either of two types of targets, system *A* should be used on the target where the highest *relative* benefit can be obtained.

Constant dollars. Dollar estimates are said to be expressed in constant dollars when the effect of changes in the purchasing power of the dollar has been removed. Usually the data are expressed in terms of some selected year or set of years.

Controllable Dollars. Budget outlays that can be increased or decreased within a fiscal period by the budget authority.

Cost. There are two major concepts of cost: *explicit* (and implicit) *costs* are the value of resources used, and *opportunity costs* are the value of alternatives foregone by the choice made. In addition, *relevant costs* define those values pertinent to a decision being made and *differential* (incremental) *costs* identify those values which differ between two alternatives in a decision. Other kinds of costs are defined in this glossary.

Cost center (expense center). If the control system measures the expenses incurred by an organizational unit but does not measure the monetary value of its output, the unit is called a cost or expense center.

Current dollars. The purchasing power of dollars prevailing in any given year.

Diminishing returns, law of. An increase in some inputs relative to other fixed inputs will cause total output to increase, but after a point the extra output resulting from the same additions is likely to diminish.

Direct labor. Workers directly engaged in or identified with the process of converting materials into finished products.

Direct materials. All of the measurable raw materials entering into or directly identifiable with a resulting finished product or job, though these may include the finished products of other jobs or of other manufacturers.

Econometrics. The branch of economics that uses mathematics and statistics to build and analyze economic models, to explain economic phenomena, and to estimate values for economic variables.

Economic analysis. A systematic approach to "choice" problems or opportunities, using economic and quantitative techniques and tools, designed to assist in problem solving. Objectives and alternatives are sought just as in Systems Analysis and their benefits and costs compared.

Economic cost. See OPPORTUNITY COST.

Economic growth. The sustained increase in the total and per capita output of a country as measured by the gross national product (in constant prices) or other output statistics.

Economic life. The period of time over which the benefits to be gained from a project may reasonably be expected to accrue to the producer. It is affected by both the physical and technological life of the item.

Economies of scale. Efficiencies, usually expressed as reduction in cost or per unit of output, that result from increasing the size of the productive unit.

Elasticity. A quantitative measure of the quantity of a demanded or supplied product in response to a change in product price. Normally a flat demand curve means an elastic demand, i.e., small change in price, big change in quantity; a steep demand curve means inelastic demand, i.e., small change in price, small change in quantity.

Fixed costs. Those elements of cost that do not vary with volume of production.

Full employment surplus. The budget surplus or deficit that would exist under current tax rates and government expenditures and policies if the country were operating at full employment— usually considered to be a maximum of 4 percent unemployed; now 6 percent.

Gross national product. Total value at market prices of all goods and services produced by the nation's economy during a period of one calendar year. As calculated quarterly by the Department of Commerce, gross national product is the broadest available measure of the rate of economic activity.

Incremental cost (differential cost). The added cost of a change in the level or nature of activity. Sometimes interpreted to be the same as marginal cost, though the latter has a much more limited meaning, referring to the cost of an added unit of output.

Index numbers. Numbers used to measure change in prices, wages, employment, and so on, by showing the percentage variation from an arbitrary standard, usually 100, representing the value of a chosen base period. A measurement of fluctuations in prices, volume, economic activity, or other variables over a period related to a base.

Indifference map. A two-dimensional graph denoting an individual's preference regarding two quantities of inputs. The body of the graph consists of a family of nonintersecting lines concave to the origin. Each line of the family represents an equally desirable mixture of the quantities involved.

Inflation. A rise in the general level of prices. Pure inflation is a rise in the general level of prices unaccompanied by a rise in output.

Information system. A combination of personnel, procedures, data, communication facilities, and equipment that provides an organized and interconnected means (automated and manual) for collecting, processing, transmitting, and displaying information.

Investment costs. Costs associated with the acquisition of equipment and real property. They include all costs beyond the Research and Development phase required to introduce the system into operational use.

Isocost. A line on an indifference map which represents various combinations of two inputs that can be acquired for a given total amount of money.

Isoquant. A curve of constant quantity, on which all points relate different combinations of input factors needed to attain the same fixed level of output.

Joint cost. Costs shared by several departments or activities and not easily attributable to one specific activity. An example would be an air base which supports both fighter squadrons and airlift units.

Long run. A period sufficiently long to allow a firm to make desired adjustments to a changed demand by varying the size of the plant.

Macroeconomics. That branch of economics concerned with the study of aggregates in an economy, such as national income and gross national product of capital formation.

*Marginal concept (marginal cost, marginal revenue). A quantity which defines the change in total value caused by the addition of one more unit. Used also to describe relationships of utility, output, cost, and revenue.

Microeconomics. That branch of economics concerned with individual firms, their output and costs, the production and pricing of single commodities, wages of individuals, and so forth.

National income. The money measure of the overall annual flow of goods and services in a nation. It is essentially equal to gross national product minus (1) allowance for depreciation and other capital consumption, and (2) indirect business tax and nontax liability to government.

Opportunity cost. The cost of opportunities given up; the sacrificed amount of other things such as equipment, training, or units of production that could have been obtained if the same time, effort, and resources had been used for an alternative course of action.

Optimization. The attainment of the best possible result, i.e., the maximization (minimization) of some desirable (undesirable) criterion measure, subject to the constraints imposed on the choice of solutions.

Overhead costs. The costs of an enterprise that cannot be attributed directly to the quantities of productive activity. They include all costs except direct labor and direct materials. Overhead costs, sometimes called burden costs or indirect costs, are not identical with fixed costs.

"Per unit" cost curves. Graphic display of curves which relate value per unit of output to different quantities of the unit (instead of total or cumulative values). Examples include average cost curve, average variable cost curve and marginal cost curve.

Production function. The technical or mathematical relationship defining the amount of output capable of being produced by each and every set of specific inputs. It is defined for a given state of technical knowledge.

Profit centers. A center of responsibility usually has revenue as a measure of monetary output, and expense as a measure of inputs, or resources used. Profit is the difference between revenue and expense. Thus, if performance in a responsibility center is measured in terms of both revenue earned and cost incurred, it is called a profit center.

*Return on investment. The desired or specified earnings, as a percentage of investment, that will accrue over a period of time as a result of the productive activity created by the investment.

Short run. A period of such duration that plant size cannot be varied and as a result some costs become a fixed commitment while other costs vary directly with the units of output.

Sunk cost. A past cost representing resources already consumed and, therefore, no longer a relevant cost in considering alternative courses of action.

Utility. The ability of goods or services to satisfy human wants. Utility expresses the relationship between productive output and the satifaction provided.

Variable costs. Those costs that vary with the volume of output as contrasted to fixed costs, which do not vary with output (in short-run analysis).

QUANTITATIVE REASONING

A posteriori reasoning. Empirical or inductive reasoning whereby knowledge of the truth or fallacy of principles concerning propositions is derived from observing such facts or propositions.

Array. An orderly grouping of values according to magnitude, usually from smallest to largest, i.e., some predetermined standard.

Asymptotic. Describes a boundary or limit which a function approaches but never crosses. A curve is said to be asymptotic to a given straight line if the curve approaches but never reaches the given straight line.

Average. The typical or characteristic value of a group of numbers. Often *average* is used interchangeably with *arithmetic mean*. Strictly, the term includes a group of measures of central tendency (e.g., median, mode, and variously computed means).

*Bayesian theory (probability). A probability theorem which explains how newly acquired sample information can be combined with prior probabilities to arrive at a revised, and more accurate, probability.

Bernoulli process. A random process that (1) yields an either-or (success-failure) outcome on each trial with known probability of occurrence, and (2) results from statistically independent trials.

Central limit theorem. If independent random samples are drawn from a sufficiently large population and the mean of each sample is used to form a distribution of sample means, this distribution will be approximately normal.

Central tendency. The tendency of quantitative data to cluster around some value. A single value which is descriptive of the entire body of data. Most frequently used values are the mean, median, and mode.

Certainty. A prevalent decision situation where the state of nature is known but the alternatives are internally complex or far too numerous for a simple judgment.

Confidential interval. A measure of effectiveness in testing, expressed in quantitative terms; e.g., the value of a specific factor (variable) lies within a specified interval a given percentage of the time.

Confidence level (confidence coefficient). A measure of the assurance with which an interval estimate may be made. It represents the likelihood that the true population value being estimated lies within the confidence interval being cited—usually expressed as a percentage.

Conflict. An uncertain decision situation in which the relative value of alternatives is affected by the possible decisions of a thinking opponent with conflicting objectives. The uncertainty resulting from the possible mixes of strategies can be reduced through the use of a minimax decision criterion—resulting in either a saddle point solution or a mixed strategy (using predetermined proportions of each alternative on a random basis).

Contribution. The additional gross revenue attained from sales after deduction of the variable costs of such sales. It contributes toward the overhead costs of the activity, often providing the financial basis upon which other products may generate profit.

*Correlation. The study of the degree of functional or close relationship which exists between two or more sets of variables in a population. A statistical tool.

Correlation coefficient. A number that attempts to measure the interdependency of variables, ranging from -1.0 to $+1.0$.

Curve fitting methods. See LEAST SQUARES METHOD.

Discrete distribution. A distribution in which the variables can assume only specific values, usually integer values (0, 1, 2, . . .). This is in contrast to the continuous distribution in which the variable can assume any value.

Dispersion, measures of. Values that measure the spread (or, inversely, the concentration) of the items in a frequency distribution. Examples are the average deviation or the standard deviation.

Extrapolate. Estimate by trend projection the unknown values that lie beyond the range of known values in a series.

Frequency distribution. An arrangement of statistical data that divides a series of items into classes and indicates the number of items falling into each class. An example is the income distribution which shows the number of persons falling within each income class.

Function. A basic mathematical concept, normally portrayed $Y = f(X)$. A variable Y is said to be a function of another variable X if a rule or relation exists whereby when a value is assigned to X, one or more values of Y are determined. X would be the independent variable, Y the dependent variable.

Histogram. A graph of a frequency distribution with rectangles whose widths represent the class intervals and whose heights represent the corresponding frequencies.

Inequalities. A mathematical relationship that expresses maximum or minimum limits of a relationship, rather than expressing an equality. The symbol $X \leq Y$ means X is equal to or less than Y, and $X \geq Y$ means X is equal to or greater than Y. Its primary application is in the description of constraints in a linear program formulation.

Interpolate. To estimate the intermediate value in a series of numbers by using a formula that relates the unknown value to the pattern of known values in the series.

Interval estimate. An estimate which states that the characteristic of interest has a value that is located somewhere within a range or interval of values.

Logarithm. The logarithm of a number is the exponent or power to which the logarithmic base must be raised to equal that number.

Logarithmic ratio scale. When the vertical axis of a chart is laid off in terms of the logarithms of natural numbers, the arrangement is known as a semilog chart and the vertical scale is called a *log* *scale.* A curve plotted on such a chart represents not the numbers in the series but the logarithms of these numbers. Changes in the slope of such a curve show changes in the percentage increase or decrease of the original series. As long as there is no change in direction, equal distances on the vertical scale correspond to the same percentage change in the original series.

Mean, arithmetic. The measure of central tendency normally synonymous with average. The result is obtained by dividing the sum of two or more quantities by the number of items.

Median. Halfway point between the two end points of an array; thus, one-half of the items have equal or greater value.

Mode. The value in a set of values that occurs with the greatest frequency.

*°**Monte Carlo methods.** Methods of taking random samples from a statistical universe with an assumed probability distribution. These methods of simulated sampling are used when experimentation is either impossible or too expensive.

Objective function. In linear programming, that which is to be maximized or minimized. It is a production function which optimally relates inputs to the output. Output may be expressed in profit, minimum cost, or maximum output for a given cost constraint.

Objective probability. Probability for which there is definitive, historical evidence and common experience to support the assignment of probability.

*°**Payback.** The length of time necessary for the sum of all the annual net cash benefits to equal the amount of the initial investment.

*°**Payoff.** The gain to be derived if a particular course of events develops. A payoff matrix displays the payoffs for a set of alternatives under various possible states of nature.

Point estimate. An estimate which states that the characteristic of interest has a single, specific value. It is the single best estimate of a population value when determined by a sample.

Probability. *Marginal probability* is a number between 0 and 1 that, when assigned to an event or occurrence, expresses the likelihood that the event will occur. *Joint probability* is the probability of two or more specified events occurring simultaneously or in sequence. *Conditional probability* is the likelihood that an event or outcome will occur, given that another event has occurred or a specific condition exists.

Random sample. A sample selected from a population to be tested, in such a manner that every element in the population has an equal chance of being chosen for the sample.

Risk. A decision environment characterized by quantified uncertainty. As used in analysis, a situation is characterized as risk if it is possible to describe all outcomes and assign meaningful objective probability to each one.

*****Sampling.** The process of determining characteristics of a population by collecting and analyzing observations from a representative segment of the population.

*****Scatter diagram (scattergram).** One of several statistical forecasting techniques involving a simple plotting on graph paper of related data with one displayed on the x axis and the other on the y axis of a 90° angle. Often the line of best fit is sufficient to reveal a positive or negative linear relationship useful enough for a rough approximation and prediction of future trend. Logic and judgment are necessary.

Slope. The measure of the steepness of a line. It is computed by calculating the number of units the line rises per unit move to the right.

Standard deviation. A measure of the dispersion of observed data. Mathematically, it is the positive square root of the variance.

Standard error. The standard deviation of a group of measures with the same characteristics (often termed a statistic or a parameter), each obtained from a distinct sample drawn from a larger universe or population.

Statistic. A measure, quantity, or value which is calculated from a sample rather than from the population.

Subjective probability. A probability for which historical evidence is not available for decision making. The decision maker must therefore rely on his own estimate of the likelihood of various possible outcomes.

Uncertainty. In a strict sense, a situation is uncertain if there is no objective basis for assigning probability to the different possible outcomes or if there is no way to describe the possible outcomes. However, in the broader context of analysis and decision making, uncertainty describes all conditions less than certainty, and degrees of objective and subjective probability do exist.

Variance. A measure of dispersion of a frequency distribution computed by summing the squares of the difference between each observation in the sample and the arithmetic mean of the sample distribution, and then dividing by one less than the number of observations.

ANALYTICAL REASONING

A *fortiori* analysis. An analysis deliberately made to favor an alternative system when compared to a judgmental best system. If the best system receives a favorable comparison under the weighted analysis, its position is strengthened. See DOMINANCE.

Alternative. One of several different ways of achieving a desired objective. Each alternative need not be an obvious substitute for the other or perform the same specific function. Thus, for example, to protect civilians against air attack, shelters, air defenses, and retaliatory striking power are all alternatives.

A priori reasoning. Deductive reasoning whereby understanding is derived from reasoning, formulating theories, hypotheses, or rules of inference prior to or instead of undertaking observations or analysis of such factors.

Assumptions. Used to deal with difficult realities that tend to upset a problem-solving routine. They infer the existence of a fact (not known with certainty) from the known existence of other facts.

Attributes. A set of values, the characteristics of which can be used to describe any of the parameters (input, process, output, etc.) of a system. The term *variable* is often used with the same meaning.

Base case. The computation of all costs generated by a past decision. Taken alone, they have little substantive value to a decision maker, but they do have a significant value when contrasting cost implications of changes to the decision.

Benefit. The degree of satisfaction of objectives achieved by selecting any one alternative. It is the result of productive output gained from a given resource utilization. Used interchangeably with the term "effectiveness."

Bias. A conscious or unconscious attitude of evaluating, interpreting, presenting, or using certain data in a subjective, rigid, or advocatory manner.

*Break-even point (break-even analysis). A specific, quantitative output level at which two alternatives become equally economical or where revenues and costs are equal for a single product output. The point where total costs equal the value of total production. A point beyond which profit is realized.

Commensurability. The capability of two qualities or values to be measured by a meaningful, relevant common index. For example, machineguns and rifles are commensurable either in dollar cost or in effectiveness (enemy casualties). However, machineguns and friendly casualties are not commensurable in terms of dollars. Incommensurability is the incapability of two values to be measured by a relevant common index.

Constraints. The conditions that limit and describe how the objective is to be attained. Constraints are dimensions of the objective; they act to confine, or to bring the problem within bounds.

Control. Any process that guides an activity toward some predetermined goal. Essentials for control include predetermined objective, means of measuring activity (criterion), means of comparing activity with criterion, and a correction mechanism.

Criterion. Test of preferredness needed to tell how to choose one alternative over another. For each alternative, it compares the extent to which the objectives are attained with the costs or resources used.

Decision criterion. The rationale by which one decides *how* a decision should be made. Several types of decision criteria can be used, depending on the decision situation (certainty, uncertainty, risk, or conflict) and the desired outcome, i.e., maximum possible return, called (maximax); avoiding maximum loss, called (minimax); or, equally likely to occur, maximum expected return, also called expected value.

Decision making. A systematic process of adapting one's judgment or conclusions about alternative solutions to problems.

Decision situation. A condition in which there is a gap between a present or existing state and a desired or proposed state, and in which there are alternative means of closing or eliminating this gap. Alternatives must exist. A decision situation may be a problem, an unfilled requirement or condition for a change or adjustment, or an unforeseen opportunity to make a choice.

Decision theory. Used to select the best course of action when information is available only in probabilistic form. (See BAYESIAN THEORY, which allows executive judgment to be optimistically brought into the analysis. Also see DECISION THEORY.)

Deductive reasoning. A logical method of working toward specific conclusions from assumed or established generalizations or conclusions. See A PRIORI REASONING.

Dependent variable. Those variables or values which change by the manipulation of the independent variable.

Descriptive standard. See NORMATIVE STANDARD.

Deterministic Model. Used to represent operations or processes in which chance plays so small a role that its influence can be ignored in formulating the model.

Dominance. When one alternative is clearly more effective than any other—at every cost. Dominance cannot always lead to a preferred alternative but it can eliminate inferior alternatives. Similar reasoning is used in *a fortiori* analysis.

Dynamic. A system or process is dynamic if its behavior over time is determined by functional equations in which variables at different points of time are involved in an essential way.

Effectiveness. The degree of performance or amount of capability to accomplish some objective. Various criteria (e.g., targets destroyed or tonnage moved) might be used to measure this amount of capability.

Efficiency. Attaining the greatest possible output from a given amount of resource input. Sometimes used as a synonym for productivity.

Endogenous variable. A variable whose magnitude is dependent on and determined by the model being studied.

Equally likely (laplace) criterion. A decision criterion under uncertainty stating that because the probabilities of future states of nature are unknown, they should be considered equal. Equal probability is assigned to each possible state of nature and the alternative which maximizes expected value is selected.

Exogenous variable. A variable which is wholly independent of the model being studied; that is, a variable determined by outside influences.

Expansion path. On an indifference map, the line which connects all points at which the isoquants are tangent to the isocosts for various budget levels. Every point on this expansion path represents the maximum output for a given cost, and likewise, the minimum cost for a given level of output.

Expected value criterion. The decision criterion that, when faced with several possible strategies, a decision maker (who is neither very conservative nor much of a gambler) must be expected to use or else choose the alternative providing the probability of highest return. Expected value is the probability of an event occurring multiplied by the payoff associated with its occurrence.

Feasible solutions. Those combinations of inputs that will produce a wide range of outputs not constrained by limitations of the system or process. Within this range of feasible solutions are found the most efficient solution (when one more unit of output cannot be produced without sacrificing another output—isoquant) and the optimal solution (where an efficient solution is produced at minimum cost—the isoquant–isocost tangent point).

Feedback. Data extracted from a process or situation and used in controlling, planning, or modifying immediate or future inputs.

Heuristics. A systematic, experimental method of approaching unstructured, symbolic, or unmeasurable problems for which solutions are found by successive identification and evaluation of the progress made toward the final solution. Additional elements of heuristic reasoning include a tradition of independent investigation, heavy reliance on common sense, and the use of intuition.

Incommensurability. The incapability of two qualities or values to be measured by a meaningful, relevant common index.

Independent variable. A variable that an analyst allows to change in some organized and controlled fashion during an analysis to see the effects it may have on the other (dependent) variables.

Input. The energizing or start-up force that provides the system or process its operating material. As a parameter of a system, it can take values of resource components, sets of descriptive information, estimating procedures for the components and other subsystems.

Iteration. A process for calculating a desired result by means of a repeating cycle of operations, which comes closer to the desired result with each repetition.

Learning curve. A cost-estimating tool which indicates how the rate of learning changes with increased practice. It is generally used to predict or describe the decrease in the cost of a unit as the number of units produced increases.

Matrix. A rectangular array of terms called elements. It is used to facilitate the study of problems in which the relation between these elements is fundamental.

Maximax criterion. A decision criterion under uncertainty that states that the decision maker should select that strategy which has for one of its possible outcomes the highest payoff value of any outcome—for any strategy.

Measures of effectiveness. Those qualities (the same used to define the criterion) which are used to indicate the degree of achievement of objectives. The *effectiveness scale* provides a range of values for these qualities and thus defines possible levels of achievement; *effectiveness* is the measured position on this scale assigned to each alternative considered.

Minimax criterion. A decision criterion under uncertainty stating that the decision maker should select the strategy whose lowest possible payoff is higher than the lowest possible payoff of any other strategy. This criterion dictates a highly conservative strategy.

***Model.** A simplified representation of an object or operation, containing only those aspects of primary importance to the problem under study. The means of representation may vary from a complex set of mathematical equations of a computer program to a purely verbal description of the situation.

Normative standard. As a basis of analysis, evaluating an alternative in terms of what it should attain relative to some predetermined standard. In contrast, a descriptive standard requires only the describing of characteristics, an estimated extent of occurrence, or predicted outcomes.

Objective. The purpose to be achieved or the position to be obtained. Objectives vary with the level of suboptimization involved in the decision structure.

Optimal solution. See FEASIBLE SOLUTION.

Output. The results of system processes. This parameter is the purpose for which the productive function was brought together; hence, output is congruent with the objective (except that subsystem outputs becomes intermediate steps to higher order subsystems and objectives).

Parameter. A characteristic considered to be essential in accurately describing a problem, population, or system and the value of which is therefore held constant during a calculation related to that problem.

Payoff matrix. A graphic presentation which depicts the output (cost, profit, etc.) resulting from the interaction of available alternatives and those states of nature that might occur.

***Present value.** The estimated present worth of a stream of future benefits or costs arrived at by discounting the future values, using an appropriate return-on-investment rate.

Saddle point. A solution to a game matrix which yields the optimum strategy for both persons (lowest element in the row is also the highest element in the column). If no saddle point exists the opponents must use a mixed strategy to obtain game value.

Satisficing. A term, advanced by Herbert Simon, which views decision making as a process of reaching satisfactory rather than optimal positions.

Spend out. The cost implications of decisions made to date regarding a given system—when spread over the planned future time horizon.

Spillover. The effects of one system or organization upon another.

States of nature. Specific, alternative sets of uncontrollable factors in the decision environment that result from natural occurrences — natural in the sense that they were not calculated by thinking opponents.

Static condition. A system or process state in which established relationships between elements of the system have the same time frame.

Stochastic process. A process in which outcomes are dependent on chance and incorporate probabilities of events occurring.

Suboptimization. The optimization of a criterion which measures performance at one level in an organization or system but which is not perfectly compatible with criteria at higher levels in the organization. Suboptimization is usually necessary because alternatives at all levels of decision making cannot be analyzed simultaneously before decisions are made at any level.

Subsystems. The interrelationship of systems, wherein the outputs of one system form inputs for other systems.

System. A composite of elemental units so arranged that they are dependent on each other to effect their purpose. Generally, this implies that a change in one element will have an effect on the others. Systems range from a simple framework or skeleton to the extreme complexity of a society.

Trade-off. An exchange of values within an analytical relationship (usually a model) to determine the impact of that change on the output, with the final objective to come closer to the most favorable solution.

Variable. A quantity or quality which may take on any one of a specific set of values. Variables have two types of relationship: Independent variables can be given different values and cause changes in the dependent variables, while dependent variables change only in response to the independent variable.

Zero-sum game. A conflict situation in which the sum of the gains for one person exactly equals the sum of the losses to another person.

ANALYTICAL PROCESSES AND TECHNIQUES

Algorithms. A systematic set of instructions which permits the manipulation of numbers using an iterative process that converges on the true value.

*****Assignment method.** A specialized form of the transportation method for solving linear programming problems.

Automatic data processing (ADP). The use of electronic computers to process data, with less cost, more speed, and greater accuracy. This includes arranging data in any form to use for different purposes. It also means that computers can be programmed to process data to perform long, complex, sequential operations rapidly for the purpose of problem solving and to aid in decision making.

*****Break-even analysis.** A method of evaluating the effect that changes in volume (output, quantity) have on costs, revenues, and profit for single output productive activities. When comparing alternate means to achieve the same objective, break-even analysis identifies minimum cost systems relative to given level of output.

Contingency analysis. Analysis that varies the qualitative assumptions about the environment (such as terrain or type of conflict) to determine their effects on the results of the initial analysis.

Cost analysis. The systematic examination of cost (total resource implications) to interrelated activities and equipments to determine the relative costs of alternative systems, organizations, and force structures. Cost analysis is not designed to provide the precise measurements required for budgetary purposes.

*****Cost-benefit analysis.** Most of the descriptions of cost-effectiveness apply. It must be added that it is the net result of productive output gained from a given resource utilization *minus* the opportunity cost incurred. Often written Cost/Benefit analysis by analysts and economists.

Cost-effective analysis. An analytical approach to solving problems of choice. It requires a definition of objectives, an identification of alternatives, an established measure of effectiveness, and the identification of that alternative which yields the greatest effectiveness for a given cost—or that alternative which produces the required level of benefits at lowest cost.

*Critical path methods.** See NETWORKS.

Cybernetics. The discipline dealing with control processes wherever they are found, ranging from the single cell through the individual animal, group, organization, business, or even entire society. Similarities in control and feedback mechanisms essential to control have been found in different environments which provide a basis for applying controls in business.

*Decision Trees.** A method of displaying the structure of a decision and the interplay between a present decision, chance events, competitors' activities, and possible future decisions and their consequences.

Decision theory. A discipline for dealing with alternative courses of action which takes into account: (1) the possible states of nature to which probability of occurrence may be assigned, (2) some method of assessing the correctness of actions and their consequences in terms of effectiveness, and (3) some criterion for determining the optimum choice.

*Delphi technique.** A series of repeated interrogations, usually by questionnaire, asked of individuals whose opinion or judgments are of value. The purpose is to arrive at a consensus regarding an issue under investigation. Each subsequent interrogation is accompanied by information regarding the preceding round of replies.

*Discounting (discounting cash flow, present value).** The method of evaluating the future earning power of capital expenditure projects by discounting at a specified rate the flow of anticipated costs or savings, so that the accumulated present values of these payments can be compared with alternative resource allocations (also discounted). By discounting (the reverse of compounding) at a specific time and rate, one can determine the present values, or the estimated present worth of a stream of future benefits or costs, as compared to other uses that could have been made with the capital. By use of the discount rate, the present worth is arrived at by reducing all values in proportion to the duration between the present and actual time of their occurrence.

*Game theory. A branch of analysis concerned with models of conflict
   between two or more opponents under specified rules. It involves
   formulating decision strategy with the aim, one assumes, of
   maximizing the return and minimizing loss. It is used to determine the optimum strategy in a competitive situation.

Gaming. A method of examining policies and strategies under the
   conditions of a particular scenario, allowing factors (human or
   chance) to vary.

Index numbers. Numbers which reflect the measurement of fluctuations in price, volume, economic activity, or other variables over
   a period of time, relative to a base. Critical elements are the
   choice of a base period, method of weighting, and selection of
   components.

Inventory models. Mathematical techniques to determine the quantity
   of materials to order and the frequency of placing orders so that
   the costs of keeping an inventory and the cost of reordering are
   minimized.

*Least-squares method. A statistical method of fitting a functional form
   to observed data. It is so called because the sum of the squared
   deviations of the calculated values from the observed values of
   the variables is minimized.

*Linear programming. A mathematical method of planning the opti-
   mum allocation and use of limited resources in situations where
   there is a wide range of possible alternatives. Mathematical
   requirements for applicability of linear programming in addition
   to those above are as follows: (1) both resources and the activities
   that use them are nonnegative quantities; and (2) both the
   objective (e.g., profit or cost) and the restrictions on its attainment
   are expressible as a system of linear equalities or inequalities.

*Marginal analysis. The process of identifying the benefits and costs
   of alternatives as a one unit change occurs in the quantity of the
   alternative. The resulting benefit-cost ratios of the various alternatives are utilized to select optimum choices—until the cost-
   benefit ratios of all alternatives are equalized.

Markov analysis. An analysis based on mathematical techniques which
   describe a series of conditions in which each condition depends
   on its forerunner, i.e., the probability of a particular outcome in
   the tenth event is determined by the outcome of the ninth event.
   Markov analysis is very useful in analyzing the current movement
   of a variable in an effort to predict the future movement of that
   same variable.

*Networks (critical path method, PERT, line of balance). A group of techniques used in planning, scheduling, and controlling complex problems related to large-scale, nonrepetitive projects which involve a great number of interrelated decision points or events. The project is displayed as a network which connects these events in such a way as to show the various alternative paths leading to completion. The total job is broken down into a number of events or milestones; the activities required to accomplish each is estimated; the time and sometimes the cost of each is estimated; a network is constructed showing relationships between activities and events and then analyzed to find which of the activities are critical in determining total time for the whole job. PERT is an evaluation application to study more efficient ways of scheduling activities, further planning, and better control.

Operations research. The application of quantitative scientific methods to problems to obtain optimum solutions. It normally includes many disciplines, combined in a team approach to provide quantitative bases for decisions.

Parametric analysis. An analysis conducted with various assumed values for the parameter instead of a constant value. Parametric analysis is used to examine a problem, to identify sensitive parameters, and to obtain reasonable approximations of final results. It answers the figurative question: "If the value of the parameter ranged from some upper to some lower limit instead of the stated constant value, what would the result be?"

*PERT (Program Evaluation Review Technique). See NETWORKS.

*Present value. See DISCOUNTING.

Probabilistic model. A computational process used to represent operations in which chance plays a major role. Consequently, this type of model is constructed to use probability theory.

*Queueing theory (waiting lines). A technique that deals with the costs incurred when people or items randomly arrive at a servicing facility which has less processing capability than the potential arrivals. Included are the costs of waiting for service and the costs of providing faster processing service.

*Regression analysis. A mathematical method used to establish the relationship, if any, between observed and quantifiable variables. More specifically, a poorly named but useful technique of determining an unknown, related variable in the future based upon a mathematical series of simple equations to plot a curve which will fit most cases.

Scenarios. Word pictures of fixed sequences of events in a defined environment. By varying the sequences and factors of the environment, comparisons and evaluation of various alternative strategies can be made.

*Sensitivity analysis. Repetition of an analysis with different quantitative values for cost or operational assumptions or estimates (e.g., hit-kill probabilities, activity rates, or R&D costs) to compare effects of substitution with the results of the basic analysis. If a small change in an assumption results in a proportionately greater change in the results, then the results are said to be sensitive to that assumption or variable.

Simplex method. A set of procedural rules for computing and finding the optimum solution to a linear programming problem in an efficient, finite number of steps. It is not limited by the number of constraints and variables, as are the graphic and algebraic methods, but only by the capacity of the computing equipment available.

*Simulation. Usually resulting from the inability to fully express a problem mathematically, a simulation is a constructed model or definition of a system that realisticallly portrays the world and can be manipulated. It is a detailed description of how the conditions at one point in time lead to subsequent conditions at a later point in time.

Strategic planning. This is the process of deciding on the changes in the objectives of the organization, in the resources a business is to use to attain the objectives, and in the policies that are to govern the acquisition and use of these resources. Long-range policy plans that change the character or direction of an organization are strategic plans.

Systems analysis. A formal inquiry intended to advise a decision maker on the policy choices involved in major decisions. To qualify as a Systems Analysis, a study must look at the whole problem. Characteristically, it will involve a systematic investigation of the decision-maker's objectives and of the relevant criteria; a comparison—quantitative when possible—of the costs, effectiveness, and risks associated with the alternative policies or strategies for achieving each objective; and, an attempt to formulate additional alternatives if those examined are deficient.

*Time series analysis. The interpretation of sales, production, price, or other variables over a period of time. A series of data over time is analyzed to find chief types of like means or fluctuations such as trend, cyclical, seasonal, or irregular.

*Transportation Method. An algorithm for solving a certain class of linear programming problems. It can be used in problems where it is necessary to fulfill several requirements from a number of sources and both requirements and resources are expressed in the same kind of units; i.e., a supply organization must provide products to several bases from several supply depots.

*Waiting line theory (queueing theory). A technique of analyzing the feasibility of adding facilities or quantities and of assessing the amount and cost of waiting time. Most models assume a specific distribution of arrivals and service times. Useful in managing processes which depend upon passing through required stages.

APPENDIX III

Some Popular Quantitative and Other Techniques and Tools Used in Analysis

There are dozens of definitions, tools, and techniques used in almost every analytical process, most of which are listed and defined briefly in Appendix II. However, it seems appropriate for a handbook on the subject of decision making to include a somewhat fuller explanation of some of the more popular techniques and tools used in analysis (often the most provocative and misunderstood). In this appendix these are included for the purpose of providing the user with a ready reference and some idea as to the "what," "where," and "how" of their use. A few are quite simple and easy to use as compared to others. Often, a single one can offer a "quick and simple" answer to a problem. *Once* a logical approach has been made to determine the exact problem; this is all that may be necessary for solution of the moment. These few have an asterisk alongside to identify them. The remainder do not. The reader should realize that it is a virtually impossible task to attempt to provide in one section of a handbook *all* the accumulated knowledge in economics, mathematics, management science, statistics, and other sources which provide us with these tools and techniques, and that this is merely an attempt to provide a handy and understandable collection of some of them. "Purists" will please excuse both the lack of complete coverage and the nuances and esoteric modifications of the techniques and tools.

The illustrations are in alphabetical order, except that many fall under a classified or generic term to which they are related, or of which they are modifications and extensions. A bibliography of some excellent texts on accounting, economics, statistics, mathematics, and management science is included at the end of this appendix.

Immediately following is a contents section for this appendix.

LIST OF TOOLS AND TECHNIQUES

1. Common Methods of Evaluation   178

    (a) Break-Even Analysis   178
    (b) Payback   181
    (c) Rate of Return   183
    (d) Discounting (Present Value)   184

2. Decision Trees   188
3. Delphi Technique   191
4. Game Theory   193
5. Linear Programming Methods   196

    (a) Linear Programming   196
    (b) Transportation Method   202
    (c) Assignment Method   205

6. Marginal Analysis   207

    (a) Marginal Concept   208
    (b) Marginal Cost   209
    (c) Marginal Revenue   210

7. Models   213

    (a) Verbal   214
    (b) Human   214
    (c) People and Computers Interacting   214
    (d) Analytical/Mathematical   215
    (e) Conceptual/Computer   215

8. Networks   215

    (a) Program Evaluation and Review Technique   215
    (b) Critical Path Method   218

9. Probability Techniques   219

    (a) Bayesian Probability   219
    (b) Bernoulli Process   220

10. Sampling   222
11. Simulation   225

    (a) Monte Carlo   226
    (b) Waiting Line Technique   229

12. Statistical Forecasting Techniques   232

    (a) Scatter Diagram   232
    (b) Correlation   236
    (c) Regression   240
    (d) Some Warnings   242

13. Time Series   243
14. Various Other Techniques   244

    (a) A Fortiori Analysis   244
    (b) Index Numbers   244
    (c) Operations Research   245
    (d) Simplex Method   245
    (e) Statistical Quality Control Charts   245
    (f) Utility Theory   245

Selected Bibliography   246

1. COMMON METHODS OF EVALUATION

*(a) Break-Even Analysis (Break-Even Point; Cost, Volume, Profit Analysis)

Cost, volume, and profit analysis is one of the most helpful tools for management when making decisions about:

1. Relation of changes in *sales* to changes in *profits*.
2. Relation of changes in *costs* to changes in *profits*.
3. Relation of changes in *scale of operation* to changes in *profits*.

The most common approach to portray these is that of the *standard graphic method*.

The standard graphic approach above is a typical representation of breakeven. The *fixed costs* of $30,000, shown by the rectangular base supporting the variable costs, are those which do not change over the short or normal run and can be calculated regardless of volume. This fixed cost base is the starting point ($30,000) for an upward curve of *variable costs* which increases as volume increases because more labor, more material, and so forth, are used. By plotting the sales

---

*Asterisk indicates one of the quick and simple methods or techniques.

revenues in dollars, starting on the same Y axis as the costs and then plotting the *volume* or *units of production* on the X axis, the point where the *total revenue* (sales) line *intersects* the *total cost* line (both fixed and variable costs) locates the *Break-Even Point*(BEP). It is at this point that total revenue is exactly *equal* to total variable costs plus fixed costs.

To use a BEP diagnostic study such as Figure III.1 displays is very easy. Any vertical distance between the total revenue line and the total cost line which lies to the *right* of the break-even point (BEP) *up* to the point where they *intersect* measures *profit* at that volume. To the *left* of the BEP, any vertical distances between those two lines measure the loss at that volume. Thus, the graph clearly reveals the close relationship between four variables: revenue, fixed costs, variable costs, and volume or output. It reveals the point of *maximum* profit. It supplies answers to the three relationships of sales, costs, and scale of operations. The break-even chart helps managers estimate what effect certain decisions regarding *each* of the relationships would have on profits. It should be noted that the limits of profits are *not* limitless simply because the right side of the BEP *may* be "open-ended." The realities of capacity, resources, the market, and other factors cause the two curves to approach each other and meet. That is, there are some *fixed variables* and other parameters that limit production and profit.

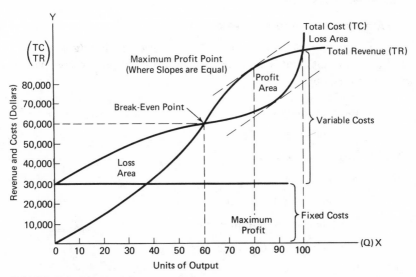

FIGURE III.1 Standard Graphic Method

Inverted Graphic Method of Breakeven

The *inverted graphic method* can be used where the fixed cost line is shown *above* the variable cost line. In such a case, the major factor is to control overhead, a fixed cost. The fixed costs may be disproportionately high while the variable costs are relatively low and stable. In charting this situation, the greater effect of overhead costs is more easily seen by plotting such costs *above* the variable costs.

To summarize these brief examples of breakeven, it is appropriate to repeat the three key variables to profits. Total dollar profits are directly affected by the interactions of *revenues, fixed costs,* and *variable costs,* and one may be able to see more clearly by either graphs or algebra that:

1. A change in the selling price of each unit, or the volume of units sold, will affect profits.
2. A change in the fixed cost total will affect profits.
3. A change in the variable cost of each unit will change the profit figure.

In conclusion, two points about the limitations of breakeven are in order: (1) A company needs good, valid cost figures or else the entire exercise produces false analyses; and (2) breakeven is not considered a good tool for long-range use, as breakeven is static in nature and therefore only useful under relatively stable conditions. However, viewed as a guide to profit variables, it is a popular method if *judgment* is also used.

Algebraic Method of Breakeven

Another method of determining breakeven is the *algebraic method,* the mathematics of which, again, are quite simple for cost, volume, and profit analysis:

Let TR = total revenue in dollars

TC = total cost in dollars

TVC = total variable costs

TFC = total fixed costs

x = volume or output in units

v = variable cost per unit in dollars

p = selling price per unit in dollars

BEP = break-even point

180

In the algebraic method, total revenue must equal the volume in units multiplied by the selling price per unit, or $TR = xp$. Also, total cost must equal total variable costs plus total fixed costs, or $TC = TVC + TFC$, or $TC = vx + TFC$.

To determine the BEP for *units*, simply equate TR to TC and solve for the volume (units of production) figure. For example, assume TFC are \$10,000 for the year, v amounts to \$2, and p is \$4. Setting up the equation TR equals TC:

$$x\,(\$4) = \$10,000 + x\,(\$2)$$

$$\$2x = 10,000$$

$$x = 5,000\,units\ (BEP)$$

To get the BEP in dollars, the 5,000 units are multiplied by \$4, giving the figure of \$20,000. The formulas for break-even points in dollars, units, and percentage of capacity are these:

$$BEP,\text{ dollars} = \frac{TFC}{(1-v)/p}\ (or)\frac{TFC}{1-v} \times p$$

$$BEP,\text{ units} = \frac{TFC}{p-v}$$

$$BEP,\text{ percent of capacity} = \frac{TFC}{(p-v)\,(\text{total capacity in units})} \times 100\%\ [1]$$

(b) Payback

A simple and useful tool is *payback*. It is the length of time necessary for the sum of all the annual net cash benefits to equal the amount of the initial investment. It is used most frequently in decisions concerning capital outlays. Assume a manager is considering the purchase of a certain machine to do a production job, perhaps to have the machine assist or replace human labor, or to replace an older machine. He knows that if purchased, it will reduce the cash outlay for

---

[1]This is a modification of a fuller treatment of cost, volume, and profit analysis given in Richard I. Levin and Charles A. Kirkpatrick, *Quantitative Approaches to Management*, 2nd ed. (New York: McGraw-Hill, 1971) pp. 21–22. The algebraic illustration is from same source and is copyrighted © 1971 by McGraw-Hill. Used with permission of McGraw-Hill Book Company.

labor and perhaps even for spoiled or wasted material, over a period of three years. He knows also that a reduction in cash outlay is as good as an increase in cash inflow, but he must consider the *time* it will take to get the purchase money back. Capital is scarce and therefore he does not wish to tie it up too long, as there are many other competing uses for such capital.

The simple formula for payback is really one which is known to almost everyone: $P = \dfrac{I}{C}$

P = payback period

I = original investment

C = annual cash inflows (after taxes)

Hence, an investment of $18,000, with

annual cash inflows of $6,000 would be

$P = \dfrac{\$18,000}{\$6,000} = 3 \text{ years}$

A mental calculation is usually enough. The more difficult part is to determine objectively the annual cash inflows. But, they too can be determined by costing the outputs of the new machine over any *former* method. This method is especially useful because it highlights the key factors of time and liquidity.

However, this method has shortcomings. First, the emphasis *is* on time and liquidity and does not necessarily indicate real profitability. It may be that the $18,000 machine is worthless after the three-year period. Also, it presupposes that *alternative* uses of limited capital have been considered, one of which may, in the long run, have proven to be more profitable. Another way of stating this is that the payback method does not in itself consider any stream of income that may continue beyond the payback period. Finally, if two different capital outlays are competing, a careful determination is needed of *when* and *how much* the paybacks occur. In other words, the outlay with a payback in earlier years is better than the other outlay (assuming all other things remain equal or of no influence) because of the *time value of money*, an important consideration which will be included in the illustration of discounting and present value.

To end on a positive note, payback is useful if the firm is short of cash and needs a quick return of any cash funds. Also, a firm which has no alternative choices and whose business is changeable, vulnerable, or short-lived may like payback simply because there is no predictable future, and hence there is no point in projecting cash flows beyond a short period of time. Finally, the payback period can also give a rough approximation of interest rates.

*(c) Rate of Return (Average or Accounting Rate of Return)

Another, easy evaluation method is the *rate of return*, often called the accounting method because it determines the return by using accrual accounting methods. By determining the accrued rate of return on an investment, the resulting percentage is a *measure of profit*. This measure of profit overcomes one of the disadvantages of the payback method.

Rate of return is defined as the percentage of *average* annual net income after taxes to the *average* investment over the life of the project. It does not depend upon cash flows but upon actual reported accounting income. The method is simple to illustrate:

Let R = the accounting rate of return

C = annual cash inflows (cash after taxes)

I = original investment

D = depreciation

The formula is $R = \dfrac{C-D}{I}$

Going back to the previous example on payback, we will recall an original investment of $18,000 for a machine and an annual cash inflow of $6,000. Let's assume depreciation to be $3,600 annually. Hence,

$$R = \frac{\$6,000 - \$3,600}{\$18,000} = \frac{2400}{18,000} = 13.3\%$$

As in breakeven, the calculation is based upon return on the original investment, but since a machine is a *depreciable* asset, depreciation is subtracted each year. In the above case, depreciation is subtracted over a useful life of five years, with no salvage value.

To obtain the rate of return as the average of the undepreciated value over its life, a straight-line method of depreciation would appear as follows:

Original Investment	$18,000
Undepreciated Balances	
Year 1 end	14,400
Year 2 end	10,800
Year 3 end	7,200
Year 4 end	3,600
Year 5 end	—
Total	$54,000
Undepreciated Average	
(divide by 6) =	$9,000

Where there is no estimated salvage value, the undepreciated average balance may be assumed logically to be one half the cost.

½ × $18,000 = $9,000, which is the same answer as above.

The *rate of return* is different, based upon an average investment. The formula is:

$$R = \frac{C-D}{(1/2)I} \text{ or } \frac{C-D}{1/2}$$

$$R = \frac{\$6,000 - \$3,600}{1/2\ \$18,000} = \frac{2400}{9000} = 26.7\%$$

As a rule of thumb, the rate of return may be relied on as a better estimate than payback if the anticipated life of the machine is less than twice the payback period.

Payback, breakeven, and rate of return are somewhat "rough and ready" (or "dirty and quick" if that is preferred) common methods of evaluation. The rate of return also has shortcomings. It still overlooks the *time value* of money. Also, if the earnings are in an *uneven* flow, the method cannot measure precise effects on profits because it *is* an averaging technique. This leads to a fourth, more precise method, that of *discounting* or discounted cash flow or the present value of money as compared to its future, which is treated next.

(d) Discounting (Discounted Cash Flow; Present Value)

Much superior to the previous methods of evaluation is *discounting*. Sometimes the technique is referred to by its real purpose, namely, to find out the *present value* of future money; and sometimes, as *discounted cash flow*. It requires a little more effort than the "rough

184

and ready" techniques, but not too much if the *principle* is grasped and prepared present value tables are used in calculations.

There is hardly any problem or decision situation in business or organizations, public or private, more prevalent than the problem of proper capital outlay. Alternative ways to reach the optimum use of capital in an environment of limited resources is the heart of the decision-making problem. It becomes especially important when those limited resources are borrowed funds. Repayment becomes a vital part of the picture. Interest rates and the time period in which the funds are committed often become deciding factors.

We begin with the idea of the time value of money. If $100 were borrowed for a year at 6 percent, $106 would have to be repaid one year hence. This means that one year's time makes a difference of $6 in the value of the borrower's money. Put another way, it means that $100 *today* is worth as much as $106 a *year* from today. Many have described the principle of time and money as "the bird in hand versus the bird in the bush." Money does change its value in time. As entrepreneurs and others well know, a dollar put to work today to earn more money is worth more than money received tomorrow simply because it *can* be put to work now. If not, the use of the money until a future year is foregone. Inflation is not the issue here, but rather an added fact of life which depreciates money. Compounding arrives at a figure, x years hence, which will be comprised of both the initial value or loan and its added value if the interest, payoffs, or dividends were not touched but left to accumulate together with the ever-growing principle base. Present value is a way to determine the amount which would *have to be invested* to attain a desired amount or percentage of return (compounded) on the original investment. That is, if we desire a given percentage return (especially when comparing the return on alternative investments) for x years hence, what is the value of that investment if made right now?

The general rule for discounting, or present value, is to compute the value *today* of $1, which is payable n years from now, by determining how much must be invested at compound interest to *become* $1 at the end of the n years. Compound interest grows exponentially, e.g., $(1 + \text{Interest rate})^n$, n being the *end* of a certain number of years. This expression only needs to be *inverted* to arrive at present value (*PV*). That is, the present value of $1 which is payable n years hence, at interest rate (*i*) is

$$PV = \left(\frac{\$1}{1 + \text{Interest rate } (i)} \right)^t$$

Thus at a compound interest rate of 8 percent for ten years the formula would yield:

$$\left(\frac{\$1}{1+0.08}\right)^{10} = \frac{\$1}{2.16} = \$0.4632$$

To look at it another way, $1 invested today at 8 percent would be worth $1.08 a year from now. Or, the present value of $1.08 a year from now is $1, discounted at 8 percent. Since this seems awkward to some, calculating the present value of $1 received one year from now, or some multiple of $1, is more apropos. Referring to a present value table (illustrated at the end of the case study), we find that the *present value* of $1 at the 8 percent interest rate for one year is only 0.926. It is worth 0.074 less in a year than it is now. If compounded by ten years (See table A at the end of Appendix I) the result is a figure of 0.463, which is what we got with the formula.

The tables which exist provide ready answers for all kinds of present discounted values, but one must be careful to use one table for annuity types, or even-flow amounts over the years, as opposed to one year, or uneven flows. A second table of present values of $1 of the nonannuity type is available for that. If uneven flows or amounts are involved, each year must be looked up separately and the totals added; whereas the annuity type reveals the compounding effect of equal amounts each year.

There is another way to illustrate present value to take annuities *and* uneven flows into account:

First we define:

B_t as benefits in time t n is the life of the project

C_t as costs in time t t is time

    i is interest

The present value of a project, then, is found by this formula:

$$\sum_{t=1}^{n}\left(B_t - C_t\right)\left(\frac{1}{1+i}\right)^t$$

If $B_t - C_t = A$ constant, one has an annuity; otherwise one has uneven flows.*

---

*Formulas involve variables and constants. A *variable* is a quantity which can take on more than one value. A *constant* always remains the same.

As a useful tool, discounting can aid in computing the return on a capital investment (capitalized cost) when the investor wishes to realize a specific percentage return below which the capital investment perhaps would not be made. It can be used to compute the return on a uniform flow of income from any source over a period of time. It can also be used to determine the return from nonuniform or *different* amounts of flow over a period of time. As pointed out, tables exist to find these returns or present value *now* of x amount of dollars y years hence, of both the annuity types and one-year different amount types. They can be found in almost any mathematics, finance, or accounting book; however, a page of each type is illustrated in Appendix I, at the end of the case study.

By reducing them all to their present values, discounting also helps in determining the service life of different equipments or services which may be used or rendered at different intervals. Still another use is in determining depreciation and taxes. In straight line depreciation, for example, the technique takes into consideration that a *deduction* is realized in a constant rate over a period of time. The present value of such "flows of depreciation" can be found by calculating cost after taxes, cost before taxes, the depreciation amount, and the tax rate (T), usually expressed in a decimal form.

In summary, while there are many uses, perhaps the most common one for managers is that of *discounted cash flow* sometimes known as the investor's method, or the interest rate of return, or the internal rate of return. It makes possible the comparison of competing profitable investments where limited resources prevail. It further makes possible the setting of a return rate goal, below which a manager may judge the investment unacceptable. This can be done in reverse also, by finding the interest rate, which when applied to the investment, will yield the *expected* annual cash flows. For example, if a new machine is expected to result in $5,000 savings each year for five years, the present value table (annuity) shows that for each $1, a 10 percent rate for five years would yield 3.791. By multiplying the 3.791 times $5,000, the total amount required to attain the expected value would be $18,955. In view of the fact that the savings are expected to be $25,000 (five years × $5,000), the purchase should be made, at least from a purely economic point of view.

The full-blown example of present value in the Downtown Parking Authority case solution in this book is a practical example of this valuable tool, whose strongest point is that it takes the *time value* of money into consideration. Its weakness is that, like other attempts to approach certainty and prediction, it is judgmental in anticipating future returns and can be affected by a not-so-certain future.

2. DECISION TREES (DECISION DIAGRAMMING)

The use of *decision trees* or *decision diagrams* often is an appropriate way of representing the elements of a decision model in a clear manner. In diagramming a sequence of decisions, events, and the consequences of their flow, a problem is clarified by virtue of the explicitness, simplicity, and visibility which a decision tree can provide. It is especially useful in multistage situations. It is a better way of visualizing consequences than the matrix* approach because it can illustrate a *series* of related decisions.

One illustration of a decisions tree for only two decisions and two events is illustrated in Figure III.2. Note that the tree "grows" from left to right, not from the bottom to the top. The two possible courses of action, or initial decisions are presented first as emanating from a point called action and labeled decision one and decision two. They divide, forklike, and lead to possible events by taking certain routes and then also including the probability of such events. Thus, the opportunity to employ known or best-judged probabilities exists. If any one of the four events should occur, the results can be shown in the final column opposite each event, called consequences. The consequences can be interpreted as profit or loss by adding the cost or profit from Decision One to Event One (calculated for its probability) and so on.

An illustration of a four-decision, multiple-event decision tree which the author considered in one of his hobbies, lobster catching, is given in Figure III.3.

These are the facts. Fifty pots (commercial license) are the limit we are able to tend. Lobster is $2 wholesale. The cost of the boat (mine) for the season's operation is $250 if only 5 pots (noncommercial limit) are set, and one-half of $1,000 if 50 pots are used. Probabilities are the key, for they are best estimates based on experiences of other lobstermen and my own. Note that where I do the work, the probabil-

---

*Matrix—A rectangular array of numbers is referred to as a matrix:

$$\begin{bmatrix} 4 & 5 & 2 \\ 9 & 6 & 1 \\ 3 & 2 & -1 \end{bmatrix} \text{(A square, or } 3 \times 3 \text{ matrix)}$$

Each number is referred to as an *element*. It has *rows* and *columns*. A calendar is an example. A matrix shows comparisons of rows versus column choices; or steps in a move; or transition from one state or value to another. It may be added or multiplied by another matrix to show transitions.

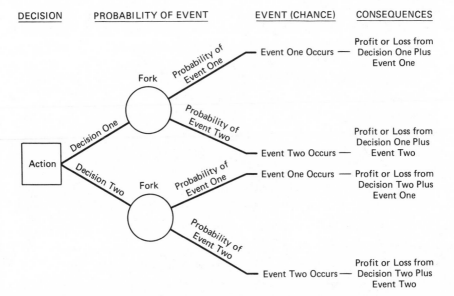

| DECISION | PROBABILITY OF EVENT | EVENT (CHANCE) | CONSEQUENCES |

FIGURE III.2 Simple Format for a Decision Tree

ities drop somewhat simply because without another "hand," the frequency of visiting and pulling the pots *will* fall off. I have not included the cost of the pots, which are $15 each, but can deduct the amount 50 × $15 = $750 after the first calculations. Also, the pots may be used for several years with proper care. A ten-week period of summer work is the limit of lobstering, as I must return to regular work in the fall.

The following alternative decisions are mine:

1. Noncommercial (5-pot) operation alone.
2. Commercial (50-pot) operation alone.
3. Commercial (50-pot) operations with Phil, who will go for half the costs, half the profits, and will work with me as a partner.
4. Commercial (50-pot) operation with Bob, who will go for half the costs, 25 percent of the profits, but cannot work with me. (He golfs.)

Thus, the payoffs are laid out for me in the simple tree illustrated. Considering profit, I should choose to go for events a2–S3 or a4–S3, which would net $4,250. or $3,625, respectively. My common sense prevails, however, and I realize that at age 60 it is too much work and too risky to attempt the job *alone*. My chances of more frequent good catches and having half the work done (to say nothing of the safety of having a companion) appeal to me more; hence, I choose a3 plus S3, lobstering with Phil, with the good probability (0.90) that we two can

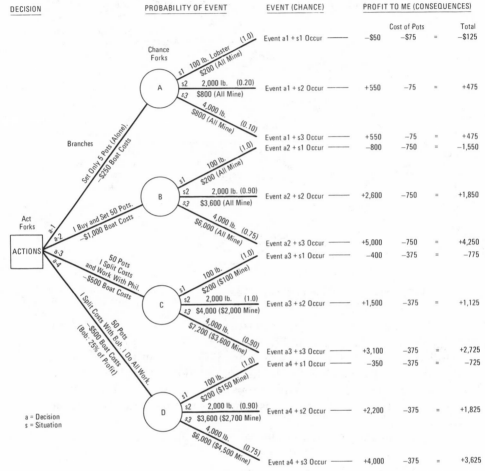

DECISION		PROBABILITY OF EVENT	EVENT (CHANCE)	PROFIT TO ME (CONSEQUENCES)		
				Cost of Pots		Total
	Chance Forks					
		s1 100 lb. Lobster $200 (All Mine) (1.0)	Event a1 + s1 Occur	−$50	−$75 =	−$125
	A	*s2* 2,000 lb. (0.20) $800 (All Mine)	Event a1 + s2 Occur	+550	−75 =	+475
		s3 4,000 lb. $800 (All Mine) (0.10)				
Branches			Event a1 + s3 Occur	+550	−75 =	+475
		s1 (1.0) 100 lb. $200 (All Mine)	Event a2 + s1 Occur	−800	−750 =	−1,550
Set Only 5 Pots (Alone). −$250 Boat Costs	B	*s2* 2,000 lb. (0.90) $3,600 (All Mine)	Event a2 + s2 Occur	+2,600	−750 =	+1,850
		s3 4,000 lb. $6,000 (All Mine) (0.75)				
I Buy and Set 50 Pots. −$1,000 Boat Costs			Event a2 + s3 Occur	+5,000	−750 =	+4,250
Act Forks		*s1* (1.0) 100 lb. $200 ($100 Mine)	Event a3 + s1 Occur	−400	−375 =	−775
ACTIONS *a-1 a-2 a-3 a-4*	50 Pots I Split Costs and Work With Phil. −$500 Boat Costs	C	*s2* 2,000 lb. (1.0) $4,000 ($2,000 Mine)	Event a3 + s2 Occur	+1,500	−375 =	+1,125
		s3 4,000 lb. $7,200 ($3,600 Mine) (0.90)				
I Split Costs With Bob. 50 Pots (Bob. 25% of Profit) −$500 Boat Costs I Do All Work			Event a3 + s3 Occur	+3,100	−375 =	+2,725
		s1 (1.0) 100 lb. $200 ($150 Mine)	Event a4 + s1 Occur	−350	−375 =	−725
a = Decision s = Situation		D	*s2* 2,000 lb. (0.90) $3,600 ($2,700 Mine)	Event a4 + s2 Occur	+2,200	−375 =	+1,825
		s3 4,000 lb. $6,000 ($4,500 Mine) (0.75)	Event a4 + s3 Occur	+4,000	−375 =	+3,625

FIGURE III.3 Decision Tree for Lobstering Profits

catch 4,000 pounds. With my deliberate choice of less profit and more safety and higher probability, my share would be $2,725.

All decision trees are not this simple, yet they are growing in popularity because they not only lay out decisions, events, and payoffs in more complex decision areas but also allow for probabilities.

Before ending this section on decision trees, mention of *expected value* should be included. The random values calculated as end positions on the tree example were affected by the probabilities given to each. That is, the random values (of profit) resulted, in part, from probabilities assigned. Expected value is a long-run average of a random variable and is obtained by multiplying each value of the

190

random variable by its probability of occurrence and then summing up the products of the multiplications. In a more complex tree, this would require two steps:

1. Select a fork which has *all* branches leading to an end position (i.e., branches not eliminated in the process before reaching a final payoff number).
2. If it is an "act" fork, select the branch that has the highest payoff and cross out others emanating from the fork. If it is a "chance" fork (probability and expected value involved), compute the *total* expected payoff by summing up the product of the multiplication of each random variable (end nuuber) by its probability, and then sum up the multiplications.

The square or circle of the fork is an end position and its value is the payoff for the end position.

3. DELPHI TECHNIQUE

As a welcome switch to another technique less quantitative than the preceding ones, it is appropriate to consider the Delphi technique at this point. This is meant to convey neither the fact that the technique may not *use* calculations, for it often does, nor that it is always simple. The author has seen it used in such simple matters as determining the number of people in the Norwegian Air Force (without the help of world almanacs or other official information), to reading of its unique use in a most complex and difficult consensus, that of the probability of a nuclear war.

Delphi is a form of organized brainstorming and consensus technique which can be used for many problems which defy quantification or preciseness. Quantified answers *are* possible, however. It is a technique of gathering information from and dealing separately with experts who have generally the same specialized capabilities. It is almost cybernetic in its handling in that "steering" of the deliberation process is through careful feedback of *anonymous* contributions by experts to each other. This process is sometimes called *cybernetic arbitration*. Feedback is the job of a *control* individual or group. The problem is presented to the chosen decision group members, which well could be a group within a given business whose different responsibilities all focus on the same problem. Or, it could be a widely dispersed group of experts in the same field whose inputs are handled by written communications. To improve upon committees or panels, the technique strives to get the players to feel free to give their best inputs by submitting them anonymously, frankly and unfettered by face-to-face meetings. The control group or person then issues the first of what may be several questionnaires. Participants give their opinions *and* the *reasons* for them. Then, in the next communication they are given feedback or refined information—the product each of them—as well as the computed *consensus*. The process goes on until further consensus is negligible. The views are documented and the consensus becomes a solution.

This example from Quade and Boucher highlights the uses and mechanics of the technique:

Example: Choosing a Number by Delphi. Consider the common situation of having to arrive at an answer to the question of how large a particular number N should be. (For example, N might be the estimated cost of a measure, or a value representing its overall benefit). We would then proceed as follows: First, we would ask each expert independently to give an estimate of N, and then arrange the responses in order of magnitude, and determine the quartiles, Q_1, M, Q_3, so that the four intervals formed on the N-line by these three points each contained one quarter of the estimates. If we had eleven participants, the N-line might look like [Figure III.4.]

Second, we would communicate the values of Q_1, M, Q_3 to each respondent, ask him to reconsider his previous estimate, and, if his estimate (old or revised) lies outside the interquartile range (Q_1 Q_3), to state briefly the reason why, in his opinion, the answer should be lower (or higher) than the 75-percent majority opinion expressed in the first round. Third, we would communicate the results of this second round (which as a rule will be less dispersed than the first) to the respondents in summary form, including the new quartiles and median. In addition, we would document the reasons that the experts gave in Round 2 for raising or lowering the values. (As collated and edited, these reasons would, of course preserve the anonymity of the respondents.) We would then ask the experts to consider the new estimates and the arguments offered for them, giving them the weight they think they deserve, and in the light of this new information, to revise their previous estimates.[2]

[2]E.S. Quade and W.I. Boucher, eds., *Systems Analysis and Policy Planning, Applications in Defense*, New York: Elsevier, 1968, pp. 334–35.

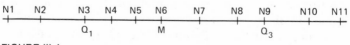

FIGURE III.4

In this example, Quade goes on to point out that the one last round might be Round 4, and that the responses to this round could be taken as representing the group's position as to what N should be.

Delphi can be used for policy decisions, for certain "numbers" decisions, for estimated cost decisions, and others which lie on the fringes of or beyond previous experience and quantifications. If the technique works for you, use it. Perhaps it does take more time and effort than a committee or a panel, but it has worked in areas where anonymity plus expertise, and the absence of one expert imposing his will on others are appropriate. It is also a lot of fun to do!

4. GAME THEORY

The generic term *games* refers to general conflict or opponent situations usually played over a period of time. Playing cards, chess, checkers, backgammon, and all sorts of athletic contests are well known. In most of them, with experience one can become more expert and more accurate at predicting opponents' reactions strategies and tactics. Competition is the norm in games and in business. Those who do well usually can select and direct the strategies and tactics and win.

In business games, as in more lethal ones such as war games, wise opponents make use of logic and quantitative techniques to help determine the best strategy. One of those techniques, the mathematics of game theory, is highly developed today and when coupled with sound judgment, is a recognized method of achieving solutions. Games are useful because one discovers that one's decisions are constantly *conditioned* by others' decisions and actions. Thus, they are not one-sided decision-making situations.

There are several ways to categorize games: (1) by numbers of competitors (usually a two-person game); (2) by competitive types of conflict, such as a duel; and (3) by the amount of information and certainty (or uncertainty, chance) available to all players. Common to most games is a sequence of moves made by the competitors until the game is over or a "play" is done. The outcome of all the plays occurs at the end. It is a highly complex result. Even in a two-person confrontation with guns, one may hit the other, or the reverse, or both can be hit, or both can miss and perhaps start over.

Usually, however, competition leads to a two-person (party) zero-sum game. It is so popular that the example of game theory will be illustrated by such a zero-sum game.

Suppose a game has two players and each player has three strategies. One player will be called A, and this player's options are *columnar*. The other player will be called B, and this player's options are in *rows*. A has three strategies open, as does B. In a simplified form, using only two of the boxes for illustration, a decision payoff matrix appears like Figure III.5.

Nine different combinations or squares are available. Payoffs are specified for each combination of strategies. The matrix helps keep track of them. Usually, the payoff to B (row) is shown first in the square, followed by A (column) payoffs. Hence B's strategies are B1, B2, and B3; A's are A1, A2, and A3. If B uses strategy B2 and A uses A3, the determined payoff is +$5.00 for B (row) and − $5.00 for A (column). Notice that one's loss is the other's gain and the sum of the payoffs is zero ($5.00 − 5.00 = 0). Hence, the name, zero-sum game.

Also, it is usual to simplify the matrix even more and to show only one number in a square, and that is the amount which would be paid from Column to Row or received from Row. The matrix would then show only −$1.00 in square B1, A1 and +$5.00 in square B2, A3 (shown in parentheses in the matrix).

Many examples of gaming could be used, but following is an illustrative and amusing one of a two-person (two-party) zero-sum game involving the payoffs of Wells Fargo versus the Bad Guys from David Heinze's management science book:

> Recall the Wells Fargo stage traveling across the Badlands. The Bad Guys, as it happens, actually have four possible strategies they might employ. These are: (1) Send no one after the stage, (2) Send one Bad Guy after the stage, (3) Send two, or (4) Send three after the stage. Wells Fargo, on the other hand, has only three strategies available: (1) Send no agent riding shotgun on the stage, (2) Send one agent, or (3) Send two agents.

A's Strategies (Column)

		A1	A2	A3
	B1	−$1.00 + $1.00 −($1.00)		
B's Strategies (Row)	B2			+$5.00 + $5.00 + ($5.00)
	B3			

FIGURE III.5 Decision Payoff Matrix

		Wells Fargo Strategies:		
		Send 0	Send 1	Send 2
	Send 0	No One Robbed.	No One Robbed.	No One Robbed.
Bad Guys' Strategies:	Send 1	Bad Guys Get Pot.	Agents Rob Bad Guys.	Agents Rob Bad Guys.
	Send 2	Bad Guys Get Pot.	Split Pot.	Agents Rob Bad Guys.
	Send 3	Bad Guys Get Pot.	Bad Guys Get Pot.	Agents Rob Bad Guys.

FIGURE III.6

Suppose it is well known that in an attempted stage holdup, one agent is the equal of two Bad Guys. Also, by Bandlands' rules all ties, as when there is one agent against two Bad Guys, result in the payload being split. Suppose also that if the agents are superior in force to the Bad Guys (i.e., more than one-to-two) the agents rob the Bad Guys. The outcome can be specified by arranging the outcomes in matrix form as shown in [Figure III.6]. The "pot" refers to the payload of gold dust. To determine the exact payoffs, it is assumed that there is $5,000 in the strongbox (pot) and that the Bad Guys normally carry $500 each. The resulting matrix is then given in [Figure III.7].

To summarize, the game matrix above shows that there are two players or competitors and that the *Row* player has four possible strategies and the *Column* player has three possible strategies. Because the gain of the Row player (Bad Guys) is the loss of the Column player (Wells Fargo) and vice versa, it is necessary to specify only one number in each square. The numbers in the squares represent the payoffs to the Bad Guys or

		Wells Fargo:		
		Send 0	Send 1	Send 2
	Send 0	0	0	0
	Send 1	5000	−500	−500
Bad Guys:	Send 2	5000	2500	−1000
	Send 3	5000	5000	−1500

FIGURE III.7

195

Row players. This game matrix is the so-called normal form representation of a two-person zero-sum game with a finite number of strategies.[3]

From this point, this type of game is developed to produce the *best* strategies for each player; however, the matrix can be the basis for a decision if the numbers of people are fixed or the amount of return or of risk is predetermined by the player. The matrix can reveal a dominant payoff which becomes the choice because it is *always* superior to the others. Or, a strategy of *maximin* or *minimax* may be planned. Maximin is the principle of considering only the minimum gains for each act and then selecting the act which has the greatest or maximum of these minimum gains. Where the consequences are gains or profits, the maximin principle is best applied. Minimax is used best in cases where the consequences are losses or costs. It requires that the maximum cost for each act be determined first; then the act which has the least or minimum of such maximum costs should be chosen. Both choices are used commonly by one who fears the worst, because the worst can be disastrous and so must be guarded or hedged against. One may well ask here, what about maximax? A principle for the incurable optimist who does not consider losses, this sanguine criterion is that for each available outcome, one must consider *only* the best possible outcome and then choose that alternative with the best of the best outcomes. (This is thought audacious by most decision makers!) [Applying these strategies to our example, for Wells Fargo the maximin would be to send 0; minimax, to send 2; and maximax, to send 2.] Game theory or gaming has many more interesting applications, which space does not permit at this point.

5. LINEAR PROGRAMMING METHODS

(a) Linear Programming

Perhaps the most widely used quantitative procedure for analyzing real-world decision problems under conditions of certainty is that of *linear programming*. The real-life problems of making the best decision are usually concerned with *choosing* a set of activities or actions because they compete with one another for scarce available resources. Linear programming is a recognized procedure by which a choice can be made when there is more than one possibility, as is the

---

[3]David Heinze, *Management Science, Introductory Concepts and Applications*, Cincinnati: South-Western Publishing Co., 1978, pp.400–401.

usual case in problem solving. It is an orderly, well-defined procedure for building and solving a mathamatical model consisting of linear *equations* and/or *inequalities*.

Generally, the form of a linear programming problem starts with statements. One kind of statement is concerned with the *objective* (or objective function). The other kind addresses *limitations* or *constraints* in attaining the objective. Let's illustrate these with an example. Profit is our objective in a cabinet-making and door-making shop, but production involves two constraints.

Product A–Cabinets	*Product B–Doors*
Each contributes $100 profit. Required time is 4 hours each.	Each contributes $80 profit. Required time is 2 hours each.
Let X_1 = number of cabinets	Let X_2 = number of doors
Total hours available = 160	

First, if we choose to make cabinets only, a *labor constraint* imposes a 160-hour availability. Each cabinet requires 4 hours, hence an output of 40 is possible. A second constraint, that of *assembly* of doors, poses no problem for cabinets made.

Result: 40 cabinets × $100 profit each = $4,000

Second, if we choose to make doors only, there is an *assembly function* constraint which imposes a total production capacity of 50. Labor is no restriction.

Result: 50 doors × $80 profit each = $4,000

Third, if we choose to produce a mix of 20 cabinets and 40 doors, we find the door assembly constraint is still 50, thus 40 doors are within the limit of that resource. As for labor, 20 cabinets use 80 hours of labor, leaving 80 hours for 20 cabinets, so the numbers we have chosen are still feasible.

(20 cabinets × 4 hours + 40 doors × 2 hours = 160 hours)

Result: 20 cabinets × $100 profit + 40 doors × $80 profit = $2,000 + $3,200
= $5,200 total

or $100X_1 + $80X_2 = total profit (the objective)

The third production scheme appears best. But now let's put the problem into standard linear programming form.

First, it should be recalled that the symbols > for "greater than" and < for "less than" may also be expanded to include ≥ for "equal to or greater than," and ≤ for "equal to or less than." The symbol ≤ is used in the example, as it is an upper limit constraint case. In some cases it may be a lower limit constraint problem for which ≥ would be used or even a mix of the two would be used.

Thus far in the example we have found that assembly time capacity had a constraint of 50 for Product B, doors. So each *unit* of Product B uses one unit of the capacity. Product A, cabinets, was not affected by the resource.

Hence, for the *assembly* resource a formula can be formed:

1 (use of the resources) times X_2 (number of doors)

+ 0 (use of the resource for cabinets) times X_1 (number of cabinets) is ≤ 50 (equal to or less than) (assembly resources).

or

$$1X_1 + 0X_2 \leq 50 \text{ (assembly constraint)}$$

The other constraint, labor, affects cabinet production by requiring 4 hours for each cabinet, and also 2 hours for each door. The total available hours are 160.

Hence, for the *labor* resources a formula can be formed:

2 (hours for each door) times X_1 (number of doors) + 4 (hours for each cabinet) times X_2 (number of cabinets) ≤ 160 (hours resource)

or

$$2X_1 + 4X_2 \leq 160 \text{ (labor hours constraint)}$$

Next, the objective (or objective function) should be stated. It is to maximize:

$$\text{Total profit} = \$100X_1 + \$80X_2$$

But within these constraints:

$$1X_1 + 0X_2 \leq 50$$
$$2X_1 + 4X_2 \leq 160$$

Now we are ready to graph these functions by:

Assembly	*Labor*
Setting X_2 to zero, $X_1 = 50$	Setting X_2 to zero, $X_1 = 80$
Setting X_1 to zero, $X_2 = 40$	Setting X_1 to zero, $X_2 = 40$

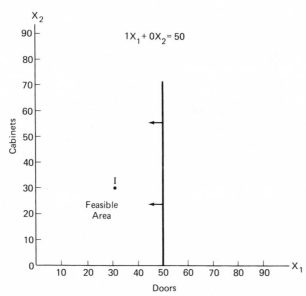

FIGURE III.8 The Assembly Constraint

1. Because X_2 is zero, there is no X_2 value or intercept. The graph is simply a perpendicular line crossing X_1 at 50.
2. The arrows indicate the direction of inequality (a "less than" inequality).
3. If we wished to produce, say, 30 doors and 30 cabinets, shown by point I, it would be feasible in so far as this resource is concerned, i. e.; *only* in terms of the *assembly* constraint.
4. Substituting 30, 30 = $1(30) + 0(30) \leq 50$

1. The difference in graphing the labor constraint is that it results in two intercepts and is an *equation* of *linear* form.
2. Note that because of the *labor* constraint, in the previous feasible point I of 30, 30 is no longer feasible.

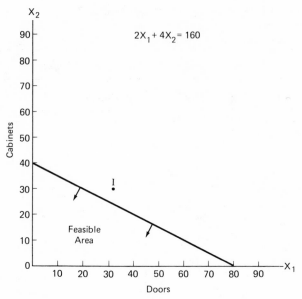

FIGURE III.9 The Labor Constraint

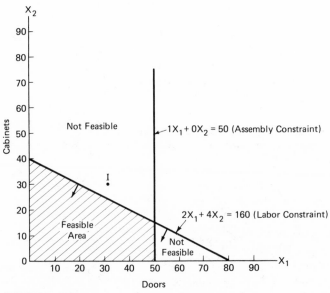

FIGURE III.10 Assembly and Labor Constraints

Next, combine two constraint graphs as in Figure III.10.

1. Note how combining the two reduces the feasible area. Next, the objective function of maximum profit (which is an equation, not an equality) is sought for the *optimal* feasible number of each product. Let's arbitrarily graph $2,000, $4,000 and $6,000 profits.

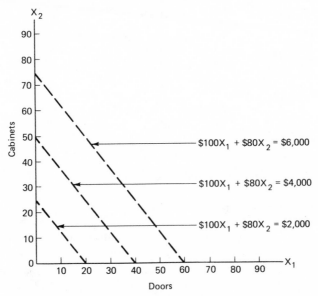

FIGURE III.11 The Objective Function

1. By setting X_2 to zero, the X_1 intercepts are 20, 40, and 60 for $2,000, $4,000, and $6,000, respectively.
2. By setting X_1 to zero, the X_2 intercepts are 25, 50, and 75 for $2,000, $4,000, and $6,000, respectively.
3. Each *point* (mix) on these lines will generate the profits shown, except we must not yet assume that they all fall within the feasible areas which the constraints have established.
4. Note that they are parallel lines, and broken, to distinguish them from constraint lines.
5. Note also that the larger the profit, the more the lines move *away* from the origin. While the objective may move outward, the constraints cannot.

Finally, superimpose the graphs of the objective function on the constraint inequalities graphs.

The last feasible point intersected by the objective function as it moves outward is 50 doors and 15 cabinets. The total profit would be $80 × 50 + $100 × 15 = $5,500, or $300 *more* than the originally selected mix of 40 doors and 20 cabinets.

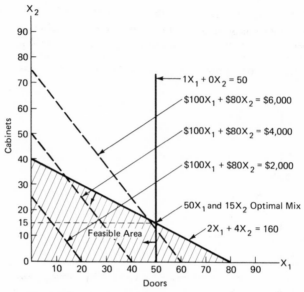

$1X_1 + 0X_2 = 50$

$\$100X_1 + \$80X_2 = \$6,000$

$\$100X_1 + \$80X_2 = \$4,000$

$\$100X_1 + \$80X_2 = \$2,000$

$50X_1$ and $15X_2$ Optimal Mix

$2X_1 + 4X_2 = 160$

Feasible Area

Cabinets

Doors

FIGURE III.12 Superimposed Graphs

Extensive treatment has been given to linear programming in this appendix, since it is one of the most popular and most useful methods in organizations and management. Its many uses and complex applications cannot all be covered in these few pages. However, it is appropriate to add in conclusion that the method is useful wherever there is an objective, wherever there are alternative courses of action, wherever limited resources exist, and wherever the objective and limitations may be expressed in mathematical equations and/or inequalities—and these must be linear equations and inequalities. Economics, management, finance, accounting, marketing, transportation, and practically all decision-making functions involving the above conditions make wide use of linear programming today.

(b) Transportation Method

Within the classification of linear programming techniques there exists a problem of "transportation" or transportation-related problems. These can be solved by linear programming, but more easily by the so-called transportation method. The term *transportation* is used because this method is the result of original studies of the most efficient transportation or delivery routes. The key decision in such problems is simply how much to transport from each place of origin to each destination or project.

202

For example, if we had a case of two factory outlets serving three separate locations, the possible number of separate routes would be six; however, the over riding requirement we wish to know is the *optimum* routes to save time and resources, and to avoid duplication. Let's call the plants X and Y and the destinations (projects) 1, 2, and 3. Plant capacity is known to be 60 (per period) at Plant X and 80 at Plant Y. The requirements for each project are 65 for I, 50 for II, and 25 for III, or a total of 140, which equals our plant outputs.

Figure III.13 shows how a transportation problem would be laid out. Following it is an explanation of the format, the squares, the numbers, and the squares or circles in which they appear.

First, add an identification to each square or cell, such as XI, XII, or XIII. Now the cell combinations are identified (Factory X to Destination I, for example).

Second, in the middle are six squares or cells. These are the alternative plant-to-destination (project) assignment squares that can be made. For example, the 60 truckloads available per week at Factory X may be used to fulfill completely the requirements for all of Destination XI or if the number were larger, to partly fill all the projects. However, any combination of shipments may not exceed 60, the factory's capacity.

Next, put the actual cost per truckload between Factory X and Destination I in a small box in the cell. The cost is $6 from Factory X to Destination I. These costs are available from our records, but keep in mind that they may vary with the total quantity distributed. Obviously, the actual costs for each truckload are most important to the delivery routes chosen.

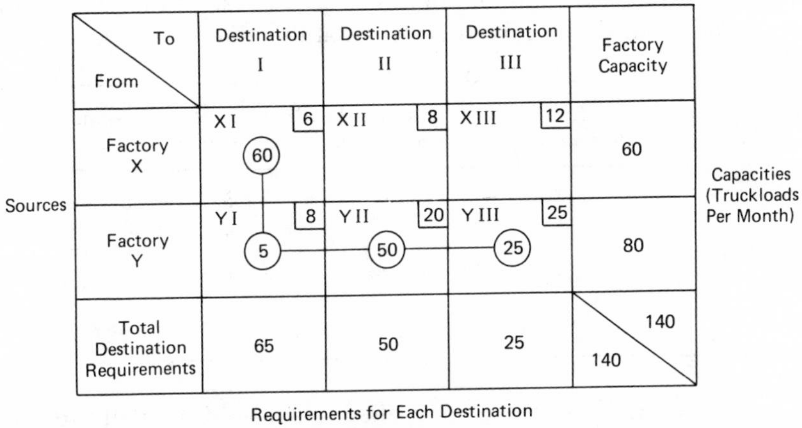

Sources	To / From	Destination I	Destination II	Destination III	Factory Capacity	
	Factory X	X I [6] (60)	X II [8]	X III [12]	60	Capacities (Truckloads Per Month)
	Factory Y	Y I [8] (5)	Y II [20] (50)	Y III [25] (25)	80	
	Total Destination Requirements	65	50	25	140 / 140	

Requirements for Each Destination

FIGURE III.13 Transportation Method Matrix

Next, insert circled amounts to represent the numbers of truck-loads shipped from factories to destinations. Hence, all 60 from Factory X will go to Destination I. The number 60 is placed in a circle in the square. The volume of the total X's should be positive or zero.

Next, a procedure known as the *northwest corner rule* is used. Systematic and easier than trial and error, it is primarily designed only to get an *initial* solution, which will be revised later. The rule is that one should start at the upper left-hand corner (the northwest corner) of the table and *exhaust* the supply available at each *row* (crosswise) before going down to the next row. The *rim requirements,* or capacity for each *row* (e.g., 60 in the Factory X row), and the same rule for each rim requirement of any *column* must be used up before moving to the right for the next *column.* Always check to see that all rim requirements have been used. The results of doing this in the example are shown in the squares.

In square XI, we next use 60 of Factory X's full capacity of 60, which entirely exhausts the factory but has satisfied 60 of Destination I requirements. This leaves Destination I 5 truckloads short. By moving down to the second row to cell YI, we see we can ship the 5 loads from Factory Y to Destination I, thus completely satisfying the requirement.

Next, Destination II needs 50 loads, and so we move to the right to cell YII and designate 50 loads to be shipped to Destination II. None remains from Factory X, but it might have, and we would have used it. This leaves Factory Y with 25 loads left after 5 are shipped to Destination I and 50 to Destination II. Destination III requires 25 loads and, of course, they are happily available from Factory Y. Again, the *northwest corner* procedure is temporary and leads to the *stepping stone* procedure for a better solution. No analyst would stop at this point. The table shows how it costs out at this point.

From Factory	To Destination	Quantity of Loads per Month	Unit Cost	Total Cost
X	I	60	$ 6 =	$ 360
Y	I	5	$ 8 =	$ 40
Y	II	50	$20 =	1,000
Y	III	25	$25 =	625
		Total Cost		$2,025

This example is greatly simplified and would normally result in only an *initial* solution. The next step would be to use a refinement such as the *stepping stone technique,* which poses the question of what the cost would be if truckloads were tentatively shipped to an *unused* square. If the costs of shipping to that unused square were less, even when combined with final destination cost, the result could be a further decrease in total cost, despite additional movements. The northwest rule alone is insufficient in most cases. Stepping stone procedure would be used by most decision makers in order to complete the method.

(c) Assignment Method

The assignment method is one of the kindred techniques concerned with real-world problems which arise when decisions must be made regarding the assignment of each of a number of different persons to different positions, or persons to machines, or machines to a number of different locations. It is closely related to the transportation method discussed earlier in (b).

The assignment of skilled help to certain jobs, for example, with the purpose of assigning the least costly skilled person to the appropriate job, or the assignment of costly equipment without tying up such equipment on jobs that could have been assigned less costly equipment, are typical uses of the method. The problem occurs when many assignments or locations or positions are possible. Obviously, with only one piece of equipment and several jobs, the decision is clear. But with multiple choices or assignments the problem can become complex; hence, we want decisions which will yield the comparative costs (or profit) resulting from all possible assignments.

As we saw in the transportation method, considering each assignee as a separate origin and each assignment as a separate destination and using the northwest corner method for decision making, an initial set of assignments of all resources could be made. If carried further, costs could possibly have been reduced by the stepping stone modification. The assignment method is considered to be easier and, at the very least, a substitute.

The general problem in assignment, therefore, is to use n resources (persons) by assigning them to n recipients (jobs or machines) and to be able to know the cost of each choice and each set of choices. The objective is to minimize the total cost of the assignments. To do such a job by enumeration would require considerable calculations. For example, only 5 workers assigned to 5 different machines have 120 combinations ($5 \times 4 \times 3 \times 2 = 120$).

The assignment method, also known as the *Hungarian method,* can solve the problem quickly, as demonstrated in this clear example by John E. Ullmann, in his *Quantitative Methods in Management.*

Four workers are to be assigned to 4 jobs, it being known that the time taken by each on each job would be as in Fig. (a). Find an assignment which would minimize the sum of the times taken. (Assume that all workers are paid at the same rate; if not, costs should be used instead.)

Jobs

	A	B	C	D
a	15	18	21	24
b	19	23	22	18
c	26	17	16	19
d	19	21	23	17

(a) (Workers)

	A	B	C	D
a	0	1	5	7
b	4	6	6	1
c	11	0	0	2
d	4	4	7	0

(b)

	A	B	C	D
a	0	1	5	7
b	3	5	5	0
c	11	0	0	2
d	4	4	7	0

(c)

FIGURE III.14

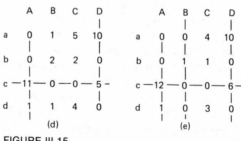

	A	B	C	D
a	0	1	5	10
b	0	2	2	0
c	11	0	0	5
d	1	1	4	0

(d)

	A	B	C	D
a	0	0	4	10
b	0	1	1	0
c	12	0	0	6
d	1	0	3	0

(e)

FIGURE III.15

1. First modify the time (cost) matrix, Fig. (a). Deduct the smallest (nonzero) time in each *column* from all entries in that column, obtaining at least one zero in each column (Fig. (b)).

2. In each row of positive entries deduct the smallest time from all entries in that *row.* In Fig. (b) this applies only to the second row because all the others already have zeros. The result is Fig. (c). If Step 1 had produced at least one zero in each *row* as well, the present step would be omitted.

3. Now draw the *minimum* number of lines which will cover all the

zeros. In [Figure III.14] (c) three lines suffice. If there are as many such lines as there are rows or columns, an optimal assignment is possible. If not, the matrix must be changed. Here there are three lines instead of four, so the next step is necessary.

4. In [Figure III.14] (c) subtract the smallest uncovered entry (which is 3) from all uncovered entries. Enter the results in Fig. (d). Then *add* the same number to the elements at which the lines of Fig. (c) cross (7 in line a and 2 in line c), obtaining 10 and 5 respectively. Enter these results in [Figure III.15] (d) and complete the figure by entering the other covered elements without change.

5. Repeat Step 3. In [Figure III.15] (d) it is again possible to cover all zeros with only three lines. Therefore repeat Step 4, obtaining Fig. (e) in which four lines are necessary. Thus it is an optimal matrix.

6. Make the actual assignments, starting with the zero which is unique in its row or column. (If no such zero exists, start with any zero.) Here this is cC. Complete the assignment; as may happen, there is more than one. The two solutions are

cC, aA, bD, dB; Time $= 16 + 15 + 18 + 21 = 70\,Ans.$

cC, aB, bA, dD; Time $= 16 + 18 + 19 + 17 = 70\,Ans.$[4]

6. MARGINAL ANALYSES (MARGINAL CONCEPT; MARGINAL COST; MARGINAL REVENUE)

The objective of almost every business is to maximize profits, or, if not profits, to maximize something, or to minimize costs. The objective may be the owner's satisfaction or ability to create or to provide work. In the military it is much harder to maximize and to measure effectiveness, or efficiency, than in the civilian sector, where the same objectives are sought, but different *kinds* of effectiveness are obtained, depending on the kind of service being rendered. In the Defense Establishment, effectiveness measures have ranged from the absence or prevention of war to more measurable things such as the greater fire power of weapon x over weapon y. In health, welfare, and education, it may be measured in diseases cured, epidemics averted, welfare recipients receipts, or members of public school graduates

[4]John E. Ullmann, *Theory and Problems in Quantitative Methods in Management.* Schaum's Outline Series in Business (New York: McGraw Hill, 1976) pp. 57–58.

compared to previous years, and so on. But when we restrict ourselves to business organizations which must survive in a highly competitive environment, objectives are more measurable and success, more visible.

Economists advise that one of the most useful ways to succeed in personal and business life is to "think and act marginally." This principle can be applied to problems of production, sales, inventory, costs, and all others which bear upon whether the most is gotten out of limited and valuable resources.

(a) The Marginal Concept

The marginal concept or *marginal approach* concerns first the problem of proper choice from among alternatives to ensure that we have made the *optimum* one. This has been discussed earlier in the section, Common Methods of Evaluation. Second, it concerns the ability to make an analysis of choice in terms of the *change* that *even one unit* can make in our calculations of inputs or costs, benefits or outputs, revenues or returns. It is this second area with which marginal analyses are concerned. The key question becomes, if we add one more unit of cost to our efforts, is the benefit worth it? Or, if we add one more unit of revenue, is the cost worth it? It is the crucial point where one more unit affects optimum profits or optimum satisfaction. For a long time, economists have shown us the base for such thinking in the classic supply-demand curve, (Figure III.16), which also can

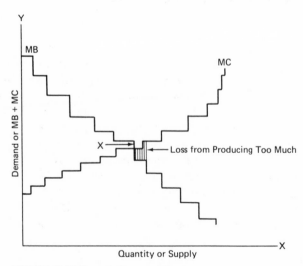

FIGURE III.16 Supply-Demand Curve

illustrate the optimum point of marginal benefit (MB)* and marginal cost (MC).

As supply rises and the demand decreases, there is a point (or area) *x* where they are equal. To supply more would not result in increased demand. The same curves show us the point at which the cost of producing one more unit equals the return on that unit. Beyond that point, one more unit costs us more than the return. Where the marginal cost and marginal benefit curves meet is that point beyond which a decision to produce more is deliberately going beyond the point of equilibrium.

(b) Marginal Cost

Marginal cost is basic to business thinking. It is, at any output level, the *extra cost* of producing *one unit more*. A more complete example of the changing effects of marginal cost was given in the section on breakeven. Here is another way of visualizing the effect if marginal revenue, which can be found by comparing total dollar costs of adjacent outputs, is known.

	Quantity Produced (Q)	Total Cost (TC)	Marginal Cost (MC)
Q	99	31,920.10	
			79.90 (given)
Q	100	32,000.00	80.00
			80.10
Q	101	32,080.10	

Accepting the numbers as given from records of costs, the marginal cost can be shown by simple subtraction. The difference in total cost in dollars by producing *one more unit* is found by using Q, which here equals 100. The MC equals $80.00 at Q 100, but rises to $80.10 when production rises by one to 101. It is at $80.10 that the MC considered is too high (above maximum profit) to produce one extra unit (or less). If we placed this information with many other Q's on a graph, we would find the MC tends to be U-shaped. It rises *ultimately* even though it falls in the initial production. The equilibrium point was reached in the example at 100 units (which is only known when marginal revenue is given).

*Marginal Utility (MU) is a similar term.

(c) Marginal Revenue (Marginal Pricing)

The profit-maximizing price for a product or service is the price which produces the *largest difference* between total revenues and total costs. One of the clearest and most inclusive examples the author has found is this, taken from Lynch and Williamson's *Accounting for Management, Planning and Control:*

TABLE III.2 Zero Company—Estimated Sales

Selling Price per Unit	Estimated Units to be Sold per Year	Estimated Sales Revenues per Year	Marginal Revenue
$2	80,000	$160,000	
			−$5
3	70,000	210,000	
			− 3
4	60,000	240,000	
			− 1
5	50,000	250,000	
			+ 1
6	40,000	240,000	
			+ 3
7	30,000	210,000	
			+ 5
8	20,000	160,000	

MARGINAL ANALYSIS AND PRICING

The profit-maximizing price for a particular product or service is that price which produces the largest difference between total revenues and total costs. It is natural, then, to begin an analysis of the profit-maximizing price by considering total revenues and total costs.

DEMAND FUNCTIONS

Suppose that the marketing division of the Zero Company estimates the relationship between the selling price of its new product and the quantity which could be sold per year is that shown in the first two columns of the above chart .... The third column of the chart indicates the total revenue estimated by the marketing division. Notice that it increases for some price increases but not for others .... This concept is known as the *price elasticity of demand*—it represents the *relative* change in quantity caused by a change in price. For example, when price is raised from $2 to $3, a 50 percent increase, quantity is estimated to decrease from 80,000 to 70,000 units per year, only a 12½ percent decrease. Since the relative price change is greater than the relative quantity change, total revenues increase. Demand at this point is considered *inelastic*. An increase in price from $6 to $7, however, gives the opposite result—a 16⅔ percent rise in price leads to a 25 percent decrease in quantity, from 40,000 to 30,000 units per year, and thus a decrease in total revenue results. The demand curve at this point would be considered *elastic*.

The elasticity of demand is related to another economic concept called *marginal revenue,* which is defined as the change in total revenue resulting from a one-unit increase in quantity. Marginal revenue is shown in the fourth column [of the chart]. When price is decreased from $4 to $3, for example, the estimated quantity to be sold increases by 10,000 units per year and total revenue *decreases* by $30,000 per year. The reason for this $30,000 decrease is that the firm's revenues are *reduced* by $60,000 because of the decrease in price of $1 on the original 60,000 units, while the firm's revenues are *increased* by $30,000 because of the extra 10,000 units sold at $3 each. Marginal revenue is computed as —$3 by dividing the net lost revenue ($30,000) by the increase in volume (10,000). This —$3 is an average amount representing the revenue lost by increasing volume from 60,000 to 70,000 units per year. It can be seen that marginal revenue will be negative when demand is inelastic because revenue will be reduced with an increase in volume. By the same token, marginal revenue will be positive when demand is elastic.

MARGINAL COST

The profit-maximizing price cannot be determined from demand data alone, of course. Cost information is equally important. Suppose that the manufacturing division of Zero Company estimates that the fixed costs of its new product will total $80,000 per year and that variable costs will amount to $3 per unit. The estimated total costs are shown in the third column of the third chart below. The fourth column of that exhibit shows marginal costs, which are defined as the change in total costs resulting from a one-unit increase in quantity. Marginal costs in this example are constant at $3, equal to the variable costs.

ECONOMIC THEORY OF PRICING

One way to determine the profit-maximizing price from demand and cost data is to compute the estimated profit at various price–output combinations. This is done in the last chart where a maximum estimated profit of $40,000 results from selling 40,000 units at $6 *or* 30,000 units at $7 each.

The more traditional economic analysis, however, considers the marginal amounts, rather than the total revenues and costs. Economic theory concludes that *the most profitable price-outputs combination will be the one where marginal revenues and marginal costs are equal.* The final chart above indicates that this is so in the case of the Zero Company.

TABLE III.3 Zero Company—Estimated Costs

Selling Price per Unit	Estimated Units to be Sold per Year	Estimated Total Cost per Year	Marginal Cost
$2	80,000	$320,000	
			+$3
3	70,000	290,000	
			+ 3
4	60,000	260,000	
			+ 3
5	50,000	230,000	
			+ 3
6	40,000	200,000	
			+ 3
7	30,000	170,000	
			+ 3
8	20,000	140,000	

Table III.4 Zero Company–Estimated Profits

Selling Price per Unit	Estimated Units to Be Sold per Year	Estimated Total Revenues per Year	Estimated Total Cost per Year	Estimated Profit per Year	MR	MC
$2	80,000	$160,000	$320,000	−$160,000		
					−5	+3
3	70,000	210,000	290,000	−80,000		
					−3	+3
4	60,000	240,000	260,000	−20,000		
					−1	+3
5	50,000	250,000	230,000	+20,000		
					+1	+3
6	40,000	240,000	200,000	+40,000		
					+3	+3
7	30,000	210,000	170,000	+40,000		
					+5	+3
8	20,000	160,000	140,000	+20,000		

Marginal revenue and marginal costs are equal at a price between $6 and $7 a unit and an output between 30,000 and 40,000 units per year."[5]

There are, of course, limitations on marginal analyses, as with all other tools and techniques. One of them is that demand and cost factors are estimated. If there were certainty about these, marginal

[5]Richard M. Lynch and Robert W. Williamson, *Accounting for Management, Planning and Control* (New York: McGraw-Hill, 1976), pp. 392–96.

analysis would be valid to apply to price-output decisions. Second, a relatively small error in estimating quantity demand can result in a large error in estimating marginal revenue. Many firms set prices without making a marginal analysis and use a simple "cost-plus" pricing method. It would be more exact to go to the trouble of determining marginal revenue as an indicator and as a bidding tool in a world of competition. Finally, to end on a positive note, marginal costs and marginal revenues are *not* the same as *average* costs and revenues, which are arrived at by dividing totals by number of units produced or sold. Therefore, marginal costs and revenues, and the marginal concept, can be viewed as incremental or differential costs and revenues.

7. MODELS. (VERBAL; HUMAN; PEOPLE AND COMPUTERS; ANALYTICAL/ MATHEMATICAL; CONCEPTUAL/ COMPUTER)

Although the technique of using models was covered in the handbook and in the case study in particular, it may be appropriate to describe other ways to use and classify a model. Because a model is often the heart of a good analysis, it is well to be aware of its range of uses.

A *model*, it was pointed out, is a simulation of reality. As such, it becomes a frame or a means of providing data in a form that permits developing the outcomes of alternatives. For example, a model can provide data in the form of measures of cost and effectiveness of several alternatives which will accomplish the same objective. Earlier, we covered *iconic* models, or those which are simply scaled down transformations (or scaled up in some cases of minute systems or organisms) of the real world. A model airplane or the table model of a plant layout are examples. Also covered were *analog* models, more abstract in that certain properties are transformed to represent the real world, such as a graph on paper representing actual occurrences or data. Last, there were *symbolic* models, in which symbols are substituted for properties. Equations, mathematical formulas, and computer programs are examples.

To view models from other perspectives and definitions and to be aware of their breadth and versatility, following is a listing by types by R.D. Specht, who classifies them in a different manner. He classifies them first as to:

Purpose—training, study, and so on.
Field of application—strategic, tactical, logistic, and so on.
Level—from national policy to base operations.
Time character—static or dynamic.
Form—two-sided or one, conflict or not.
Analytical development—degree to which mathematics is used.
Use of computers—how much and how.
Complexity—detailed or aggregated.
Formalization—the degree to which the interactions have been planned
for and their results predetermined.[6]

He goes on to adapt these classifications to categories into which
he pigeonholes the many and varied kinds of models.[7] Using his
categories as a base, with some amplification and modification to
emphasize nonmilitary uses, the result is this categorization with
examples.

(a) Verbal Models

Verbal models range from a scenario for a competitive war game
or business game to the Delphi method. Delphi is in large part verbal
as it approaches solutions of nonquantifiable problems. The philosophy, purpose, policies, and entire manual of operations for a firm are
really verbal models of what they "stand for" or how they operate.
Most models include both verbal and some of the other categories
which follow.

(b) Human Models

Human models exist because people are involved in every model,
as creators or users. But what is meant here is those models in which
humans play an integral and necessary part. War games, business
games, political and other crises models are examples. They require
human actions and reactions to the working of a model.

(c) People and Computers Interacting

This has become quite popular in recent years. Both people and
computers are embedded in the model. Systems development, simulation exercises, and competitive games are examples where computer
calculations and printouts, followed by human reactions and a repeat
of the process, are examples.

[6]Quade and Boucher, eds., *Systems Analysis and Policy Planning*, p. 221.
[7]*Ibid.*, pp. 222–23.

(d) Analytical/Mathematical Models

Models which exclusively use techniques of linear programming, dynamic programming, queueing or waiting line theory, network theory, and other problems requiring vast numbers of calculations, or multiple plays of situations while changing variables, are those categorized as analytical/mathematical. But one must remember that, originally, someone had to perform and structure the mathematics in creating these seemingly nonhuman models.

(e) Conceptual/Computer Models

Perhaps this category could be combined with (d), but because some problems have become so large and so complex and are so far beyond the time man can afford to devote, this category refers to problems which have been programmed to do the *whole* task of operating the model by computers. Once instructions have been written for the machine, the machine takes over the model, and it apears to be totally a computer model.

A final word of caution about models. Do not permit them to become the *end* rather than the *means* to the end. The end is a systematic analysis which will yield alternatives and compare those alternatives and not the working of a model. Above all, don't let someone convince you that *your* problem can be *fitted* to his or her ready-made model, or become so enamoured with a model that the real objective is not reached.

8. NETWORKS. (PROJECT ANALYSIS; PROGRAM AND EVALUATION REVIEW TECHNIQUE; CRITICAL PATH METHOD)

(a) Program Evaluation and Review Technique (PERT)

Networks, or project analyses as they are sometimes called, are techniques which help solve problems involving complexity, varied tasks, varied times to complete tasks, and interdependency of one task upon another. Undertakings consume time. They also create crises, bottlenecks, critical points for completion, coordination of subtasks, all requiring solution in order to complete an undertaking by a given time. Happily, project undertakings do have an end by definition, or they would be ongoing and therefore provided for differently.

215

Many projects can be helped through their critical points by two analytical techniques, the Program Evaluation and Review Technique (PERT) and the Critical Path Method (CPM). Both are similar, yet in some respects different, ways of formalizing project planning and operations, rather than leaving them up to less formal ways, including "horsesense" and trial and error. Both have *time* as the critical factor. PERT began on a noticeable scale probably with weapons systems projects, perhaps the most famous being the building of the first nuclear-powered submarine.

As mentioned, a project entails jobs or tasks, any one or several of which must be completed by critical times in order to complete the whole project on time. The real problems arise because these jobs or tasks require unequal times and differ in their importance to the entire project, especially in timing. One job may not even be begun until another or others *behind* it are done. If all could be accomplished simultaneously, the problem would not be as critical. But it is the nature of different tasks and the difference in time allotments which forces careful advance planning.

Usually, a *project diagram* is made, showing each job and the time required to complete it. Next, those which are necessary for completion before others are undertaken are identified. Here is a greatly simplified diagram for a small building construction, such as a school, required by a certain date. Construction engineers and contractors may question a layman's idea of the specific tasks but will agree that these are the kinds of scheduling problems which must be considered.

From Figure III.17 it is apparent that only *after* the foundation is done, the basement and basement plumbing may be begun. The walls can go up only after the basement and basement plumbing work is done. Hence, the foundation and basement affect the *commencement* of building walls and floors, at least the main floor. Further, the two electrical systems must be coordinated with the erection of the walls and the basement, respectively. Otherwise, the all-too-often situation of undoing work already in place may be experienced. Does this sound familiar to those of you who have experienced this, especially in streets being torn up repeatedly as each task is undertaken? Finally, plastering and painting depend on everything being done.

The point is that we are interested in total *terminal* time. Thus, if we look to what might be done simultaneously, such as floors and walls, we can cut total time by *scheduling* them simultaneously. It is not a matter of adding all the days shown on the diagram (roughly 60) but one of trying to reduce them by indentifying key start-stop jobs

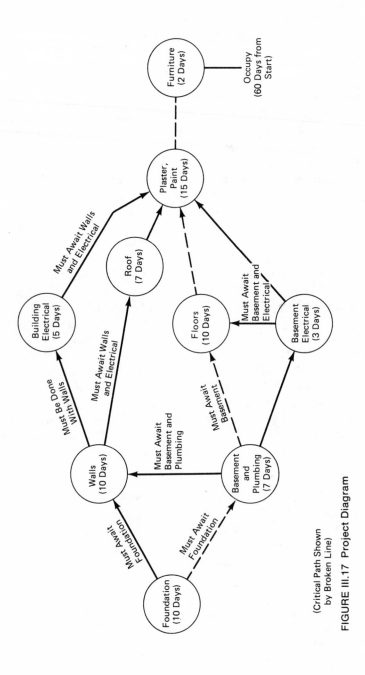

(Critical Path Shown by Broken Line)

FIGURE III.17 Project Diagram

217

which affect the *next* job, and also by identifying simultaneous jobs which could reduce total time.*

(b) Critical Path Method (CPM)

The *critical path method* is just what the name implies, namely, that there are *certain* task paths and points which affect the entire task *more* than others. One of the main points of CPM is to identify these critical *subtasks* and also those with *slack time* so that we can isolate within a total project those tasks which *must* be completed at a certain time or those which may be delayed.

For example, by adding optimal *times* to the chart on PERT, (Figure III.17) such as indicating "foundation *can* be started in 0 to 5 days," and "*can* be finished in 5 days," or for the basement task, "*can* be started in 5 days," or "*must* be started in 7 days," we can deduct each task from the total in order for them to be ready for "floors" or "walls." Working *backward* from right to left is the best method. If we begin with the last job, "plaster and painting," (15 days) we note that it *can* be finished in 10 days. Thus, it *must* be finished in 10 days to meet the target date. Hence, we subtract the 10 from 15 and find that the job may be started 5 days from its beginning ($15-10=5$) and we can pick up 5 days of "slack time." We can examine all the other tasks and subtract the real completion time from the number of days it normally takes. If it takes the full time on the original diagram, so be it. After the chart has been completed, working backward, the critical path of the entire project can be laid out and timed. For example, one critical path appears to be one which flows from the foundation to basement to walls, and so it should be indicated by another line (a broken line or some other device).

"Time" could have been incorporated in PERT also, but in CPM it is used primarily to highlight the really critical paths to completion. Also, CPM is deterministic, while PERT is probabilistic.

If we were to chart the slack times for all the tasks in our building by using the above procedure, we *might* come up with:

Start	Earliest Start	Latest Start	Slack Time
Foundation	0	5	5
Basement	5	7	2
Walls	5	5	0
Plastering and Painting	15	10	5

*Complex diagrams and applications are available for reference in the excellent texts in the bibliography.

From this we can identify as a critical point any job with a zero slack time; while those with positive slack time become points of possible pick-up time, and all directed toward the task of finishing certain tasks *and* the overall task (occupancy) on time or ahead of time. One must always allow for "Murphy's Law"!*

9. PROBABILITY TECHNIQUES. (BAYESIAN PROBABILITY; BERNOULLI PROCESS)

(a) Bayesian Probability (Bayes' Theorem)

Bayesian probability, or Bayes' theorem as it is sometimes called, is one of a set of techniques dealing with probability. Bayesian probability is considered as a law of probability which is useful because it can incorporate probabilistic *additional* information into the decision-making process. Specifically, it provides a way of revising or changing the probabilities of conditions, states, or outcomes on the basis of new information becoming available after the original information has been used, to determine a previous state of probability.

Condensing a practical application taken from Gerald E. Thompson's[8] chapter on Bayesian probabilities, suppose a copying machine is known to make defective copies 50 percent of the time. In other words, the probability is 0.50 of a copy being made *defective* each time one is made. Thus, in making the first *two* copies, the probability of each of *four* events, "good-good," "defective-good," "good-defective" and "defective-defective" is 0.25. Now suppose the copies come up good-good, good-defective, and defective-good during three simple events which take place in that order. This is really saying that at least *one* of the copies will be a good one. The unconditional probabilities comprising the multiple event (0.25 + 0.25 + 0.25 = 0.75).

How about the probable event that the *last copy* will be defective? Again, this is a compound-event example and the "last copy defective" could occur only if either good-defective or defective-defective happened. The probability of this event is 0.50 or the sum of good-defective 0.25 and defective-defective 0.25 = 0.50.

It has been shown that the probability of at least *one* of the copies being good is 0.75. This is called the *prior* probability for the case. However, other, *posterior* probabilities are concerned in most out-

---

*If something can go wrong, it will. And it will be the worst thing that can go wrong.

[8]Gerald E. Thompson, *Management Science, An Introduction to Modern Quantitative Analysis and Decision Making* (New York: McGraw-Hill, 1976), pp.57–59.

comes. Suppose we are interested in the probability of two good copies and suppose we could actually look at the *last* copy and see that it is defective? It would mean that this additional observation precludes our having two good copies (one already being defective). Instead of the 0.25 probability of two good copies in the original case (good-good as one set of four possibilities), the occurrence of two good copies is now impossible or down to 0.00. This is called *a posterior conditional probability.*

To return to the main issue, we are really interested in obtaining at least one good copy and now that we know the last copy is defective, we must revise *downward* the prior probability of 0.75 that we started with. How much it should be lowered is the result of applying full Bayesian procedure, which is a more involved one of summing up the remaining key probabilities. The facts now are that if the last copy is defective (known to have occurred), the only simple events that can take place are good-defective or defective-defective, the events that made up the same 0.50 probability calculated earlier.

The probability of at least one *good* copy can occur now only if good-defective happens. Since good-defective has a probability of 0.50, the probability of one good copy also is 0.50. The revision of the prior probability of 0.75 is now down to 0.50 (given that the last defective copy occurred). To summarize, the first or prior unconditional probability of at least one good copy was 0.75, or P = (at least one good copy) = 0.75. But if we add something to our knowledge, in this case knowledge that the last copy is defective, the posterior conditional probability is revised downward to 0.50, or P = (at least one good copy) (last copy defective) = 0.50. (Which happens to be the same 0.50 probability originally stated because of the machine.)

To conclude, it should be emphasized that this process has become more and more useful in determining probabilities. It also is not always as simple to apply as in the example given. The reader is encouraged to refer to a fuller treatment in any good management science or quantitative text when considering the process.

(b) Bernoulli Process

The *Bernoulli process*, is yet another way to assess probabilities. It is concerned about the outcome of a *sequence* of experiments or events in which the outcome of each experiment is *independent* of the outcomes of all other experiments. Flipping a coin to determine "heads" and "tails" is an example. If one flips an "honest" coin, the probability of heads is 0.5. If one flips it again, the probability of 0.5 for heads again holds, and so on. The two events are independent, since the first flip does not change anything that shapes the outcome of the second flip. It is called *statistical independence.*

All probability situations are not as neat as coin flipping. There are those whose outcome depends upon the outcome of an event or experiment immediately *preceding* it. This involves mathematical techniques generally known as *conditional probability,* of which Bernoulli is a popular one. An example of this kind of probability would be to make artificial (yet probable) choices or decisions based upon schemes ranging from chance events, like flipping a coin, to conditional events, like a deliberate decision *not* to repeat the last decision even though it was arrived at fairly or to follow a scheme which would depend only on the last event and nothing previous, and so on. In other words, this technique involves a deliberate decision to manipulate probabilities by deciding that the outcome of each event would be dependent only on the event immediately preceding, even though several are associated in a series.

To illustrate the Bernoulli process, Levin and Kirkpatrick offer a basic example in applying it to the chances of getting good parts produced out of a given number. The process, joined to their preceding explanation of the formula, is shown by this modified example.

Suppose we were studying a process in which historically nine-tenths of the parts produced were good ones (successes). If we wanted to compute the probability of getting exactly two good parts out of six, we would first define our symbols:

$p = 0.9 =$ process characteristic or proportion of success

$q = 0.1 = 1-p =$ proportion of bad parts

$r = 2 =$ number of successes desired

$n = 6 =$ number of trials undertaken

and then use the formula for *binomial probability distribution.*

$$\text{Probability} = \frac{n!}{r!\,(n-r)!}\,p^r q^{n-t}$$

Although this formula may look somewhat complicated, it can be used quite easily if one remembers that the symbol ! means *factorial;* 6! means $6 \times 5 \times 4 \times 3 \times 2 \times 1$, or 720; and when we calculate 2! it means 2×1 or 2.0 (0! is defined as equal to 1).[9]

[9]Levin and Kirkpatrick, *Quantitative Approaches,* p.57.

$$\text{Probability} = \frac{n!}{r!\,(n-r)!}\, p^r q^{n-t}$$

$$= \frac{6!}{2!\,(6-2)!}\,(0.9^2)(0.1^4)$$

$$= \frac{6\times5\times4\times3\times2\times1}{(2\times1)\,(4\times3\times2\times1)}\,(0.9^2)(0.1^4)$$

$$= 15\,(0.81)\,(0.0001)$$

$$= 0.001215\ \text{(probability of getting 2 good parts out of 6)}\ [10]$$

As the authors point out, a problem such as this could have been solved by *probability trees*, but they become too complex for large problems. The formula itself is not so easy, either, if one is computing the value of 35! or 45! This formula is known as the *binomial probability formula*, and tables exist by the same name to provide the results of such computations.

10. SAMPLING

Sampling is a useful and economical way of getting information about populations (things in number) without having to observe the entire population. Obviously, it saves time, effort, and resources, and if correctly done, can provide sufficient accuracy for most purposes. Technically, sampling means obtaining a *random* selection of a part of the population under consideration to yield an accurate picture of the whole. Randomness means unbiased in any way, shape, or manner, either deliberately or accidentally. Manufacturers take samples of production line or end items using all sorts of sampling techniques, for the purpose of quality control during production and to predict the quality of the end product. Marketing managers take samples of potential markets prior to the introduction of a new product. Pollsters take random samples of the voting population to predict actual voting behavior. Sampling is indeed a way of life and prediction.

Its value lies in the fact that masses of data or populations are too great to count or analyze as a whole; hence, valid sampling makes it possible to generalize about the whole based on a few. An example of sampling is the problem of trying to obtain the average gasoline price per gallon in a major metropolis. The costs of visiting all the gas

[10]*Ibid.*, pp.56–57.

stations is prohibitive for our purposes and resources. If we went only to the major oil companies, the data could be biased. If we went only to the independents, again it could be biased. Yet we desire a limited, unbiased sample. One method to draw our sample would be to divide the city deliberately into homogeneous sections and to call at random on a few stations in each section. This would give us what is called a *stratified* sample, which one hopes would include all kinds of neighborhoods and incomes. In short, we would be attempting a more random approach to more uniform areas and then trying a combination of all. In a stratified random sample including each observation is an attempt to achieve a constant for each segment or stratum of a population, but this varies, of course, from stratum to stratum.

Another method would be to deliberately select a sample, *manipulated* in such a way as to obtain a representative cross section of the entire city. This is called a *purposive* or *judgment* sample. In any deliberate manipulation the technique is just that, a judgmental decision, and it requires special techniques to achieve validity.

For most truly random sampling methods there are techniques which can be applied to determine the validity and significance of the sample. One of these is the *standard error*. Assume that 100 samplers went out to 1,000 gasoline stations, one each to ten stations, to get a fast sample of the prices. The prices could then be arranged in a frequency distribution which, if plotted on paper, would probably be found to be a "normal" distribution. Our sheer size of the number of prices would be large enough to reveal an *average* price the same or very near the *true mean* of the data. It would look something like Figure III.18.

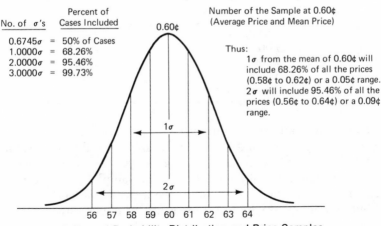

No. of σ's	Percent of Cases Included
0.6745σ =	50% of Cases
1.0000σ =	68.26%
2.0000σ =	95.46%
3.0000σ =	99.73%

Number of the Sample at 0.60¢
(Average Price and Mean Price)

0.60¢

Thus:
1σ from the mean of 0.60¢ will include 68.26% of all the prices (0.58¢ to 0.62¢) or a 0.05¢ range. 2σ will include 95.46% of all the prices (0.56¢ to 0.64¢) or a 0.09¢ range.

56 57 58 59 60 61 62 63 64

FIGURE III.18 Normal Probability Distribution and Price Samples

The more we approach infinite numbers, the more the *true mean* is also the *average* of a distribution. But even in a curve or distribution which clusters about a narrower range (as with gasoline prices), there are samples that are different distances from the mean. The rule is, however, that the more a distribution approaches infinity, the more the distribution approaches normality. In a normal curve or distribution one can determine the *standard deviation* from the mean with some accuracy. It is done in terms of standard deviations.

$$\text{The formula is } \sigma = \sqrt{\frac{\Sigma(x^2)}{N}}$$

(or)

$$\sigma = \sqrt{\frac{\sum\limits_{i=1}^{N} (x_i - \bar{x})^2}{N - 1}}$$

(where N is not "large," $N-1$ is needed in the denominator)

N = the number of cases

x = deviation from the arithmetic mean

$\bar{x}$ = mean

σ = standard deviation

In other words, the standard deviation is the square root of the deviation from the arithmetic mean. Here are the standard deviations for a normal distribution as shown in sigmas and the percentage of cases which will fall within the plus *and* minus standard deviations:

Number of Standard Deviations (*plus* and *minus* from the mean)	Percentage of Cases Included
0.6745	50%
1.000	68.26%
2.000	95.46%
3.000	99.73%
And so on to infinity.	

Hence, we can say that in a normal distribution, 99.7 percent of the cases will be included within a distance of only three standard deviations from the true mean. Knowing this, and knowing our sample, can give us quite a bit of confidence in the sample's being error free if cases fall within the above confidence areas or, indeed, if they are distributed more or less within three standard deviations.

The standard deviation of a distribution of means is termed the *standard error of the mean* ($\sigma\bar{x}$), or the standard error of other statistical measures.* Its formula is $\sigma\bar{x} = \dfrac{\sigma}{\sqrt{n}}$

In our example, reliability can be computed from one sample of prices, taken from the above probability distribution.

If our sample $\bar{x}$ = $0.60

One standard deviation (σ) = .05

$$\sigma\bar{x} = \frac{0.05}{\sqrt{1000}}$$

$$= \frac{0.05}{31.6}$$

$$= 0.00158, \text{ the standard error} \atop \text{of our mean (average)}$$

Further, it can now be assumed that the error of our average of $0.60, even if three standard deviations away from the true average, would only be 0.0047 (3 × 0.00158 = 0.0047). In short, our sample result of $0.60 ± 0.0047 gives us a good confidence level about the low outer limits established in our study.

There are, of course, more ramifications to the subject of sampling, and its applications to analysis and management problems are valuable because information can be obtained at little cost and with good reliability, if used properly.

11. SIMULATION (MONTE CARLO; WAITING LINE TECHNIQUE; QUEUEING PROBLEMS)

Simulation is the technique of analyzing a system by imitating its behavior in an experiment. Another method for making predictions and decisions, it is closely allied with the use of models by its definition, and it is an important supplement to mathematical analyses.

---

*An error which is not exceeded by 50 percent of the cases is called the *probable error*. It is equal to 0.6745 σ times the standard error. Its formula is:

$$PE_x = 0.6745 \frac{\sigma}{\sqrt{n}}$$

One can simulate by experimenting directly with a given situation, manipulating an element and observing the results. One can also conceivably construct a model of almost anything in the real or imagined world. The author recalls a debate at one time between advocates of modeling during which some maintained an operating model of the world could be constructed but it would probably be larger than the Empire State building! At any rate, to return to reality, once a model is constructed, mathematical analysis can be applied and experimentation carried out with elements just as if the real situation were being manipulated. If one could, the best way would be to manipulate reality itself, but that would pose problems.

Simulation can even pick up where some analyses end. Even though not as efficient, simulation can indicate optimal courses of action which may not fit conventional analysis. To illustrate, let's first examine the technique of Monte Carlo.

(a) Monte Carlo

Monte Carlo is one of several forms of simulation applicable to those "beyond analyses" areas mentioned above. In Monte Carlo the behavior of some parts of the model are determined probabilistically. Highly complicated inventory problems, queueing or waiting line probabilities, and replacement problems are a few among the many possible applications. To approach these, specific tables have been constructed to give any fixed selection procedure one might wish to use, ranging from the use of five successive random numbers, or every other number, or every fifth number, in columns, diagonally, and so on. These have been constructed by the long procedure of preparing what are called *randomly generated numbers.* Such numbers are generated by a simple but tedious task. Suppose a jar contains ten identical poker chips numbered 0 to 10, one number to a chip. These chips are then mixed up. One is withdrawn by someone who is blindfolded and the number recorded. The chip is returned and the act is repeated over and over again. From the record, a table of *strictly random* numbers is prepared, usually with five digits as the units. Each five digit number series drawn would differ (by most odds) in its sequence. However, over *time,* there would be as many 1's as there are others. No pattern is possible and the table produced is exactly what its name describes, a table of random numbers. An example is shown in this section. This table is the heart of Monte Carlo simulation.

Now for an example of Monte Carlo. The problem is whether or not to procure a new machine. The facts, records, or estimates of management point to an *expected* profit of $100 (thousands if the

Table of Random Numbers

73310	60288	63577	73455	37934	03129	40925	78395
01847	56844	08198	78401	86756	77247	92110	36216
✓11415	✓60919	37282	58414	17041	46406	65948	33433
59904	14566	17560	01207	08524	78466	54385	85977
91949	26871	24194	23557	03087	73521	57892	17521
23508	00921	41837	91474	02823	54046	60816	30407
61959	24468	29867	28336	58566	06874	55020	32109
25331	71533	13363	41962	63996	22425	74337	00253
65397	87789	17863	13223	14485	51935	12155	86530
57357	84246	35832	75425	99208	67379	66887	58634
56889	70257	45315	41428	50166	32962	71446	73229
75802	24387	52183	02935	94143	68424	94263	64390
04778	93048	51135	28714	25696	22690	52141	68005
37211	67903	49585	32749	97035	53820	29382	38981
57133	17416	19555	22474	42718	33142	59996	52763
86062	21176	37823	47127	36676	07243	23397	43173
61226	03677	00086	22723	57463	63959	59465	49627
40075	12613	09780	87206	90447	41887	06312	83332
61073	58323	59741	70270	18884	85794	32504	47781
34624	10187	80102	91149	12205	67151	39922	78558
79690	31099	40885	50813	00054	21900	36653	86715
28587	24620	72831	08156	79211	70752	59096	84209
07064	91427	16180	21018	46865	04522	36743	07116
77293	08441	51742	74868	06431	77105	90106	01449
42198	42693	14800	25939	84468	48466	06070	94096

reader wishes). Using Monte Carlo, this figure can be approximated by simulation; that is, an *approximated expected profit* can be determined.

Course of action decided upon: buy a new machine	
Profit expected	$100
Probability	0.50
Probability of quality–Good	0.50
Probability of quality—Poor	0.50
Profit for good quality	$150
Profit for poor quality	$50

The use of a random device is sought that will produce good quality 0.50 of the time and poor quality 0.50 of the time. We could flip a coin and let heads equal good, tails equal poor. One of these may follow the other or it may not. If the first flip is a head, it equals $150 profit,; if the second is a tail, it equals $50 profit; the third, if a tail, is $50; the fourth a tail, $50; and the fifth a head, $150. We have a total of $150 + 50 + 50 + 50 + 150 = $450. We duplicated our effort five times to get this by simulating five events. If we have faith that these five events would happen with the machine, an average profit of $90 is obtained (450 ÷ 5). This is $10 different from our initial projection. It also leads to two conclusions about simulations; namely, that they will deviate by *some* amount from expected returns and that, generally, the more simulations carried out, the smaller will be the average deviation from the expected one. Suppose we had done six flips and there were three goods and three poors, the results would have been $600 ÷ 6 = $100 average profit, which is the same as our initial expected profit.

However, what we want is a flexible *random* device that permits *simulation* of chance processes with numerous events. This can be done using numbers which are generated randomly and placed in a table as described above. There are, of course, computer routines for doing the same thing. If we use the table, and assign a fifty–fifty chance for each possible event or profit outcome, we can deliberately assign digits 1 through 5 to "good" and 6 through 9 plus 0 to "poor." We have a representation of each current probability having a one-tenth chance. The probability of 1 or 2 or 3 or 4 or 5 is the sum of their individual probabilities, or 5/10. The same holds for 6–0. Referring to the table of random numbers, the numbers 1, 1, 4, 1, 5, 6, 0, 9, 1, and 9 are drawn from adjacent columns. In profit dollars this would give seven goods and three poors or 1200 ÷ 10 = $120 average profit. Thus, assigning these new random numbers results in a new average of $120, which deviates from the mathematical one of five flips, which gave us $100. So it is evident, depending upon the assigned profit figures of each occurrence ($150 and $50) that changing the simulated profit figures results in a Monte Carlo profit in excess of the mathematically computed ones.

Monte Carlo is thus a random method of approximating solutions of problems in almost all areas by sampling from simulated random numbers. It is a technique that appeals to those who would like to inject random chance into a decision, and random chance is a likelihood.

As mentioned in the beginning, simulation can continue where analysis leaves off. It is appropriate to consider for use in practical problems that cannot be handled satisfactorily with current analytical procedures. This is especially true when a mathematical model contains uncertainty, risk analysis, questionable availability of equipments, actual delivery, time factors, unknowns, and nonlinear relationships. Simulation, in an explicit manner, puts uncertainty *into* the model.

(b) Waiting Line Technique (Queueing Problems)

The problem of waiting lines of products about to enter a production process, or services to be performed, is fairly well known. A simple example is the waiting period for a barber (for men, usually) in a shop where there are no appointments. The customers may or may not wait and the barber is usually faced with an uneven flow of customers. The problems of whether he can afford an extra barber or suffer the loss of business from those who will not wait become determining factors for his business. In industry, particularly of the process and assembly types, the problem of waiting lines or queueing-up components in an assembly line is a very real one which can be measured in actual costs.

To eliminate these queueing up and waiting line kinds of problems, we would immediately have to know of the actual demand plus actual resources to meet that demand. Unfortunately, the demand cannot always be determined with accuracy, and the cost of enough resources or capabilities to react to such unknown demands and peak periods is a critical factor. To be ready for any and all customers would be ideal, but it is unlikely in most cases.

To define, a waiting line is simply the formation of a line-up of people or units which have not been serviced at once. The line-up usually accumulates and is based on a first come, first serve basis.

However, in manufacturing, priorities or random methods can be used to accommodate the critical, demanding situations or products. In production industry more than in most service enterprises, it is possible, with time, experience, and scheduling, to plan for everything to arrive at fixed times, but even in industry the unknown quantities of orders and unforeseen priorities may affect the process. Thus, in both types of enterprise, it is usually an average situation that determines planning and resources.

Actually, queueing *theory* is not a simulation technique, but using simulation to approach a waiting line problem is sometimes helpful. The idea is to get some measure of the expected cost of waiting. Here is a clear example of a truck-loading problem condensed from one by Gerald E. Thompson which demonstrates the problem and technique of waiting line calculations.[11] The classic waiting line problem model is illustrated: the number of servers must be scheduled before the actual (future) arrivals are known.

Let's assume a 20-hour period of operation (a simulation) for a trucking company. The number of arrivals per hour to be unloaded is uncertain; however, they all require unloading (or servicing). The *probabilities* of their arrival range from 0.05 to 0.25 for 0 to 5 trucks, numbers of trucks arriving per hour, for a total of 1.00. If this were shown in graph form as a general relationship between the waiting

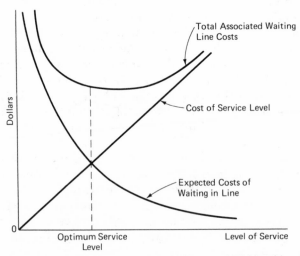

FIGURE III.19 Level of Service and Expected Waiting Line Costs.

[11]Thompson, *Management Science*, pp.410–15.

line costs and the level of service, the graph would appear as in Figure III.19.

Prior to further simulation discussion, we should note that the optimum service level essentially depends on the relative magnitude of the service level costs and the expected costs of waiting in line. Total service level costs typically *rise* as more servers are scheduled. However, expected costs of waiting *decrease* as the service level increases. Table III.5[12] illustrates this common sense relationship, using three selected service levels where the number of services is *assumed* to be 2, 3, and 4, and the average cost of waiting is $22.50, $4.50, and $1.00 per hour.

TABLE III.5 The Optimum Service Level

Service level (number of persons in the dock crew)	Cost of service level (dock-crew cost per hour)	Expected cost of waiting (expected cost per hour of driver delay)	Total associated waiting-line costs per hour
2	$14	$22.50	$36.50
3	21	4.50	25.50 (minimum)
4	28	1.00	29.00

Next, to obtain a measure of the expected cost of waiting we proceed in our simulation problem using probabilities and random numbers. Let's assume the detailed possibilities are 0 to 5 with the assigned probabilities of 0.15 for 0 trucks per hour, 0.25 for 1 truck per hour, 0.25 for two, 0.20 for 3, 0.10 for 4, and 0.05 for 5 trucks arriving per hour.

Next, assume the assignment of a random number to each arrival as shown in Table III.6.[13]

The service time for each truck is one hour for one server. Idle drivers cost $10 per hour while waiting to be served. If we employ three servers (dock crew), the problem is to estimate the number of

[12]*Ibid.*, p.409.
[13]*Ibid.*, p.411.

TABLE III.6 Assignment of Random Members to Arrival Possibilities

Number of trucks arriving per hour	Probability of this number of trucks per hour	Random numbers assigned to simulate the occurrence of this number of trucks per hour
0	0.15	01–15
1	0.25	16–40
2	0.25	41–65
3	0.20	66–85
4	0.10	86–95
5	0.05	96–100

trucks each hour where unloading is delayed an hour. This will result in the waiting line which occurs for each hour. By making a simulation run for three servers, Table III.7 would give us answers to both questions:[14] ($90 cost of waiting ÷ 20 hours = $4.50)

It would now be appropriate to repeat the 20-hour simulation for two servers and for four servers. For two servers it amounts of $22.50 for the expected cost; for four servers it would be $1.00. This would show that the average costs of waiting clearly decline as the level of service is increased, as one would expect. But it would also show that the cost of too many servers would offset this savings and that the *minimum total cost* is what is important. Thus, we find by returning to the chart and calculations shown in Table III.9, (same as Table III.5) that the minimum total cost is $25.50 per hour for the optimal number of three servers. That is, *total associated* waiting time costs are minimized at that number.

12. STATISTICAL FORECASTING TECHNIQUES (SCATTER DIAGRAMS; CORRELATION; REGRESSION)

(a) Scatter Diagram (Scattergram)

Often a simple plotting of related data on graph paper can provide management with a fairly accurate basis upon which to forecast, *provided* the variables continue to operate in the same pattern and that the ultimate, fixed capabilities have not yet been reached. As an

[14]*Ibid.*, p.414.

232

TABLE III.7 Simulation Results in the Truck-Unloading Problem

Hour	Random number (From Table III.8)	Simulated number of trucks arriving this hour	Number of trucks ready to be unloaded this hour	Capacity of the dock crew (number of trucks that can be unloaded this hour)	Number of trucks actually unloaded this hour	Waiting-line length: number of trucks where the unloading is delayed until the next hour	Cost of waiting ($10 per hour of delay)
0						2	
1	35	1	3	3	3	0	$ 0
2	86	4	4	3	3	1	10
3	78	3	4	3	3	1	10
4	16	1	2	3	2	0	0
5	05	0	0	3	0	0	0
6	44	2	2	3	2	0	0
7	96	5	5	3	3	2	20
8	23	1	3	3	3	0	0
9	17	1	1	3	1	0	0
10	92	4	4	3	3	1	10
11	09	0	1	3	1	0	0
12	07	0	0	3	0	0	0

TABLE III.7 (continued)

13	63	2	2	3	2	0	0
14	96	5	5	3	3	2	20
15	18	1	3	3	3	0	0
16	04	0	0	3	0	0	0
17	94	4	4	3	3	1	10
18	53	2	3	3	3	0	0
19	91	4	4	3	3	1	10
20	41	2	3	3	3	0	0
				60	44		$90

$$\frac{\$90}{20} = \$4.50$$

TABLE III.8 Random Numbers

3509
8607
7863
1696
0518
4404
9694
2553
1791
9241

TABLE III.9 Identifying the Optimal Service Level[15]

Service level (number of persons in the dock crew)	Cost of service level (given dock-crew cost per hour)	+	Expected cost of waiting (expected cost per hour of driver delay)	=	Total associated waiting-line costs per hour
2	$14		$22.50		$36.50
3	21		4.50		25.50 (minimum)
4	28		1.00		29.00

example, assume that Figure III.20 is a plot of admissions to a new wing of a hospital which opened on the 10th of the month.

A line drawn to have roughly as many differences above the original starting point as there are below—i.e., as near average or

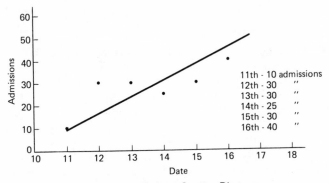

11th - 10 admissions
12th - 30   ''
13th - 30   ''
14th - 25   ''
15th - 30   ''
16th - 40   ''

FIGURE III.20 Hospital Admissions Scatter Diagram

[15]*Ibid.*, p.409.

middle, as is obvious from the data points—considering the magnitude of the differences gives some fairly good indications. First, the trend of admissions is upward; second, it varies; third, 40 or more might be expected on the 17th, 18th, and so on.

More accuracy can be attained in the forecast by using mathematical calculations such as correlation, or regression analysis (or the least-squares method). At this point the usefulness of a simple scatter diagram may be quite adequate for the purposes of visualizing admissions, or for such forecasts as sales and discharges, without employing algebraic methods to refine the forecast.

Another aspect of visualizing trends and the relationship of two variables, such as the number of sales to numbers of salesmen or the numbers of hospital beds to turnover, is to determine if there *really is* a relationship and, if so, what kind. Consider the following four scattergrams without being concerned about *what* is being projected. As they are plotted on paper indications of *correlation,* or the lack of it, appear. Correlation means that as one variable changes, so too does a related one in some ratio; this is a cause and effect relationship. One must be careful, however, not to be deceived by a *positive correlation* between two *unrelated* phenomena or variables. It can happen, but it is simply "happenstance" or a spurious relationship.

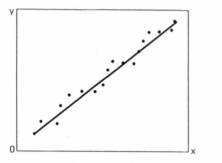 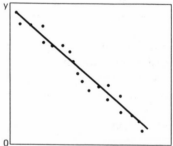

FIGURE III.21(*left*) A *positive* correlation. Note clustering and direction; hence, they relate in a positive way. (*right*) A *negative* correlation. Note clustering, but direction is negative. Still meaningful.

(b) Correlation

It is important in most every endeavor to measure the association between two (or more) variables which have a real relationship and predictability. To review from the section on sampling the usefulness of such paired data obtained from random variables, we can expect a normal probability curve of those variables if they have a *bivariate*

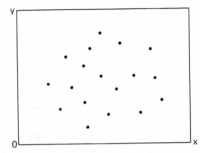 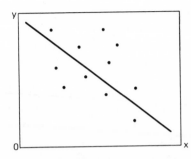

FIGURE III.22 (*left*) No correlation. Note no line either positive or negative is possible. (*right*) Weak correlation. Note the lack of real denseness of data around the line.

distribution. The curve, with its normal number of cases that fall on each side of the mean, looks like Figure III.23.

To continue with correlation, it is first necessary to know if there really is a relationship between the variables or data. If so, the relationship of the two can be measured, given the proper data. Scattergramming was pointed out as one method not employing calculations but simply data and judgment. It is usually necessary to obtain a more precise measuring technique. Thus, correlation or other methods may be required.

Correlation is a method of helping measure the *validity* and *reliability* of a relationship of variables. As in sampling, by applying dispersion or standard deviation (the sigmas (σ) shown below) and using a standard error of estimate an attempt is made to isolate how great or how little the measurements may be in error.

Standard deviations (to either side of the mean) in a normal curve are really measures of data dispersion, or how much they cluster about the mean. Correlation is based on the assumption that variations will

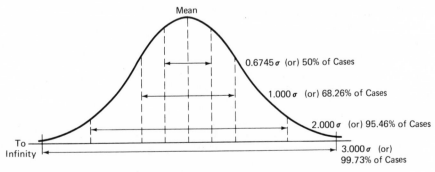

FIGURE III.23 Normal Probability Curve

237

follow the normal curve of events and that the percentage of cases falling within the *n* standard deviations will be of the percentages shown in figure III.19. It is also a way to measure the "fit of the line" when superimposed on a curve (line) prepared from plotting two related variables. Instead of the freehand method, correlation is a better indicator of *how much* the observations fall into place on either side of the line, thus giving more preciseness.

As a basis for an illustration of correlation, let's assume we have made a scatter diagram from observations of airline passengers arriving at a municipal airport and the airport hotel registrations (Figure III.24). The line shows what we would hope for, a positive relationship, i.e., a trend toward more registrations as more airline passengers arrive. The equation for such a line is $Y = a + bx$, which will be treated later. For now, we are interested in determining the number or percentage of registrations which may fall within our prediction area and the percentage which may not. Not necessarily to be memorized, but simply for awareness, these two equations would be used to find the sum of a and b:

1. $\Sigma (Y) = Na + b \Sigma (x)$
2. $\Sigma (xy) = a \Sigma (x+b) \Sigma (x^2)$

Using these we can determine the number of instances which would fall within one, two, or three standard deviations of the mean.

Briefly, the mathematics of measuring the deviation of *each* observation from the line is done by (1) computing the sum of the squares, (2) dividing by the number of observations, and (3) taking the square root of that number. This produces the *standard error of estimate*, which is the number of variations or scatter about the line. The formula is as follows:

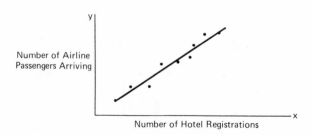

FIGURE III.24 Hotel Registrants/Airline Passengers Scatter Diagram

$$Sy = \sqrt{\frac{(y-ya)^2}{N}}$$

or

$$Sy = \sqrt{\frac{y^2}{N}}$$

The standard error of estimate can vary from 0^n to 1, and the smaller the standard error, the closer the relationship.

The calculation of a *correlation coefficient* is another tool which shows the degree of relationship of data. It is a percentage (decimal) ranging from $-1.$ to 0 to $+1$.

A minus one would be a perfect negative correlation, while a plus one would be a perfect positive correlation. Correlation is a measure of whether or not a significant portion of the variation of y has been explained. The equation for a correlation coefficient is as follows:

$$r = b \sqrt{\frac{\sum x^2}{\sum y^2}}$$

Where r is the coefficient we seek, the difference of an actual value b is multiplied by the sum of x^2 divided by y^2, and the square root is taken of that sum. The coefficient takes on the same sign as b, which may be positive or negative.

At the risk of some repetition but in the interest of clarity, here are perfect coefficients as graphs (Figure III.25, III.26, and III.27 would portray them, assuming the data gathered is exactly as plotted.

There can also be *curvilinear* and exponential relationships which could look like Figure III.28.

FIGURE III.25 Positive Perfect Correlation or $+1$.

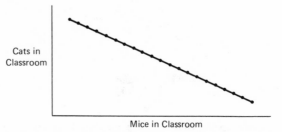
FIGURE III.26 Negative Perfect Correlation or −1. (Rarely)

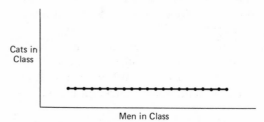
FIGURE III.27 No Correlation or 0.

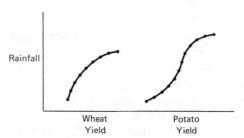
FIGURE III.28 Curvilinear and Exponential Correlation.

(c) Regression

Regression is a method which uses a format and certain algebraic equations to approach more precise relationships and forecast variables. Regression is such a popular technique that it will be demonstrated in this next illustration. Returning to our hotel registration/airline passenger example, we find by plotting the past data that a trend is observable. The question is, precisely where will it lead next? As we plan to increase the size of the airport and anticipate more landings, we would like to get a good estimate of the needed capacity of the hotel in order to accommodate the passengers and plan accordingly. The scatterplot with data shown (Figure III.29) is followed by the regression technique.

240

While the calculation may be a fairly sound quantitative projection, it still may not satisfy our *observed* knowledge that the increase in earlier years was less than in recent years. Thus, squaring and averaging may not be enough to correct this fact. Also, the confidence we can place in forecasting must take into account (1) the size of the data base, (2) data dispersion and correctness, and (3) a future which may not conform to past assumptions.

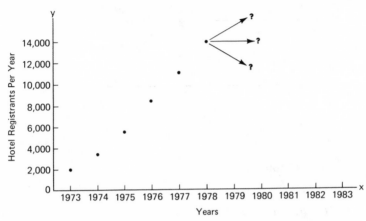

FIGURE III.29 Scatterplot

Year	Registrants	Year	Registrants
1973	2,000	1976	8,500
1974	3,500	1977	11,000
1975	5,500	1978	14,000
		1983	?

This is the format for a regression line:

List of x values	List of y values	$(x)\cdot(y)$	(x^2)
and Σx values	and Σy values	$\Sigma(x)\cdot(y)$	$\Sigma(x^2)$

(sum of each)

$\bar{x} = \Sigma \dfrac{x}{n}$ (n = number of pairs of x/y values) and (Average of the x's)

$\bar{y} = \Sigma \dfrac{y}{n}$ (average of the y's)

b (slope of the regression line) $= \dfrac{\Sigma(x)\cdot(y) - n\,(x)\cdot(y)}{\Sigma(x^2) - n\,(\underline{x}^2)}$

a (intercept point) $= y - b\bar{x}$

Equation of a regression line: $Y = a + bx$

This is the calculation of the regression line for the example:

x Year	y No. of Registrants	$(x) \cdot (y)$	(x^2)
1973	2,000	146,000	5,329
1974	3,500	259,000	5,476
1975	5,500	412,500	5,625
1976	8,500	646,000	5,776
1977	11,000	847,000	5,929
1978	14,000	1,092,000	6,084
453 (last 3 digits) $\Sigma (x)$	44,500 $-(y)$	3,402,500 $\Sigma(x)\cdot(y)$	34,219 $\Sigma (x^2)$

$$\bar{x} = \frac{\Sigma x}{n} = \frac{453}{6} = 75.5$$

$$\bar{y} = \frac{\Sigma y}{n} = \frac{44,500}{6} = 7416.6$$

$$b = \frac{\Sigma (x) \cdot (y) - n\,(x) \cdot (y)}{\Sigma(x^2) - n\,(x^2)}$$

$$b = \frac{3,402,500 - 6\,(75.5)\,(7416.6)}{34,219 - 6\,(75.5)^2}$$

$$b = \frac{3,402,500 - 3,359,718}{34,219 - 34,200} = \frac{42,782}{19} = 2252$$

$$a = \bar{y} - b\bar{x} = 7417 - 2252\,(75.5) = 7417 - 170,026 = -162,609$$

$$y_i = -162,609 + 2,252(x_i)\ (x_i = \text{the year 1983}) \text{ or } (x_i = x \text{ in year } i)$$

Number of rooms required in 1983:

$$y = -162,609 + 2252x$$
$$y = -162,609 + 186,916 = 24,330 \text{ registrants in 1983.}$$

(d) Some Warnings

This is one section of appendix III which must be concluded with some practical warnings about any forecasting technique. First, always consider the logic of a relationship. Is there a good reason why

242

one factor should be related to another? Be careful of what statisticians call "spurious relationships." Often the use of common sense is the best way to avoid them. Correlation and regression, in themselves, do not prove causability relationships among phenomena. It is perfectly possible, as examples, that imports of rum to the United States might relate precisely with the number of new ministers appointed in Massachusetts, or lightning flashes with martinis consumed, and so on—but valid inferences from these are nonsensical.

Second, much data may look like the relationship of trousers to men, or cats to mice in the classroom, which appears to be a straight line relationship and all variables of x and y fall exactly on the line. But a prediction of fewer mice if more cats are used does not rule out the possibility of clever mice or of *friendly* cats and mice in the future.

After World War II prices rose dramatically instead of falling as predicted by some leading economists. Badly needed new buildings were postponed by those in charge to await the lesser costs anticipated. The reverse took place and we found ourselves building new schools at three to four times the amount it would have cost if started earlier, when needed. Stock market predictions are just as vulnerable to time, circumstances, and above all, to the human equation.

13. TIME SERIES

Becoming increasingly popular because of the need to evaluate many events or phenomena over a period of time to make comparisons and extensions is the technique of *time series* or longitudinal time series. A time series simply consists of the values of a variable associated with successive periods of time. Easy to visualize is the increase in sales over a period of time. Time is shown on the x axis in plotting a trend, while sales is shown on the y axis. An "ideal" line or straight line (linear) is usually superimposed to accent the peaks and valleys of the actual sales.

Any function that changes with time is a candidate for this easy charting. For example, actual stock market averages can be compared to the past, present, and future of one's own forecasts. The major benefit of such charting is to show more vividly than do numbers the fluctuations and results over a period of time. It is especially useful to chart observations of a function or perhaps a group profile of individuals. For example, the actual number of business school or medical school graduates who remain in the business world or in medicine and in what sectors is of interest to society and the schools. The series

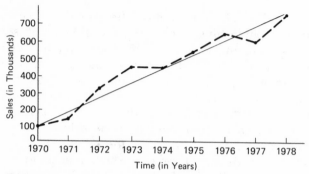

FIGURE III.30 Simple Time Series Projection

can be refined to reflect years, seasons, smoothing out seasonal fluctuations, quarters, days, hours, and so on. It only requires that time be
one of the variables.

14. VARIOUS OTHER TECHNIQUES (A FORTIORI ANALYSIS; INDEX NUMBERS; OPERATIONS RESEARCH; SIMPLEX METHOD; STATISTICAL QUALITY CONTROL CHARTS; UTILITY THEORY)

Space and the large number of available techniques and tools
preclude further detailed explanations, even though brief at best. Here
are a few more which can be described in only a paragraph or two to
make the reader aware of additional tools of analysis.

(a) A Fortiori Analysis

This is a technique which deliberately favors alternative systems
when compared to a best system or solution. The alternatives are
deliberately weighted to attempt to make them dominant. But, if the
best choice still remains the best against the weighted alternatives, it
is determined to be dominant and it's position is further strengthened.

(b) Index Numbers

There always is a need for some base against which to compare
changes. Index numbers are base period numbers, deliberately chosen,
and the selected factors to be included in such numbers, plus their
proper weighting. They reflect measured fluctuations in price, volume,

244

upward or downward trends, consumer economics, growth, loss, or any other measurable variables which change over time relative to the base originally selected. The government uses them extensively in setting large scale economic policy. Industry and other enterprises use them for more particular trend recording.

(c) Operations Research (OR)

A "school" or discipline in its own right, operations research is a purely quantitative approach to obtaining optimum solutions. It uses several disciplines as its method of research and analysis, usually making use of a team *approach* of experts to provide quantitative solutions. Problems of sales, operations, production, inventories, allocations, waiting time, replacement, competitive processes, and so on, i.e., almost every function that lends itself to a mathematical/statistical approach, are areas where OR has proved its value.

(d) Simplex Method

The graphic and algebraic methods of linear programming treated earlier have limitations when *several* constraints or variables are introduced. Simplex (really quite complex mathematics) is a method which can be used to find the most efficient, finite answer or solution. It is limited only by the capacity of computers to handle a series of mathematical formulas required for large and complex numbers of calculations.

(e) Statistical Quality Control Charts

As a result of the statistical projections described earlier, most businesses prepare quality control charts, made from samples, means, averages, or ranges, for the purpose of setting upper and lower control limits. If their sampling techniques produce samples which fall within such limits, the production and quality functions are considered under control. If outside the limits, management looks for causes of the variations. In effect, this distinguishes variations due to chance from those due to assignable causes.

(f) Utility Theory

Most businesses use expected monetary value (profit, for example) as a decision criterion. There are situations where *value* is used as a decision criterion. These are situations where the profit-versus-risk equation is not acceptable. The risk of one dollar to get ten is not too painful even if the one dollar is lost. But when thousands and perhaps millions of dollars of risk are involved, the *utility* factor enters. Utility means the pleasure of displeasure one can experience from different outcomes. For instance, the *displeasure* of losing $1,000 is a greater value than the *pleasure* of winning $10,000. To display utility differences, a simple chart can be used to plot one's point of profit versus loss, beyond which the attractiveness of the enterprise falls sharply, even negatively, and can fall below the positive segment of a normal graph down to the lower opposite, negative segment. If a utility line is *linear* is is more likely to result in a continuous picture of monetary value which can be predicted. If it is *curved,* the utility criterion takes over more rapidly and the possible loss is magnified.

SELECTED BIBLIOGRAPHY

The sources quoted or referred to in the preceding pages which I consider excellent are listed below. In addition, a few other useful mathematics, statistics, finance, economics, and management science texts are included. For a much more complete treatment of the tools and techniques illustrated in this appendix, the reader is encouraged to refer to these works. The list is made up of several sources concerned with the more quantitative aspects of analysis and is not meant to duplicate all the sources listed at the end of each chapter.

ANDERSON, DAVID R.; SWEENEY, DENNIS J.; and WILLIAMS, THOMAS A. *An Introduction to Management Science: Quantitative Approaches to Decision Making.* St Paul, Minn: West, 1976.

AWAD, ELIAS M. *Business Data Processing.* 4th ed. Englewood Cliffs, New Jersey: Prentice-Hall, 1975.

ARKIN, HERBERT, and COLTON, RAYMOND R. *Statistical Methods, As Applied to Economics, Business, Psychology, Education and Biology.* New York: Barnes and Noble, 1963.

BATY, GORDON B. *Entrepreneurship: Playing to Win.* Englewood Cliffs, New Jersey: Prentice-Hall, 1974.

HAYNES, W. WARREN; MASSIE, JOSEPH L.; and WALLACE, MACJ., JR. *Management: Analysis, Concepts and Cases.* 3rd ed. Englewood Cliffs, New Jersey: Prentice-Hall, 1975.

HEINZE, DAVID *Management Science, Introductory Concepts and Applications.* Cincinnati, Ohio: South-Western Publishing Co., 1978.

HINRICHS, HARLEY H., and TAYLOR, GRAEME M. *Program Budgeting and Benefit Cost Analysis: Cases, Text and Readings.* Pacific Palisades, Calif.: Goodyear, 1969.

HINRICHS, HARLEY H., and TAYLOR, GRAEME M. *A Primer on Benefit Cost Analysis and Program Evaluation. Systematic Analysis.* Pacific Palisades, Calif.: Goodyear, 1972.

HORNGREN, CHARLES T. *Accounting for Management Control: An Introduction.* 3rd ed. Englewood Cliffs, New Jersey: Prentice-Hall, 1974.

JOHNSON, ROBERT W. *Financial Management.* 4th ed. Boston, Mass.: Allyn and Bacon, 1971.

LEVIN, RICHARD I., and KIRKPATRICK, CHARLES A. *Quantitative Approaches to Management.* 2nd ed. New York: McGraw-Hill, 1971.

LEARNER, EUGENE M. *Managerial Finance, A Systems Approach.* New York: Harcourt Brace Jovanovich, 1971.

LUMSDEN, KEITH, and BACH, GEORGE LELAND. *Microeconomics, A Programmed Book.* 3rd ed. Englewood Cliffs, New Jersey: Prentice-Hall, 1974.

LYNCH, RICHARD M., and WILLIAMSON, ROBERT W. *Accounting for Management, Planning and Control.* 2nd ed. New York: McGraw-Hill, 1976.

QUADE, E.S., and BOUCHER, W.I., eds. *Systems Analysis and Policy Planning: Applications in Defense.* New York: Elsevier, 1968.

ROUECHE, NELDA W. *Business Mathematics.* 2nd ed. Englewood Cliffs, New Jersey: Prentice-Hall, 1973.

Spectrum Books.
Each of the following is a publication of Prentice-Hall, Englewood Cliffs, New Jersey. ALBRECHT, KARL G. *Successful Management by Objectives.* COVENTRY, W.F., and BURSTINER, IRVING. *Management, A Basic Handbook.* DAY, WILLIAM. *Maximizing Small Business Profits.* KIMBLE, GREGORY. *How to Use (and Mis-Use) Statistics.*

THOMPSON, GERALD E. *Management Science: An Introduction to Modern Quantitative Analysis and Decision-Making.* New York: McGraw-Hill, 1976.

ULLMANN, JOHN E. *Quantitative Methods in Management.* New York: McGraw-Hill, 1976.

APPENDIX IV

Two Case Studies
for Analysis

I. THE DEEPWATER PORTS CASE

As part of the President's April 19, 1973 energy message, an analysis group was working on options for a deepwater ports delivery system in the U.S. This system was postulated on the use of supertankers for the delivery of U.S. petroleum. U.S. ports were able to handle ships of only around 65,000 DWT [Deadweight tons]. Economies of price scale were very significant as one exceeded 100,000 DWT, but U.S. ports could not accommodate ships of this draft.

ISSUES FOR ANALYSIS

In examining alternatives for a U.S. deepwater port, dredging was judged to be prohibitive. Other alternatives were examined which include: sailing supertankers to the Bahamas and transferring cargo to the U.S. by 65,000 DWT tankers; sailing supertankers to the shores of the U.S. where they could off-load by either small tankers; or by constructing a deepwater transfer system. The analysis problem in this case focuses on alternative transfer systems for the northeast of the U.S. While many forecasts were utilized, this case will assume that

This case was prepared by William E. Turcotte, Chairman, Department of Management, U.S. Naval War College and is published with his permission. While it in no way represents exact data or any government policy or position, it is typical of the more important and complex problems to which the SA approach may be applied. The teaching note for the case may be obtained upon proper identification and need from the author of this handbook. See Preview of Appendices in the Preface for details.

1980 petroleum throughput requirements in the northeast will be approximately 200 million tons per year (barrels of oil can be converted to long tons by dividing by 7.4).

OFFSHORE TRANSFER

Offshore transfer concepts present several competing alternatives. One form of offshore transfer involves utilization of non-U.S. deepwater points such as Nova Scotia or the Bahamas. Bulk crude would be carried by VLCCs [very large crude carriers] to these points and thence carried by 65,000 DWT tankers or smaller tankships to U.S. distribution centers. These alternatives give impetus to the construction of refineries at the point of bulk receipt, require the costs of intermediate processing, entail low economy vessels on the transfer leg, and impact adversely on the balance of payments.

U.S. offshore terminal options include a North Atlantic Deepwater Oil Terminal (NADOT) about 8.5 miles off Cape Henlopen, Delaware. (Previous studies have established this site as best situated for distribution centralization.) NADOT involves an artificially created island with multi-berthing and oil storage. The facility would be connected to land by either a tug-barge or pipeline feeder system. Estimated throughput is 200 million long tons per year with growth potential to 300 million long tons per year.

A second offshore terminal system concept involves a proposed Mono-Mooring Buoy System. This system can be located at any point just off the continental shelf. It would be connected to land by pipeline. Estimated throughput is dependent on the number of buoy systems, one of which can handle at least 50 MTY [million tons a year].

THE NADOT

Construction costs for NADOT at a 200 MTY throughput are estimated to be $747.7 million, while annual operating costs at the same throughput level are estimated to be $60.2 million.

The life span of the terminal was estimated to range from 15 to 25 years. To be conservative, a life span of 15 years was chosen for the purposes of analysis. An annual cost of capital recovery factor was chosen at an 8% interest rate. (The capital recovery factor for 8% over 15 years is .11683.)*

*Capital recovery factor $= \dfrac{i(1+i)^n}{(1+i)^n} - 1$ where

(Present Value of a sinking fund)

i = interest rate and n = years to recover investment.

NADOT TRANSFER CHARGES

Two principal transfer options from NADOT to the mainland exist. Pipeline is one and feeder vessels (tug-barge combinations) are another. Pipelines are fixed and offer environmental protection. Feeder vessels are thought to increase the risk to the environment. Feeder vessels are thought to increase risk of spillage but offer more flexibility, since, unlike pipelines, their route can be altered. Using 48-inch diameter pipelines, the annualized cost (annual capital recovery, interest and annual operating costs) of transporting 200 MTY to the mainland was estimated to be $78 million. The alternative of utilizing feeder vessels at a 200 MTY rate was estimated to be $92 million (capital recovery, interest and operating costs) annually. This cost assumed a 30,000 DWT tug-barge carrier and would be reduced considerably if the DWT was increased to 65,000 DWT, the largest size which can enter most U.S. ports now.

In addition to transportation to the refinery, the product required off-loading and handling from the supertanker prior to its entry to the pipeline or to the feeder vessel. Annualized cost for both of these methods was estimated at 30 cents per long ton. For the feeder vessel (tug-barge) alternative, there was also the requirement to unload the delivered product at the mainland refinery. This cost was calculated to be approximately 30 cents per long ton.

MONO-MOORING BUOY TERMINAL ALTERNATIVE

The monobuoy concept involves a deepwater mooring facility at which a tanker can connect with pipeline distributing oil to mainland

TABLE IV.1 Annual Downtime (days) for Monobuoy Operation

Days	Probability of Occurrence
Less than 5	.0
5	.1
10	.2
15	.3
20	.2
25	.1
30	.1
Greater than 30	.0
	1.0

storage facilities and refineries. Downtime because of weather is likely for the monobuoy alternative. Weather can limit the capability to moor but, except in very extreme conditions, is not thought to be a deterrent to pumping once the moor is completed. After a ninety-nine year data review of meteorological data, expected sea states were represented by a cumulative probability distribution of occurrence. Utilizing the Monte Carlo technique, a cumulative distribution of downtime in days was arrived at. Approximate data read from this distribution is shown in Table IV.1.

The monobuoy project has numerous variations. Sites may differ, the number of hook-up buoys are variable, distance from shore and refineries must be considered, and so on. In the course of the study the analyst was to examine over 20 combinations of sites, hookups, and numbers of mooring buoys. He was also confronted by differing construction periods during which only part of the capacity could be utilized and during which transfer substitutes for the final configuration had to be dealt with. Costs of one composite and very simplified alternative are shown in Table IV.2.

Table IV.2 4 Buoy* Monobuoy System-Composite Capacity 210 MTY**

Capital Cost Port Component & Pipelines	Annual Maintenance Expense	Annual Operations Expense
$1,045 million	$18.9 million	$33 million

*This is constructed to involve four different locations. If one location were utilized as in the NADOT example, then the pipeline component costs would be less than in this example.
**This does not include downtime for weather.

The life of the project was conservatively estimated to be 20 years. The discount rate of 8% (capital recovery factor of 8% over 20 years is .1018) used in the NADOT alternative was chosen for use. Choice of the 8% rate created considerable controversy among the working group.

SHIPPING ALTERNATIVES

To simplify the analysis, it was assumed that all shipping would originate in the Persian Gulf area. If U.S. superport capability did not exist, supertanker voyages could be made to offshore deepwater points such as Nova Scotia or Freeport in the Bahamas. At those points, the cargo or a refined version of the cargo could be transferred at an estimated cost of 30 cents per long ton to 65,000 DWT tankers with drafts suitable for entry into U.S. terminals. With either NADOT or monobuoy capability, the supertanker could be sailed directly to U.S. offshore deepwater terminals.

COSTS OF OCEAN SHIPPING

The various shipping alternatives were examined for costs utilizing voyage analysis computer programs available at the Maritime Administration.

TABLE IV.3 Costs of Ocean Shipping for Oil Imports
(Dollars per Long Ton)

	Size of Tankers (DWT)			
Persian Gulf to:	65,000**	250,000	326,000	500,000
Delaware Bay Area	$11.00	$8.00	$7.35	$6.35
Nova Scotia	10.70	7.75	7.15	6.20
Freeport, Bahamas	10.85	7.90	7.20	6.25

**Maximum present U.S. entry draft.

The alternative of sailing a primary route to a foreign superport involves the incremental costs of transshipment shown in Table IV.4.

In addition to shipping costs, it was estimated that unloading costs in the U.S. would average about $.30 per long ton.

ENVIRONMENTAL PROTECTION

The Environmental Protection Agency was requested to draw up standards necessary to prevent, contain, and clean up spills, resulting from each type of facility operations. The supertanker component must have double bottoms. For the port component, provision was made in the cost estimates for curtains, screens, and other devices for preventing and containing spills. Data collected by the Coast Guard concluded

TABLE IV.4 Transshipping Costs to U.S.
(Assuming a 65,000 DWT—Foreign Flag)

	Dollars per Long Ton	
From:	Nova Scotia	Freeport
To: Delaware Bay Area	$1.25	$1.30

that offshore bulk operations would tend to lessen the incidence of groundings, collisions, and other minor accidents that have contributed so much to reported tanker oil spillages. There remains, of course, the matter of assessing the probability and environmental consequence from catastrophic accidents such as *Torrey Canyon* in 1967.

COMPETING FOREIGN SUPERPORTS

We have touched on but a few of the domestic alternatives for addressing the superport issues. There are foreign superport developments prepared to substitute or compete with American projects. Point Tupper in Nova Scotia can now accomodate tankers up to 330,000 DWT. Freeport in the Bahamas can presently handle tankers up to 330,000 DWT; however, plans have been finalized to improve the freeport harbor so that it can handle ships up to 350,000 DWT. This project is expected to be completed sometime in 1979. These sites can serve as superport terminals for further distribution by 65,000 DWT tankers to American markets. All of these places have, or will soon have, refinery capacity. It is logical to expect that, absenting a superport, it will be increasingly attractive to accomplish much of the crude refining offshore, with subsequent distribution of final cracking products. Were this to happen, American jobs would be lost, the balance of payments would be further aggrieved, and national defense interests jeopardized.

What superport alternative would you recommend (for simplification focus on comparison using 65,000 DWT and 250,000 DWT tankers)? What is the basis for your recommendations? What risks/limitations are attached to your recommendations?

II. SWIMMING POOLS: PROVISION OF
SWIMMING OPPORTUNITIES IN THE
DADE COUNTY MODEL
NEIGHBORHOOD

In July, 1968, a team of three analysts representing the Dade County (Florida) Park and Recreation Department, the Department of Housing and Urban Development, and the Dade County Community Relations Board were conducting an analytic study to determine the best method of providing swimming opportunities for residents of Dade County's Model Neighborhood. The decision to undertake this analysis had been made following a request by residents of Brownsville (a community within the Model Neighborhood) for construction of a swimming pool in Brownsville.

Neighborhood pool	Average daily attendance (summer)	Population living within 1½ mile radius of pool	Type of neighborhood
Bunche Park	150	18,000	poor; black
Richmond Park	200	5,750	upper-middle; black
Cutler Ridge	350	10,000	upper-middle; white

The population of the Model Neighborhood, as determined by a 1964 study, was 75,000; it was expected that this would rise to 80,000 by 1985. The area of the rectangularly-shaped Model Neighborhood was 9 square miles, consisting primarily of single-family dwellings on

This case was prepared by Graeme M. Taylor, Management Analysis Center, Inc., with the cooperation of Dade County, Florida, on behalf of the Ford Foundation and the State-Local Finances Project, George Washington University. This case is intended for class discussion only, and certain names and facts may have been changed which, while avoiding the disclosure of confidential information, do not materially lessen the value of the case for educational purposes. This case is not intended to represent either effective or ineffective handling of an administrative situation, nor does it purport to be a statement of policy by the County involved.

The author wishes to acknowledge his debt to Gloria Grizzle, Budget and Analysis Division, Dade County, and J. Robert Perkins, Chief, Planning and Research, Park and Recreation Department, Dade County, for their cooperation and assistance in the preparation of this case.

Distributed by the Intercollegiate Case Clearing House, Soldiers Field, Boston, Mass., 02163. All rights reserved.

small lots. The population was predominantly black; average family income was $3,000.

National recreational organizations had issued "rules of thumb" concerning the percentage of the population living near a pool that would use the pool on an average day; these estimates ranged from 1% to 5%. Various standards had been established for the minimum acceptable surface area of water per swimmer per day, ranging from 15 square feet to 30 square feet, with 19 square feet approximating Dade County's own experience. It was estimated that 1½ miles was the maximum practical distance that any potential swimmer would walk to use a pool.

The analytic team had gathered cost information on two sizes of swimming pools— "standard" and "olympic."

- *Standard:* A standard pool had 5,000 square feet of water surface, and would require a total of two acres of land. Construction costs were estimated at $127,900, including equipment. Operating expenses, including lifeguards' wages, were estimated at $20,800 per year.
- *Olympic:* An olympic pool would be 11,700 square feet, and would require five acres of land. Construction and equipment costs were estimated at $278,900, and annual operating expenses at $39,100.

Land costs in the Model Neighborhood area were estimated at $120,000 per acre, including acquisition, demolition, and relocation. Each acre of land, on average, contained property returning $656 per year in property taxes to Dade County. The "life" of a pool was estimated to be 17 years.

It was possible to construct a pool at each of three locations in the Model Neighborhood area, selected [so] that all residents would be within a 1½ mile radius of a pool. Several other sites were available. Six pools, for example, could be located so that all residents of the Model Neighborhood would be no more than ⅔ mile from a pool. County-operated swimming pools were normally open from March 15 to November 15.

BUS SWIMMERS TO CRANDON PARK

Another possibility considered by the analytic team was to bus swimmers to Crandon Park, a Dade County beach park located approximately an hour's bus ride from the Model Neighborhood area. This would operate each day during the four summer months, and on 20 weekends during the remainder of the year, for a total of 162 days of operation. Crandon Park contained a zoo, various amusement rides, and other attractions such as miniature golf and skating. Buses and drivers could be hired for $44 per bus per day; each bus could carry 72 passengers. It was considered desirable to have one adult recreation leader for every 30 children; the leader's wages would be $18.25 per day. Admission to the beach and all amusement attractions was free. The beach was supervised by lifeguards employed by the County: it was anticipated that no additional lifeguards would be necessary if children were bused from the Model Neighborhood. Public transportation operated between the Model Neighborhood area and Crandon Park; however, service was limited and several changes were necessary.

QUESTIONS

1. Analyze the alternatives presented in the case.
2. Which method of providing swimming opportunities to the residents of the Model Neighborhood would you recommend based on the information in the case?
3. What additional information would you want before making a final decision if you were the responsible Dade County official?

Index

Ackoff, R. L.; Arnoff, E. L. and Churchman, C. W., *Introduction to Operations Research*, 77–78, 83
a fortiori analysis, 164, 166, 244. *See also* Dominance
Albrecht, Karl G., *Successful Management by Objectives*, 247
algorithms, 170
allocation, 154
alternative cost. *See* Opportunity cost
alternatives, 57–59, 164
  in Downtown Parking case study, 59–76
analog models, 77, 213
analysis:
  a fortiori, 164, 166, 244
  break-even, 164–65, 170, 178–81, 184
  contingency, 170
  cost, 170, 178–81
  cost-benefit, 121, 123, 170
  cost-effective, 5–6, 8–9, 85–86, 171
  economic, 7–8, 156
  marginal, 172, 207–13
  Markov, 172
  parametric, 173
  regression, 173, 240–42, 243
  sensitivity, 174
  time series, 174–75, 243–44.
  See also Systems Analysis
analyst: role of, 106–7, 113
analytic processes and techniques, 170–75
analytic reasoning terms, 164–70
Anderson, David R.; Sweeney, Dennis J. and Williams, Thomas A., *Introduction to Management Science . . .*, 246
Anthony, Robert N., *Management Accounting Principles*, 152–53
a posteriori reasoning, 159
a priori reasoning, 164
arithmetic mean, 159, 160, 162
Arkin, Herbert and Colton, Raymond R., *Statistical Methods, As Applied to Economics . . .*, 246
Arnoff, E. L.; Churchman, C. W. and Ackoff, R. L., *Introduction to Operations Research*, 77–78, 83
array, 159
assignment method, 170, 205–07

assumptions, 7, 29, 53–54, 164
  in Downtown Parking case study, 54–55, 61–76
asymptotic (curve), 159
attributes, 164.
  See also Variables
automatic data processing (ADP), 170
average, 159
average deviation, 161.
  See also Standard deviation
Awad, Elias M., *Business Data Processing*, 246

Bach, George Leland and Lumsden, Keith, *Microeconomics, A Programmed Book*, 247
balance of payments, 155
Barnard, Chester, 12
base case, 164
Baty, Gordon B., *Entrepreneurship: Playing to Win*, 246
Bayesian probability, Bayesian theory, 159–60, 165, 219–20
benefit, 164.
  See also Effectiveness
benefits, 154–55
Bernoulli process, 160, 220–22
bias, 164
Bierman, H, Jr., et al., *Quantitative Analysis for Business Decisions*, 37
binomial probability formula, 222
Bishoprick, Dean W. and Rice, George H., Jr., *Conceptual Models of Organization*, 18, 19–20, 37
bivariate distribution, 236–37
Boucher, W. I. and Quade, E. S. (eds.), *Systems Analysis and Policy Planning: Applications in Defense*, 2–3, 8, 15, 17, 49, 56, 82, 84, 103 n, 117, 127, 128, 131, 134–35, 192–93, 214 n, 247
break-even analysis, break-even point, 164–65, 170, 178–81, 184
budgets, budgeting, 155
burden cost, 158
Burstiner, Irving and Coventry, W. F., *Management: A Basic Handbook*, 1, 15, 55, 247

257

capital, 155
case studies. *See* Dade County Model
    Neighborhood; Deepwater Ports;
    Downtown Parking Authority
causality, 243.
    See also Correlation
central limit theorem, 160
central tendency, 160
certainty, 160
chance, 169, 173, 229.
    See also Certainty; Uncertainty
Changing Times, 17 n, 26
Churchman, C. W.; Ackoff, R. L. and Arnoff,
    E. L., *Introduction to Operations
    Research*, 77–78, 83
Cleland, David E. and King, William R.,
    Management: A Systems Approach, 37,
    77 n, 83, 100
closed systems, 18–19
Colton, Raymond R. and Arkin, Herbert,
    *Statistical Methods, As Applied to
    Economics . . .* , 246
commensurables, commensurability, 122, 165
comparative advantage, 155
computer models, 214, 215
confidence level, confidence coefficient, 160
confidential interval, 160
conflict, 160
constant(s), 186 n
constant dollars, 155
constraints, 3, 165
    administrative, 24–25, 119–20
    distributional, 120
    financial, 120
    legal, 119
    in linear programming, 197–98, 199–201
    physical, 119
    political, 120
    religious, 120
    social, 120
    traditional, 120–21
contingency analysis, 170
continuous distribution, 161
contribution, 160
control, 28, 165
controllable dollars, 155
Cornell, A. H., *Analysis of International
    Collaboration in the Organization and
    Management of Weapons Coproduction*,
    128 n
correlation, 160, 236–40, 243
    curvilinear, 239, 240
    exponential, 239, 240
    negative, 236
    positive, 236, 239
    weak, 237
correlation coefficient, 160, 239
    negative perfect, 240
    positive perfect, 239
cost(s), 29–31
    burden, 158
    differential, 155, 157
    explicit, 155
    fixed, 156, 158, 159, 178
    implicit, 155
    incremental, 155, 157
    indirect, 158
    investment, 61–62, 157
    isocost, 157
    joint, 157
    marginal, 157, 158
    opportunity, 61, 155, 158
    overhead, 158

relevant, 31, 155, 159
    sunk, 31, 159
    variable, 159, 178
cost analysis, 170, 178–81
cost-benefit analysis, 121, 123, 170
cost center, 155
cost-effective analysis, 5–6, 8–9, 32, 85–86,
    171
cost-plus pricing, 213
Coventry, W. F. and Burstiner, Irving,
    Management: A Basic Handbook, 1, 15,
    55, 247
Coventry: bombing of, 46 n
criterion, 32–34, 85–87, 165
    and objective, 87, 89.
    See also Decision criterion
critical path method (CPM), 171, 173, 216,
    218–19
current dollars, 155.
    See also Present value of dollar
curve fitting methods. *See* Least squares
    methods
cybernetic arbitration. *See* Delphi method
cybernetics, 171

Dade County Swimming Pools case, 253–56
    costs and alternatives, 254–56
    questions, 256
Day, William, *Maximizing Small-Business
    Profits*, 247
decision(s), 9–10, 86
    revocability of, 103
decision criterion, 109, 110, 165, 245–46
    equally likely, 166
    expected value, 166–67
    Laplace, 166
decision diagramming. *See* Decision trees
decision making, decision makers, 1–15,
    28–29, 34–35, 38–40, 165
    as challenge, 11–12
    creative nature of, 11–12
    definition, 7–11
    implementation of, 35
    in management, 101–2
    models in, 10, 12–14
    need for, 1–2
    problems in, 3
    recommendations in, 108
    report in, 108–10
    role of, 105–6
    styles of, 107–8.
    See also Analyst; Systems Analysis
decision rule(s), 32–34, 86.
    See also Criterion
decision situation, 28–29, 46–47, 57, 83, 165
decision theory, 165, 171.
    See also individual theories
decision trees, 171, 188–91
deductive reasoning, 166.
    See also A priori reasoning
Deepwater Ports case, 248–53
    costs in, 249, 251, 252, 253
    issues and alternatives, 248–53
    questions, 253
delegation, 39–40
Delphi method, Delphi technique, 58–59, 171,
    191–93, 214
demand functions, 210–11
dependent variable, 166, 167, 170
depreciation, 183–84, 187
descriptive standard, 168
deterministic model, 166

Dewey, John:
decision theory, 10, 12
How We Think, 10
differential cost, 155
diminishing returns, law of, 155–56
direct labor, 156
direct materials, 156
discounted cash flow, 184–87
discounting, 31, 123, 125, 184–87.
See also Present value
discrete distribution, 161
dispersion, measures of, 161, 237
average deviation, 161.
See also Standard deviation; Standard error
distribution:
continuous, 161
discrete, 161
frequency, 161
dollars:
constant, 155
controllable, 155
current, 155
present value of, 152–53
dominance, 166
dominant variable, 79
Downtown Parking Authority case, 45, 46,
136–51
alternatives in, 59–76, 79, 81, 89–97
assumptions in, 54–55, 61–76
cost/benefit comparisons, 91–92, 94–95
cost/effectiveness computation, 59–76
discussion of, 132–34
evaluation and ranking phase in, 89–97
implementation phase, 115–16
interpretation phase, 115
latitude in, 41–42
models in, 78–81, 92–93
objectives in, 50–52
present value in, 187
search phase, 57–83
side effects and spillovers in, 124–25
systems characteristics, 40–44
dynamic (system or process), 166
dynamic programming, 215

econometrics, 156
economic analysis, 7–8, 156
economic cost. *See* Opportunity cost
economic growth, 156
economic life, 156
economic reasoning terms, 154–59
economies of scale, 156
effectiveness, 86, 164, 166, 168
measure of, 29, 31–32, 49, 82–83, 87, 168
effectiveness scale, 168
efficiency, 166
elasticity, 156, 210–11
elements:
of matrix, 167, 188 n
of model, 226
endogenous variable, 166
Enthoven, Alain C., 106, 117
equally likely criterion, 166
exogenous variable, 166
expansion path, 166
expected value, 165, 190–91
expected value criterion, 34, 166–67
expense center. *See* Cost center
explicit cost, 155
extrapolate, extrapolation, 161

feasible solutions, 167
feedback, 28, 167

Fisher, Gene H.:
Analytical Bases of Systems Analysis, 100
Cost Considerations in Systems Analysis, 83
fixed costs, 156, 158, 159
Ford Foundation, 254 n
forecasting techniques, 178–246
warnings about, 242–43.
See also indiv. methods
frequency distribution, 161
full employment, 156
full employment surplus, 156
function, 161

game theory, 172, 193–96
gaming, 172
George Washington University State-Local
Finances Project, 254 n
glossary, 154–75
analytic processes and techniques, 170–75
analytical reasoning terms, 164–70
economic reasoning terms, 154–59
quantitative reasoning terms, 159–64
Grizzle, Gloria, 254 n
gross national product, 156, 157
group methods:
Delphi method, 58–59, 171, 191–93, 214
operations research, 25, 36, 173, 245

Harrison, E. F., *Managerial Decision-Making
Process, The*, 37, 100
Haynes, W. Warren; Massie, Joseph L. and
Wallace, MacJ., Jr., *Management:
Analysis, Concepts and Cases*, 246
Heathrow Airport:
air-freight handling problems, 26
Heinze, David, *Management Science,
Introductory Concepts and
Applications*, 194–96, 246
heuristics, 167
Hinrichs, Harley H. and Taylor, Graeme M.:
*Program Budgeting and Benefit Cost
Analysis . . .*, 55, 110, 115, 116, 134 n,
247
Systematic Analysis: A Primer . . ., 55,
103–5, 119, 123, 124, 126, 247
histogram, 161
Hitch, Charles J., 106 n, 117
Decision Making for Defense, 3, 4–5, 15, 83
and McKean, Roland N., *Elements of
Defense Economics*, 37
Horngren, Charles T., *Accounting for
Management Control . . .*, 247
Hungarian method. *See* Assignment method

iconic models, 77, 213
implicit cost, 155
incommensurables, incommensurability,
35–36, 122, 165
incremental cost, 155, 157
independent variable, 166, 167, 170
index numbers, 157, 172, 244–45
indifference map, 157, 166
indifference principle, 33
indirect cost, 158
inequalities, 161
inflation, 157
information system, 157
input, 9, 12, 28, 167
International Business Machines, 26
interpolate, interpolation, 161
interval estimate, 161
intuition, 58, 59
inventory models, 172

investment cost, 61–62, 157
isocost, 157, 167
isoquant, 157, 166, 167
iteration, iterative process, 12, 29, 103–5, 167

Johnson, Lyndon B., 16
Johnson, Robert W., *Financial Management*,
    247
joint cost, 157

Kahn, H. and Mann, I., *Ten Common Pitfalls*,
    128, 135
Kahn, Robert L. and Katz, Daniel, *Social
    Psychology of Organizations, The*, 37
Kassouf, Sheen, *Normative Decision Making*,
    84, 102–3, 116
Katz, Daniel and Kahn, Robert L., *Social
    Psychology of Organizations, The*, 37
Kimble, Gregory, *How to Use (and Mis-Use)
    Statistics*, 247
King, William R. and Cleland, David E.,
    Management: A Systems Approach, 37,
    77 n, 83, 100
Kirkpatrick, Charles A. and Levin, Richard I.,
    *Quantitative Approaches to
    Management*, 181 n, 221–22, 247

Laplace criterion. *See* Equally likely criterion
Learner, Eugene M., *Managerial Finance, A
    Systems Approach*, 247
learning curve, 167
least-squares method, 172
Levin, Richard I. and Kirkpatrick, Charles A.,
    *Quantitative Approaches to
    Management*, 181 n, 221–22, 247
linear programming, 172, 196–207, 215
    assignment method, 170, 205–07
    constraints in, 197–98, 199–201
    transportation method, 175, 202–05
    uses of, 202
logarithm, 161
logarithmic ratio scale, 161–62
log scale, 161–62
long run, 31, 158
Lumsden, Keith and Bach, George Leland,
    Microeconomics, A Programmed Book,
    247
Lynch, Richard M. and Williamson, Robert W.,
    *Accounting for Management, Planning
    and Control*, 210–12, 247

McKean, Roland N. and Hitch, Charles J.,
    Elements of Defense Economics, 37
McNamara, Robert S., 16, 106 n, 117
macroeconomics, 158
management functions, 14, 28, 101–2
"managerial revolution," 1–2
Manhattan Project, 33, 89
Mann, I. and Kahn, H., *Ten Common Pitfalls*,
    128, 135
marginal analysis, 172, 207–13
    and pricing, 210–13
marginal benefit, 207
marginal concept, 7–8, 158, 208–09
marginal cost, 157, 158, 209, 211–13
marginal revenue, 158, 209, 211–13
marginal utility. *See* Marginal benefit
Markov analysis, 172
Massie, Joseph L.; Wallace, MacJ., Jr., and
    Haynes, W. Warren, *Management:
    Analysis, Concepts and Cases*, 246
matrix, 167, 188 n.
    See also indiv. methods

maximax decision criterion, 33, 165, 167–68,
    196
maximin decision criterion, 33, 34, 196
maximum expected return. *See* Expected
    value
mean:
    arithmetic, 159, 160, 162
    true, 223–24
measure of effectiveness (MOE), 29, 31–32,
    49, 82–83, 87, 168
measures of costs (MOCs), 29–31, 32, 49,
    82–83
median, 159, 160, 162
microeconomics, 158
Miner, John B. and Steiner, George A.,
    Management Policy and Strategy, 15
minimax decision criterion, 33, 160, 165, 168,
    196
mixed strategy, 160
mode, 159, 160, 162
models, 77–81, 83, 213–15, 225, 226
    analog, 77, 213
    analytical/mathematical, 215, 245
    computer, 214, 215
    conceptual/computer, 215
    defined, 77, 168, 213
    deterministic, 166
    human, 214
    iconic, 77, 213
    inventory, 172
    people and computers interacting, 214
    probabilistic, 173
    symbolic, 77, 213
    verbal, 214
    See also indiv. models and techniques
Monte Carlo methods, 162, 226–29
most efficient solution, 167
"Murphy's" law, 219

national income, 158
networks, 173, 215–19
    critical path method (CPM), 171, 173, 216,
        218–19
    line of balance, 173
    PERT (Program Evaluation Review
        Techniques), 173, 215–18
New York State:
    Radio City Music Hall subsidy, 92
N.I.H. syndrome, 128
normal probability curve, 223, 237–38
normative standard, 168

objective(s), 47–52, 55, 82, 87, 89, 168
objective function, 162
open systems, 19–20
operations research (OR), 25, 36, 173, 245
opportunity cost, 61, 155, 158
optimal solution, 167
optimism index, 33–34
optimization, 158
optimum service level, 231, 235
Optner, Standford L., *Systems Analysis for
    Business Management*, 15
output, 12, 28, 168
overhead costs, 158
overspecification, 34

parameter, 168
parametric analysis, 173
payback, 162, 181–83, 184
    advantages of, 182–83
    shortcomings of, 182
payoff, 83, 162, 168, 189–90

payoff (*continued*)
  dominant, 196
payoff matrix, 162, 168
Peck, Paul L., Jr., "Management and the
  Systems Analysis Mystique," 109,
  116–17
Perkins, J. Robert, 254 n
PERT (Program Evaluation Review
  Technique), 173, 215–18
"per unit" cost curves, 158
planning, 9.
  See also indiv. techniques
point estimate, 162
Polaris Missile program, 33, 89
present value, 152–53, 168–69, 171, 184–87
pricing, 210–13
probabilistic model, 173
probability, probability theories:
  Bayesian, 159–60, 165, 219–20
  Bernoulli process, 160, 220–22
  conditional, 162
  joint, 162
  marginal, 162
  models in, 173, 188–91
  posterior, 219–20
  posterior conditional, 220
  prior, 219
  subjective, 102–3, 163
probability trees, 222
probable error, 225 n
production function, 158
profit, 159, 207, 245–46
profit analysis, 178–81
profit centers, 158–59
project analyses. *See* Networks

Quade, E. S. and Boucher, W. I. (eds.),
  *Systems Analysis and Policy
  Planning* . . . , 2–3, 8, 15, 17, 49, 56, 82,
  84, 103 n, 117, 127, 128, 131, 134–35,
  192–93, 214 n, 247
quality control, 222, 245
queueing theory, 173, 175, 215, 229–32

Radio City Music Hall, 92
Raia, A. P., *Managing by Objectives*, 37
randomly generated numbers, 226–27, 228–29,
  235
random sample, 163, 222–23.
  See also Sampling, sampling methods
rate of return, 183–84
  shortcomings, 184
regression analysis, 173, 240–42, 243
relevant cost, 31, 155, 159
research and development, 157
responsibility center, 158–59
return on investment, 159
Rice, George H., Jr., and Bishoprick, Dean W.,
  Conceptual Models of Organization, 18,
  19–20, 37
Roueche, Nelda W., *Business Mathematics*,
  247

saddle point solution, 160, 169
sampling, sampling methods, 163, 222–25, 245
  judgment, 223
  purposive, 223
  in quality control, 222, 245
  random, 162, 163, 222–23
  stratified, 223
  validity of, 223–25.
  See also Monte Carlo methods
satisficing, 169

scatter diagram (scattergram), 163, 232,
  235–36, 237, 238
scenarios, 174
Schlesinger, James R., " 'Soft' Factors in
  Systems Studies, The," 130
Schmaltz, Robert E.:
  "Semantics," 56
  "Systems Evaluation," . . . , 44n
semilog chart, 161
sensitivity analysis, 174
short run, 31, 159
side effects, 122, 123
Simon, Herbert A., 169
  New Science of Management Decision, The,
  101–2, 117
simplex method, 174, 245
simulation, 174, 225–32.
  See also indiv. methods
slope, 163
Smalter, Donald J., "Influence of Department
  of Defense Practices on Corporate
  Planning," 14
Smith, T. Arthur (ed.), *Economic Analysis and
  Military Resource Allocation*, 109 n, 117
Specht, R. D., 213–14
spend out, 169
spillovers, 35–36, 122, 123, 124–25, 169
spurious relationships, 243
standard deviation, 161, 223, 224–25, 238
standard error, 163, 223, 238–39
  of mean, 225
states of nature, 169
static condition, 169
statistic, 163
statistical quality control charts, 245
Steiner, George A. and Miner, John B.,
  Management Policy and Strategy, 15
stepping stone technique, 204–05
stochastic process, 169
strategic planning, 174
subjective probability, 102–3, 163
suboptimization, 29, 168, 169
subsystems, 39–40, 169
sunk cost, 31, 159
Sweeney, Dennis J.; Williams, Thomas A. and
  Anderson, David R., *Introduction to
  Management Science* . . . , 246
symbolic models, 77, 213
system, 28, 39–40, 169
Systems Analysis, 16–36
  advantages of, 2, 3–4, 5, 6–7, 9, 15
  alternatives in, 29
  applications of, 4, 16–17, 22–27, 36
  assumptions in, 29
  conceptual model, 13, 14–15
  constraints in, 118–20
  costs in, 29–31
  as cycle, 18
  decision in, 34–35
  decision situation in, 28–29
  definitions, 2–3, 174
  effectiveness in, 31–32
  evaluation phase, 32–34
  examples, 21–22, 23–24, 26–27
  focus and scope in, 22, 26–27
  formulation phase, 28, 38–56
  future of, 134–35
  goal of, 17–18
  history of, 16–17, 25–26
  implementation phase, 113–14, 125–26
  interpretation phase, 34–35, 100, 101–17
  measurables and unmeasurables in, 121–22
  objective (problem) in, 29

Systems Analysis (*continued*)
    and open and closed systems, 18–20
    pitfalls and limitations in, 127–31
    recommendations and reports in, 108–12
    search phase, 29, 57–83
    unknowns in, 122–24
    verification phase, 35–36, 118–26.
    See also Downtown Parking Authority case

Taylor, Graeme M., 136 n, 254 n
    and Hinrichs, Harley H., *Program
        Budgeting and Benefit Cost
        Analysis* . . . , 55, 110, 115, 116, 134 n,
        247
    and Hinrichs, Harley H., *Systematic
        Analysis: A Primer* . . . , 55, 103–5, 119,
        123, 124, 126, 247
team approach. *See* Group methods
Thompson, Gerald E., *Management Science:
    An Introduction to Modern
    Quantitative Analysis* . . . , 219–20, 230,
    231n, 232 n, 247
Tibbetts, Larry N., "Practitioner's Guide to
    Systems Analysis," 126
time series, time series analysis, 174–75,
    243–44
time value of money. *See* Discounting; Present
    value
trade-offs, 118, 169
transportation method, 175, 202–05
Tucker, Samuel A. (ed.), "Modern Design for
    Defense Decision—A
    McNamara–Hitch–Enthoven Anthology,
    A," 106, 117
Turcotte, William E., 248 n

Ullmann, John E., *Quantitative Methods in
    Management*, 206–07, 247
uncertainty, 29, 38–39, 122–23, 163
U.S. Department of Commerce, 157
U.S. Department of Defense, 16, 27, 106
    costing format used by, 110–13
    *Economic Analysis and Program Evaluation
        for Resource Management*, 83

"Economic Analysis and Program
    Evaluation for Resource Managers,"
    110–12, 117
U.S. Department of Health, Education and
    Welfare, 27
U.S. Post Office, 27
unknowns, 35–36, 122–25
unmeasurables, 35–36
utility, 159
utility line:
    curved, 246
    linear, 246
utility theory, 245–46

value, 245–46.
    See also Profit
variable(s), 29, 164, 169–70, 186 n
    dependent, 166, 167, 170
    dominant, 79
    endogenous, 166
    fixed, 179
    independent, 166, 167, 170
variable costs, 159
variance, 163–64
Vietnam War:
    truck breakdown problem and solution,
    44–45

waiting lines. *See* Queueing theory
Wallace, MacJ., Jr.; Haynes, W. Warren and
    Massie, Joseph L., *Management:
    Analysis, Concepts and Cases*, 246
war games, 193, 214
Williams, Thomas A.; Anderson, David R. and
    Sweeney, Dennis J., *Introduction to
    Management Science* . . . , 246
Williamson, Robert W. and Lynch, Richard M.,
    *Accounting for Management, Planning
    and Control*, 210–12, 247
World War II:
    Coventry decision, 46 n

zero-sum game, 170, 193–96